Studying Cities and City Life

Studying Cities and City Life is a textbook designed to provide an introduction to the major methods of obtaining data for use when analysing cities and social life in cities. Major chapters focus upon best practices in:

*   field studies (participant observation)
*   natural experiments and quasi-experiments
*   surveys employing probability and non-probability samples
*   secondary analyses of previously published documents.

A separate chapter examines a full range of questionnaires and interviews. Each chapter includes discussion of several case studies, and recently published research employing the method being discussed. This discussion highlights the issues and choices made by investigators in actual studies conducted in cities throughout the world.

This unique book is designed for use in research methods courses that primarily enroll students majoring in Urban Sociology, Urban Studies, Urban Geography, Urban Planning, and related areas.

Mark Abrahamson is Professor of Sociology (Emeritus) at the University of Connecticut.

"This book provides an accessible and engaging introduction to the wide range of methods used in urban research. Students will benefit from the author's ability to convey complex ideas succinctly and with clarity, and understanding is aided by numerous relevant examples drawn from classical and contemporary literature."

Graham Crow, *Professor of Sociology and Methodology, University of Edinburgh*

Studying Cities and City Life

An Introduction to Methods of Research

Mark Abrahamson

Routledge
Taylor & Francis Group

LONDON AND NEW YORK

First published 2017
by Routledge
2 Park Square, Milton Park, Abingdon, Oxon OX14 4RN

and by Routledge
711 Third Avenue, New York, NY 10017

Routledge is an imprint of the Taylor & Francis Group, an informa business

© 2017 Mark Abrahamson

British Library Cataloguing-in-Publication Data
A catalogue record for this book is available from the British Library

Library of Congress Cataloging in Publication Data
Names: Abrahamson, Mark, author.
Title: Studying cities and city life: an introduction to methods of
research/by Mark Abrahamson.
Description: Abingdon, Oxon; New York, NY: Routledge, 2016. |
Includes bibliographical references.
Identifiers: LCCN 2016022794| ISBN 9780415738002 (hardback) |
ISBN 9780415738019 (pbk.) | ISBN 9781315817637 (ebook)
Subjects: LCSH: Sociology, Urban–Methodology. | City and town
life–Research–Methodology.
Classification: LCC HT110.A27 2016 | DDC 307.7601–dc23
LC record available at https://lccn.loc.gov/2016022794

ISBN: 978-0-415-73800-2 (hbk)
ISBN: 978-0-415-73801-9 (pbk)
ISBN: 978-1-315-81763-7 (ebk)

Typeset in Amasis
by Sunrise Setting Ltd, Brixham, UK
Printed and bound by CPI Group (UK) Ltd, Croydon, CR0 4YY

Contents*

---

* Note: the front page of each chapter contains a more detailed outline of the chapter's contents.

Illustrations

Figures

Tables

Preface

Over the years I have known, and taught, hundreds of students majoring in Urban Studies, Urban Planning, and related programs. They were almost always required to take a research methods course, and that course typically received very mixed reviews from the students. The most discontent resulted from the students feeling that the content of the course was too far removed from what they saw as their future profession. That was surprising to me, given that many of them knew they would later be involved somehow in conducting research, and virtually all of them knew that their future roles would likely require them to be sophisticated consumers of research conducted by others.

After some probing, it appeared that one major problem with the research methods courses the students were taking was that the students could not readily translate the texts' topics and examples into the kind of research questions that seemed relevant to them. Principles of probability involved red and black balls coming out of a box. Experimental design was illustrated with studies of small groups of students communicating with each other by passing written messages through slots in the partitions that separated them. What did any of this have to do with studying cities and city life?

From the above paragraphs, the reader should be able to infer what prompted me to write this book. I wanted urban students to share my passion for research methods; to appreciate how much the knowledge they obtained from this book would be central to their future careers as city managers, urban planners, and so on.

What title to give to this book posed a problem. *Urban Research Methods* was initially considered, but rejected, because it implied that there are lots of methods that are unique to the study of cities and city life. There are not. A sample survey is conducted largely in the same manner, regardless of whether one is studying attitudes toward the Middle East or people's willingness to commute to work using public transportation. The difference is that when the latter is discussed, the relevance of the methodology to urban students is more apparent because they can readily imagine addressing public transportation issues in their professional roles. Similarly, an ethnographic field study essentially involves the same procedures whether an investigator is studying passengers on a cruise ship or youth gangs in a public housing project; but the latter example makes the relevance of the method more apparent to students of cities and city life. I could go on with other examples, but I think the point is clear.

This book is much like the research methods texts used in many social science courses except that almost all of its applications and examples are relevant to urban students. Another difference is that in the chapter on experimental design, natural experiments are emphasized and laboratory studies are not – for obvious reasons. In addition, because students in Urban Studies, Urban Planning, and so on, are ordinarily in interdisciplinary programs, this text incorporates methods and examples from across the social sciences, from Social Psychology to Geography.

In terms of immediate goals, this text is designed to help students to conduct the research projects that are often part of the methods sequence. In addition, and very importantly, the text is designed to impart the basic principles of the major methods so that in their future roles, these students will be informed consumers: they will be able to critically evaluate studies that purport to inform the professionals who plan and manage cities.

Examples and applications are also taken from cities across the world so that the text will be accessible to students and instructors in most English-language nations. However, more cities from the US than anywhere else are discussed because there are more cities in the US than anywhere else and because social scientists from Canada, the UK, Australia and other English-language nations often study US cities while social scientists in the US less often study cities in their nations. The literature, as a result, is dominated by studies of US cities.

Research methods courses utilizing this text need not have a statistics pre-requisite. A course in statistics would be helpful, but is not required. Where some statistical procedure is an integral part of a research method – for example, calculating confidence intervals for a sample survey – the statistics are explained in the most non-technical terms possible, with additional (optional) information provided in a statistical appendix.

While this text provides complete coverage of the topics conventionally included in a research methods text, it has deliberately been kept as brief as possible. This is to enable students to get out of the classroom and into research projects quickly in those courses which require students to conduct projects. For courses that are not designed as immediate precursors to student research projects, the relative brevity of the text enables instructors to assign additional readings that can provide students with greater depth in areas that are considered particularly important by the instructor.

Introduction

PART ONE: INITIAL CONSIDERATIONS

What do you suppose are the chances of sighting a colony of giant albino alligators in the New York City sewers or a vampire lurking in the Victorian gardens of London's Highgate cemetery? These are examples of urban legends: stories that have been widely circulated for many years, but are almost certainly untrue. So, how come a lot of people believe any of them? There are probably many reasons. For starters, people have heard the stories frequently repeated in informal conversations where an experience or sighting is specifically attributed to "a friend of a friend." An actual person is alleged to have seen the albino alligators in the sewers or the vampires in the cemetery. Those concrete-sounding details make the stories being passed along seem plausible, and as more people hear them, they in turn help to further spread the tales.

Both the conventional and social media are also sources of information that is sometimes untrue or of very limited validity, but is nevertheless repeated so often that people assume it must be true. The content can involve urban legends, as described above, or can be less fantastic, such as claims that outbreaks of some illness in a metropolitan area have reached epidemic proportions or that the rate at which children in a city are being abducted has dramatically increased. Presumed to be accurate hospital rates of admission or police statistics typically accompany these stories, adding to their apparent authenticity. However, careful analyses would frequently fail to support the assertions of these stories.[1] To be more precise, skeptical conclusions come from careful assessments by trained analysts with access to the requisite data. By contrast, when most people hear about the outbreak of an illness or about children being abducted in a distant city, they do not ascertain the veracity of the stories. They may not have access to relevant data, they may lack the analytical skills if they have the data, or they may be unwilling to take the time that would be required to conduct their own analysis.

People who hear questionable stories from their friends or from media sources may also lack relevant personal experiences with which to evaluate the claims. They have never walked through Highgate Cemetery at night; they have never searched through the New York sewers. But suppose they did have some relevant personal experience upon which they could rely. How much should they trust it in reaching conclusions?

The limitations of personal experience

Much of what people believe to be true, as a result of their personal experience, is in fact true; but some is not, and the problem is that it can be very difficult to tell, for sure, exactly which conclusions based upon everyday experiences to trust. There are a number of reasons why observations from everyday lives lead all of us to hold some erroneous beliefs. One of the main culprits is the inadequacy of what may be termed *informal sampling*: we do not carefully select our observations, and we do not take enough of them.

Virtually everything we have come to accept as true is a result of drawing an inference from some sample. We reach conclusions, from our personal experiences, about the differences between small towns and large cities, or between men and women, or the like. However, all of us have encountered an extremely limited sample of all of the small towns and large cities, and the men and women that we have met come from a very small slice of the world. Our samples are, therefore, very limited. If they were expanded, perhaps it would result in new information that would lead us to change our minds.

Furthermore, we almost always enter any situation with some preconceived notions about what to expect. As soon as we see evidence that is consistent with our initial assumption, we tend to stop looking for additional evidence. Or, at least, we do not keep looking very hard. The tendency to rely upon very limited observations, especially when those observations are congruent with preconceived beliefs, is referred to as *confirmation bias*, and most people can recall many everyday instances in which they too hastily reached a false conclusion due to confirmation bias.[2] On the other hand, there are probably many other instances in which they are unaware that this bias was operating and that it led them to be in error.

Related to confirmation bias is a tendency to "cherry pick" observations. Many situations are complex and in order to simplify them people typically focus upon some aspects of the situation and ignore others. They are especially inclined to see things that are consistent with their preconceived notions, and then to stop critically observing. So, if people who believed there were alligators under New York's streets began trudging through the sewers, they would be more inclined than non-believers to see what they thought *might* be alligator droppings, then after reflection assume that they were definitely from an alligator, and climb back up to the street certain that their belief had been confirmed by what they had seen.

In order to clarify some of the differences between conclusions based upon personal experience and those based upon systematic research, let us consider a more mundane, but still important, issue: private automobile ownership in cities. Within most large cities, there are policies and practices designed to discourage private automobile ownership. Logistical problems, notably insufficient parking, also discourage ownership, but constraints of this type are also affected by local governments as they set minimum street-width standards. The wider that minimum is, the more on-street parking there will typically be, though it is not always free and it may be restricted. Nevertheless, variations in street-width minimums raise an interesting question: Do wider streets, associated with more on-street parking, encourage residents to own automobiles? Or, is self-selection involved such that people who are committed to owning one or more automobiles choose residential areas, at least in part, by the amount of street parking they provide? Which comes first? The way an answer to the question was arrived at through systematic research is illustrated in Box 1.1.

Role constraints entail the final limitation of personal experience that we will discuss here. In any social situation, each person occupies a specific role, such as: student, husband, mother, employee, member of a religious organization – or a combination of those roles. That role or role combination affects what a person is exposed to, and how the person interprets what he or she sees. In addition, how others respond to a person varies according to the person's role(s), so husbands and wives, teachers and students tend to experience the "same" situation in different ways. Alternatively, we might state that it is not the identical situation for each of them.

There are a variety of simple examples that illustrate the constraints of people's physical or social positions on their perceptions. Could the fastest runner in a marathon accurately describe how much the slowest finishers ran or walked? No, because they could only observe others who were running fast. Could people who wait every day at a bus stop for a northbound bus be relied upon to describe the relative frequency of north- and southbound buses? No, because as soon as a northbound bus came, they would get on it, so they could only observe southbound buses going past them.

In sum, personal experiences can lead people to false conclusions because their samples are incomplete and flawed, they tend to rush to

Box 1.1 On-street parking in New York City

Enormous variations in street widths in New York City make it an ideal place to study the relationship between the availability of on-street parking and automobile ownership. But, consider the problem we are trying to unravel. Could walking the city's streets and observing the number of automobiles parked on the street and the width of those streets answer the question of which came first? Obviously not; an answer would require data and systematic study.

A professor of urban planning, Zhan Guo, began with Google and Bing photos of city streets. From these photos he measured the level of crowding of on-street parking around household residences. He also measured the availability of off-street parking, by measuring the width of garages, if the residence had one, and the space available for parking on a driveway area, again, if the residence had one. Then he obtained data on household car ownership, from zero to three or more cars.

His subsequent analysis revealed a number of perhaps surprising findings. For example, on streets that offered more parking, households were more likely to own a car regardless of whether they had access to off-street parking. In effect, more on-street parking increased the total supply of parking so people were apparently more inclined to buy more cars than their off-street parking could accommodate. Further, even those persons with garages or driveways were more likely to park on the street, when on-street parking was available, rather than use their own off-street space. This preference surprised Guo because the streets were typically narrow, often crowded, and required parallel parking; nevertheless, on-street parking was preferred. In sum, more on-street parking spaces led to more automobile ownership.

Finally, Guo tried some statistical extrapolations from his observations. He estimated that if on-street parking was markedly reduced, it would decrease car ownership by about 9 percent. On the other hand, if parking was markedly expanded, it could increase car ownership by as much as almost 18 per cent. These findings have clear policy implications, suggesting that local governments wishing to discourage private automobile ownership should reconsider minimum width standards.[3]

judgment and they are limited in what they see (and how they interpret it) as a result of the constraints of their positions. The limitations of personal experience are particularly pronounced when people rely upon it to make inferences about the way social systems are organized. Even passengers who ride a bus every day for years may not, as a result of their experience, understand very much about their city's bus routes.

Using systematic research

In order to move beyond erroneous rumors and surmount the limitations of everyday experience, people rely upon the established methods of gathering data and the techniques of data analysis that have been developed in the social sciences, as illustrated in Box 1.1. That is certainly true for academics and others who are professional researchers; but it also pertains to people whose positions in city governments, NGOs, planning agencies, and so on, require them only sporadically to be involved in gathering data. Many other people in similar positions may never be called upon to participate in conducting a study, but in order to carry out their planning or administrative tasks, they must be sophisticated consumers of social science research: they must know how to distinguish between the results of well-conducted studies and the claims of pseudo-science.

This book is intended to provide an introduction to urban research methods for people who will ultimately pursue all of the above career lines. It is organized around the principal social science methods, with individual chapters devoted to a review of each of the major types of methods used to collect or compile data. Included in the discussion will be the best practices associated with each method, the theoretical assumptions that typically underlie its usage, and the ideal conditions under which to employ it. Ways of analyzing the collected data will only be briefly noted in most instances.

Scientific research methods

We have seen a number of reasons why people ought to hesitate before assuming that no systematic research is necessary in order to answer a particular question. Much of what everyone thinks they know is dubious information that is passed on by others without much scrutiny, or information derived from their personal experiences which is confounded by their roles as participants. What are most missing are systematic sampling and observation, and formal rules for making inferences; and those are precisely what the research methods that have been developed in the social sciences provide to people, whether they are urban planners working for a city government or students preparing a research report.

Defining the problem

The first step in a systematic research project is to try to formulate the question to be examined as clearly as possible. The researcher often begins with a vague conception of what she or he would like to know about, but systematic research requires more precise specification. It is usually helpful to begin with a literature review. How have previously reported studies dealt with the issue? What have theories had to say about the phenomenon? From this literature review it is often possible to formulate the question to be examined more clearly, and to define the key terms to be examined in the research. The objective is to develop a definition of each term that is sufficiently unambiguous that multiple people independently utilizing it could agree when the phenomenon is present or absent, or present to varying degrees.

To illustrate, consider urban blight. This issue is widely mentioned in the Urban Studies literature and in the popular media; but is it sufficiently clear for independent observers going through the same parts of a city to agree on whether or not they are blighted? In searching for useful definitions, investigators and theorists have examined a large number of possibilities. In this literature, blight has been treated as involving such characteristics of an area as its amount of: abandoned buildings, vacant lots, noisiness, graffiti, litter, housing code violations, etc. Other researchers have assumed that blight was a reflection of the socio-economic attributes of the area's residents, and they have focused upon the percentage of residents: living in poverty, with less than high school educations, unemployed, etc.[4]

In this instance, a literature review might yield too many alternatives, that is, more potential ways of defining blight than a researcher could use. There are statistical techniques for reducing the number and they are discussed in subsequent chapters, but researchers frequently decide how to define terms based upon the theories that have influenced them. In other words, how do they think about, or conceptualize, blight? For starters, do they think of it more as a physical characteristic of a neighborhood or as a quality of a neighborhood's residents? This decision moves an investigator toward a more limited set of potential characteristics.

Selecting any of the characteristics noted above, or utilizing several in combination, would result in a definition capable of producing consistent results that would not be dependent upon the role or experience of the observers. The residents of an area and motorists driving through the area, for example, could agree on its number of abandoned buildings, the amount of graffiti, and so on. By virtue of their different roles and experiences, they might feel differently about the manifestations of local blight that they observed, but an investigator may consider such feelings to be a separate matter.[5]

While many investigators will consider this "separate matter" to be irrelevant and disregard it, people's feelings may be of substantial importance to some investigators. In fact, the primary objective of a study could be to discover just how residents of an area feel about local blight.

If so, then the research project might deliberately begin without a rigid definition that would restrict the inquiry. The focus instead would be upon learning what the residents pointed to as reflecting blight, and how they felt about it. The distinction among these different types of research is further examined later in this chapter.

For most research purposes, investigators would like to employ an *operational definition*, which is one that specifies the operations to be performed in order to produce a measure of the phenomenon. In other words, the definition itself implies the procedures to be followed in creating a measure. To illustrate, with respect to urban blight, an investigator might count the number of abandoned buildings in an area. That number, by itself, could constitute an operational definition of blight that different investigators could employ with identical (or at least very similar) results. Alternatively, one might want to combine two or more characteristics of blight into a single measure, as illustrated in Box 1.2. When a measure combines scores on two or more variables, the measure is frequently described as an *index*. In this example, blight is operationally defined as the number of abandoned buildings in a neighborhood plus the number of times buildings in the area were cited for code violations. The two variables are combined to create a single index, or measure, of blight in a procedure described more fully in Box 1.2.

Box 1.2 Creating a measure

Suppose one wished to measure the "blightedness" of neighborhoods in a city by combining the two variables with which we have operationally defined it, namely abandoned buildings and housing code violations. Step one requires assigning numerical values to each of the variables in every neighborhood:

1) *Abandoned buildings.* A researcher might walk through each of the neighborhoods, noting which buildings appear to be abandoned. This might require some additional operational definitions. For example, a building might be considered abandoned if its doors and windows were boarded or sealed such that it would not seem possible for anyone readily to enter or exit.
2) *Code violations* refer to property conditions that do not comply with municipal regulations concerning sanitation, safety, and so on. Many cities have a department that keeps track of all open property code violations, their initial date and location. Utilizing this list, an investigator could set a time period – e.g. all cited violations between January 1, 2014 and December 31, 2015 – and then count the number of properties that were cited for violations in each of

the city's neighborhoods. (It would be ideal to count abandoned buildings during the same time period.)

To illustrate the process, consider a hypothetical city that contains ten neighborhoods that can be arranged from north to south, and labeled A (1) to J (10). Suppose an investigator took a sample of the city by selecting five of the neighborhoods: A, C, etc. Sampled neighborhoods were found to have the set of scores indicated in Table 1.1.

Each neighborhood's score on both of the defining variables are then added together to produce that neighborhood's total blight score. Thus, adding 4 (the number of abandoned buildings) plus 2 (the number of code violations) results in a (total) blight score of 6 for neighborhood A. This same procedure is followed to assign a blight score to each of the neighborhoods.

After the index is constructed and each neighborhood is given a score, those scores could be used to rank neighborhoods. So, neighborhood E with a blight score of 7 would be considered more blighted than neighborhood D with a score of 6. Alternatively, based upon how one thought about blight, one might want to employ "cut-offs" for determining when any specific area would simply be classified as blighted or not blighted. For example, any neighborhood with a score above 10 might be considered to be blighted. If so, then in the hypothetical city described in Table 1.1, neighborhood B would be classified as blighted, and A, C, D and E would be considered not blighted. Any score could, in principle, be used to dichotomize neighborhoods into blighted and non-blighted categories. If possible, however, one would want to refer to some theoretical view of blight or follow the cut-offs used in past research in order to make the classification of these neighborhoods less arbitrary and more congruent with other studies.

Table 1.1 Hypothetical neighborhood scores

Neighborhood	#Abandoned buildings	#Code violations	Blight score
A	4	2	6
B	10	15	25
C	0	1	1
D	3	3	6
E	4	3	7

In conclusion, it is instructive to compare the way an index of blight was constructed in the above example to the way people, based upon everyday experiences, might reach decisions concerning whether particular areas in their city were blighted or not. The example described in Box 1.2 is characteristic of all scientific research in that it:

1) self-consciously tried to minimize the influence of personal experience
2) sampled cases systematically rather than haphazardly, and
3) operationally defined the variable being studied so that different observers' assessments of neighborhoods would be congruent and comparable.

Introducing reliability and validity

There are two major criteria that are utilized to evaluate any measure: its reliability and its validity. There are a number of ways in which each is assessed, depending upon the particular research design. A sample survey, for example, would not ordinarily employ the same techniques as an experiment in assessing the reliability and/or validity of measures. These procedures will be discussed at length in relation to the research designs that are discussed in the chapters that follow. Here we will briefly introduce reliability and validity, and focus upon the core meanings of each. (Types of reliability and validity are discussed, in detail, in Chapter 7.)

Reliability

Reliability refers to the consistency over time of the scores produced by a measure, in the absence of change in the phenomenon being measured. To illustrate, if a man stood on a bathroom scale, noted his weight, stepped off, waited five minutes, then got back on the scale and again noted his weight, the two measures of his weight would be extremely close to each other – if the scale was reliable. If he weighed himself again in six months, however, there could be a substantial difference in the two readings, and that would not necessarily reflect negatively on the scale's reliability. Over six months, his actual weight could have changed. In other words, how much consistency is expected of a measure depends upon: (1) how much time elapses and (2) our thinking about how the phenomenon being measured might itself be changing. Like weight, we usually think of people's intelligence or of neighborhood blight as not changing much over short periods of time. Any measure of intelligence or blight, to be considered reliable, would therefore have to produce highly consistent results if repeated over a short period of time. By contrast, people's moods are much more changeable, so a measure of mood could be reliable even if its results fluctuated over short periods of time more than measures of weight or blight.

Validity

Validity refers to the degree a measure is congruent with the concept it is intended to measure. A bathroom scale would therefore be a valid measure of weight if it actually measured a person's weight, conceptually defined as the force exerted on an object due to gravity. Hence, the validity of a measure depends upon what it is supposed to be measuring, according to a theory. If one thought the bathroom scale was actually a measure of people's intelligence, then further examination would likely show that the scale did not provide a valid measure.

If a measure is not reliable, it cannot be valid. If it does not correlate with itself (low reliability), it cannot correlate with an underlying concept either. Reliability does not guarantee validity, though; a bathroom scale may give highly consistent results, but would not provide a convincing measure of people's intelligence. Thus, the reliability of a measure is necessary, but not sufficient, for a measure's validity.

Theory and research

There is an ongoing interplay between theory and research regardless of whether one is working squarely within a discipline (such as Urban Sociology) or is examining a set of issues from an interdisciplinary perspective (as in Urban Studies). Simply stated, theories very often inspire research as investigators try to assess how well a theory can account for some observable events. Moving in the opposite direction, the feedback from the results of research studies often modify, or lead to new, theories.[6]

Types of theory

In the physical and biological sciences, theories are frequently comprised of inter-related axioms, and expressed in mathematical terms. In the social sciences, such theories are referred to as formal theories, and although they are generally considered desirable, most social science disciplines contain very few that fit this form. More typically in the social sciences, the term theory is used to refer to any abstract idea, or set of ideas, and theories are routinely presented in diverse forms that can include:

1) Classifications which describe categories of a phenomenon and how the categories are arranged in some type of hierarchy. Thus, a theory of urban blight could entail placing neighborhoods into categories (e.g. blighted/not blighted) based upon their stock of derelict housing. Similarly, a theory of the dominance of cities has involved placing cities into a number of hierarchically arranged categories based upon

their population size relative to other cities in their nation. (Relative population size has provided the operational definition of dominance.) The greater the relative size of a city, the greater its presumed access to resources and control over activities within its nation.

2) Informed speculations, resembling hypotheses, that have not yet been adequately tested, but seem promising because there is some basis for anticipating the theory's applicability. For example, neighborhoods that were once highly dependent upon manufacturing jobs have been found later to have high unemployment. By extension, one might also expect that neighborhoods of this type would also have more vacant buildings and code violations, and this extrapolation could lead to a theory of blight that ties it to labor force changes and unemployment.

3) Models that describe how some phenomenon occurs, often using metaphors that liken the issue of interest to some other phenomenon that is better understood. To illustrate, one might propose that neighborhoods go through stages that resemble people's lives. In this theory of stages, blight to a neighborhood would be likened to the deterioration that is associated with old age in people.

Regardless of the form in which a theory is expressed, it can be highly useful in providing an abstract perspective that (1) provides a consistent explanation for past research findings and (2) gives direction to future research by providing hypotheses and calling attention to important issues left hanging in prior studies. Thus, theory and research are linked together in an ongoing, inter-connected chain:

Research <------------> Theory

Concepts and variables

Irrespective of the form of a theory, its main components are usually *concepts*: abstract ideas or mental images. Blight is an example of a concept, as is social class, personality, etc. The main defining features of concepts are that they are abstract and inclusive. Pointing to "that table" or "that person," by contrast, would not denote a concept. That table is merely one concrete representation, but a concept – more abstract and inclusive – would entail all tables or all wooden tables or all tables of a certain height, etc. Similarly, that person is not a concept, but all persons over age 21 or everyone under 6 feet tall, or the like, would be a concept.

In most types of research, it is concepts that are operationally defined, as in the preceding example involving blight. This introduces another important feature of operational definitions, namely, that they are frequently evaluated according to their "faithfulness" to the concept for which they are supposed to provide a measure.[7] The more abstract a concept, the more useful it may be in integrating the results of highly diverse studies, but the more difficult it is likely to be to operationally define. To illustrate, the prestige of people's occupations is a concept. It is often incorporated into still more abstract conceptions of socio-economic standing which also include such concepts as income and level of education. Thus, socio-economic standing is a more abstract and more inclusive concept than occupational prestige, and as a result it is likely to be more difficult to operationally define.

Simply defined, *variables* are concepts that are expressed in terms that are capable of assuming different values. They are created from the characteristics or attributes of a concept, and can be distinguished in qualitative (non-numeric) or quantitative (numeric) terms. Gender, for example, is a concept and also a variable because it can be expressed in two or more qualitative values (e.g. male and female). Blight, as initially introduced, was a concept, but not a variable. In other words, blight, per se, is abstract and inclusive (a concept), but it does not necessarily denote any attribute that varies, so it was not initially a variable. It was transformed into a variable with the term *blightedness*, which was expressed in quantitative terms.

As the above examples illustrate, it is usually not very difficult to translate concepts into variables, and it is important to do so because research typically involves searching for relationships – for example, between the age of neighborhoods and their degrees of blightedness or between the availability of on-street parking and automobile ownership – and relationships presuppose variables. Constants cannot be related to each other. By definition, they do not vary, hence they cannot vary in relation to each other. Concepts and variables will be further discussed, at length, in the following chapters.

Induction and deduction

Deduction in any context typically involves reasoning from the more abstract to the more concrete. It could, for example, describe the work of a criminologist who follows a theory describing what type of people commit murder and how they carry it out. The criminologist could deductively apply this theory to a particular murder scene in order to try to solve the crime. *Induction* involves reasoning in the opposite direction and could describe a detective at the scene of a murder collecting evidence. From the observed evidence, the detective could build a theory of how the crime occurred and what sort of person might have committed it. Sherlock Holmes, from this vantage point, was more a master of induction than deduction.

As we are using the terms here, inductive and deductive reasoning correspond with the different starting points in moving between research and theory. *Inductive*, or "bottom-up," reasoning begins with the observation of a concrete event (e.g. this old neighborhood has a lot of abandoned buildings) and attempts to generalize from the specific observation to a more inclusive concept (e.g. blight) or to a more general pattern (e.g. older neighborhoods are more blighted). Thus, induction describes the movement from research to theory. *Deductive*, or top-down, reasoning goes in reverse. It begins with a theory (or concept) and attempts to find appropriate observations or events that will test the explanatory power of the theory (or the applicability of the concept). Could a theory of neighborhood stages be reasonably examined by observing the number of abandoned buildings? Thus, deduction describes the movement from theory to research.

Over the long term, as we have noted, research and theory mutually impact each other. Correspondingly, induction eventually tends to lead to deduction, and vice versa. The detective inductively building a theory of what sort of person could have committed a crime will later deductively apply it to determine who is the guilty party. However, despite the ongoing interplay between research and theory involving both induction and deduction, it is also true that some research designs are more aligned with either induction or deduction, as we will note in the following chapters.

Research designs: An overview and preview

A research design can be thought of as an all-encompassing strategy for conducting a research project. While it involves a blueprint for every aspect of the entire study, for ease in presentation, designs can be divided into three major components which involve how the investigator is going to: approach the topic, collect the data and then analyze them. (Do not be confused by the plural reference to data as "them." Data are plural, though they are sometimes referred to improperly. The singular is datum.)

Approaching the topic

A basic choice to be made here concerns whether the topic to be examined will be thoroughly defined (and operationalized) before any data are collected, or whether the investigator expects clarification to emerge, piecemeal, after data collection has begun. The latter strategy is employed when the phenomenon of interest is not yet well understood, and the investigator wants to explore and begin to describe how it occurs or how it is manifested. This type of research starts with the careful selection of a site, chosen because it provides a good place to study the phenomenon of interest. So, a street corner in a low-income city neighborhood might be a good place to go in order to study street gangs.

With this type of exploratory study, investigators assume that definitions of terms, hypotheses and possibly even a theory, may later emerge from their observations; in other words, inductively. As they become more familiar with a research site, investigators may develop and distribute a questionnaire, search for documents, conduct some natural experiments, or the like. However, the researcher will make these decisions, based upon what seems relevant at the time, as the research process unfolds. The creative selection of specific methods and techniques, after an investigation has begun, is sometimes referred to as *bricolage*.[8]

By contrast, many research projects begin with a fully developed blueprint, though everyone recognizes that changes in circumstances or preliminary findings may require some modifications of the design. These are deductively developed research designs. They typically begin with a theory whose key concepts are operationally defined. Testing this theory while creating new knowledge are the twin objectives of these deductive inquiries.

At the onset of a deductive design, an investigator also selects a primary method of data collection, such as: a sample survey, an experiment, or the like. The appropriateness of the method as a way of testing the theory is the main criterion in the selection. (Some illustrations follow below.) Quantitative or qualitative analysis is typically the last part of the deductive research design, and from within those categories, investigators also tend to select in advance the particular mode of data analysis that will be employed.

Data collection

A wide range of data collection choices are available to a researcher, though the nature of the research question to be investigated often suggests which would be the most appropriate. For example, if the objective is to explore and describe a part of a city that is not well known, then field work – immersing oneself in the setting of interest – may seem best. By contrast, if the investigator begins with an established theory, then an experiment might be indicated as the best way to carefully test a hypothesis deduced from the theory. If the objective of the research is to generalize about the attitudes of a population, to illustrate further, questioning a carefully selected sample may represent the best approach. It also sometimes happens that the data of interest have been collected some time in the past, for some other purpose, by an agency of a city government, or are included in a special census, or the like. If so, then primary data collection is skipped, and the researcher goes directly to data analysis, though the previously collected data must frequently be modified in order to be used successfully in the later inquiry.

Whenever it is possible, it is also highly desirable, within the same study, to utilize different methods of data collection in order to benefit from each method's relative advantages. In addition, the simultaneous use of different methods of data collection enables investigators to ensure that their findings are not an artifact of the particular method they employed. Each of the major methods of data collection, briefly noted above, are examined at length in the chapters immediately succeeding this one, and they are followed by a chapter that discusses mixed methods.

Data analysis

Data generated in a deductive design, frequently relying upon a sample survey or an experiment, are typically quantitative in form, or can rather easily be converted into numbers. For example, checked boxes showing how strongly a respondent agreed with a question on a questionnaire are typically given numerical values such as 5 (strongly agree), 4(agree) and so on. Such data are highly amenable to statistical analyses. In addition, the hypotheses being explicitly tested in a deductive design are often expressed in causal terms: one variable is thought to lead to, or produce, another; and to demonstrate such connections often requires extensive statistical analyses.

When an investigator is proceeding inductively, data are more likely to be qualitative, i.e. non-numerical, consisting of field notes describing the investigator's observations, or consist of photographs, recorded interviews, etc. Description of a social context tends to be emphasized over testing causal hypotheses, and analysis often takes the form of creating qualitative categories, such as noting when some phenomenon occurs (day, night, after meals), where it occurs (homes, stores, street corners), and so on. These categories may later be amenable to some forms of statistical analysis, but that is not typically of importance to these research projects, unless they are being conducted as pilot studies.

This is a book about research methods, and as such it will emphasize modes of gathering data, and ways of assessing their value, rather than techniques of data analysis. As we have noted, however, data collection and data analysis are linked in a number of ways, and their connections will typically be noted in the text, but not extensively

Introduction

pursued. A number of elementary techniques of data analysis are briefly discussed in several chapters.

PART TWO: RESEARCH ETHICS

Ethical constraints

Let us begin by noting what should be apparent: researchers are not exempt from their nation's criminal laws. Being engaged in a research project – even one whose results are potentially of great value – does not, for example, give anyone a license to break into people's homes to obtain personal information. Nor does it permit an investigator to abuse or deceive subjects in a way that would not be acceptable if it occurred outside of a research context.

Similarly, if subjects are asked to provide information about their past behavior that may have violated some laws, investigators are not necessarily able to prevent disclosure which could lead to the prosecution of those subjects, even if they were promised confidentiality by the investigator. In most nations, information provided to a researcher (unlike an attorney or barrister) is not legally considered fully privileged, and hence investigators may be served with subpoenas and forced to turn over subjects' questionnaires, observations of subjects or other research data. Where any privilege is accorded to researchers, it tends to be quite limited. Therefore, people doing research, whether they are students or professionals, must begin by recognizing the potential legal restraints under which any investigation operates.[9]

Apart from legal statutes that everyone in a nation must adhere to, there are also special ethical considerations with which investigators are obligated to comply. There are two major types of organizations that define what constitutes ethical conduct in research involving human subjects: (1) review boards found in almost all colleges, units of many city governments that conduct research (e.g. Departments of Public Health) and in many private research firms; and (2) principles of ethical conduct in research expected of members are also found in most codes of ethics formulated by professional organizations and societies.

Some of the principles of acceptable research practice formulated by review boards and professional associations entail proscriptive rules whose violations can result in the withholding of permission to conduct the study, or disciplining by the sanctioning organization (e.g. censure, loss of license, etc.). Other of the proposed ethical principles are better described as prescriptive norms that describe what an investigator ought to do (i.e. what is desirable), but violations of these norms do not usually entail punishments beyond the possibility of informal peer disapproval.

Review boards

In all English-speaking nations in which social research is actively occurring, most colleges and many city governments and private research firms have committees or boards that evaluate, in advance, all research involving human subjects, proposed by anyone affiliated with the college, city or firm. A few types of research can be exempt, such as plans to re-analyze previously collected data and some field studies in which there is virtually no interaction between an investigator and the subjects being observed, and all the observed subjects remain anonymous. Such exemptions are obviously quite limited.

While the review boards throughout the world all operate similarly, they do have somewhat different names. A few examples of units that review and evaluate research in universities include:

• Institutional Review Boards (IRBs) – in the US
• Research Ethics Boards (REBs) – in Canada
• Institutional Ethics Committees (IECs) – in New Zealand

Their typical operating procedure requires that an investigator fill out forms summarizing the proposed research project, and specifically describing how subjects will be recruited, the risks to which they may be exposed, and the way confidentiality (if promised) will be maintained. If there are unanswered questions about any of the proposed procedures, the investigator can be asked to appear before the review board and may be asked to modify the proposed research design. Until the approval of such a board is obtained, universities will not ordinarily permit an investigator to begin collecting data. In addition, government agencies will not consider funding a research proposal that involves human subjects if the design has not been formally reviewed. And a growing number of social science journals will not publish the results of studies whose protections of human subjects have not been reviewed.

The research projects of students, interns and other non-permanent staff are all typically subject to review by institutionalized boards applying the same regulations and procedures. Within colleges, depending upon the student's role and circumstances, a student planning a research project may be regarded as an investigator, and required to submit the same forms as faculty and other staff. Alternatively, when class projects are involved, the instructor of record may be the responsible party in the eyes of the college review board and be required to submit forms on behalf of the class, and monitor the way students conduct the research. In either case, students should assume that if their research projects involve human subjects, they will need to obtain some form of institutional approval before they begin to collect data.

Assessing review boards

The impetus to the development of contemporary review boards stems from some experiments conducted during the twentieth century that later were widely condemned as unethical. In the worst of these studies, ill-informed healthy subjects were injected with serums known to cause serious diseases, and left untreated in order to study the "natural" course of the disease. In other studies with the same objective, subjects who were seriously ill, but did not fully understand their medical condition, agreed for the sake of the research to forego prescribed medical treatments that may have cured them. There were also a number of social psychological experiments in which investigators, while not jeopardizing the lives of subjects, did treat them harshly, taking advantage of volunteers who agreed to participate without appreciating the kind of abuses to which they might be exposed. In other experiments, investigators pressured the subjects to behave cruelly to other volunteers, leading these subjects later to experience guilt and regret.[10]

On the plus side, there is no doubt that review boards have sometimes prevented researchers from exposing unaware subjects to the types of serious risks described above. These boards have also sometimes forced investigators to modify their research designs in ways that offered additional protection to subjects without adversely affecting investigators' ability to obtain the type of information that they desired. And some boards have allowed a degree of flexibility in their decisions by permitting exceptions to the usual standards when an objectionable practice was deemed to be vital to the research and appeared potentially to be offset by the substantial benefits that could result from the research. In such instances, boards attempt explicitly to estimate a risk-reward ratio in deciding whether to permit a questionable part of a research design.

Nevertheless, on the debit side, there is also ample basis for arguing that the routine operation of review boards has sometimes led social scientists to alter their designs solely to accommodate review boards, quite possibly to the detriment of their research. Such boards may even have sometimes discouraged investigators from undertaking studies that could have been of genuine theoretical or practical value because they anticipated review board opposition.

Pertinent data come from Toronto Sociologist Will van den Hoonaard's observations of research ethics boards at five Canadian universities, and his extensive discussions with both researchers and ethics board members and staff. His observations and discussions led him to conclude that the review process was typically *ad hoc*, lacking clear principles for determining how subjects might actually be affected by any practice in a proposed research design. The net result of these boards, he concluded, is a constraint upon research freedoms without much demonstrable benefit. Furthermore, the boards entail bureaucratic structures that are expensive to maintain, costing millions of dollars annually. The money could be better spent, van den Hoonaard argued, to support research rather than to bureaucratically monitor it.[11]

The harsh critique of ethics boards offered by van den Hoonaard may have been at least partly influenced by his personal research preference for inductive field studies. The proponents of such studies have often felt particularly disadvantaged before review boards because of the difficulty of telling in advance how such field work might unfold, and that is what such boards expect. In other words, they tend to implicitly or explicitly favor deductive designs. We will return to this issue later in the chapter in the discussion of informed consent. For now, it seems reasonable to conclude that review boards have institutionalized concern for the treatment of human subjects and served as advocates for subjects where otherwise there would be none – and those are desirable accomplishments. At the same time, we should recognize that the review process sometimes seems capricious and may adversely affect certain types of research.

Professional codes of ethics

All of the associations linked to academic disciplines (Psychology, Sociology, etc.) whose members are involved in social or behavioral research have codes of ethics, or statements of ethical practice, that contain normative statements meant to serve as guidelines for researchers in that discipline. There are also professional associations organized not about an academic discipline, but about a field of inquiry, such as market research or public opinion research, that also have their own codes that describe desirable research conduct. Unlike institutional review boards which tend to emphasize proscriptive rules (i.e. conduct that must be avoided), the codes of professional and discipline-based associations tend to be more prescriptive (i.e. emphasizing what is desirable to do). In addition, the review boards of universities, city governments and research firms are usually permanently in place and automatically activated before any data collection begins. Evaluations by committees of professional associations, by contrast, do not typically occur unless they are triggered by formal after-the-fact complaints.

Either implicitly or explicitly, students conducting research on human subjects as part of a course or degree requirement are expected to adhere to the standards of the relevant association(s) in their nation. So, if a US student was carrying out a project as part of a Political Science course, or designing a study that would be part of a Master's degree requirement in Political Science, then the applicable code would be that of the American Political Science Association. Across professional and discipline-based associations and across national lines, there are substantial differences in how deviant research behavior is sanctioned, but there are extensive similarities among the various codes of ethics in describing what is appropriate research conduct. For two examples of associations with well-developed codes of research ethics, see:

- The British Sociological Association's *Statement of Ethical Practice*.[12]
- The American Psychological Association's *Code of Conduct*.[13]

Subject protections

Both institutional review committees and associations' codes of research ethics tend to identify similar sets of issues or potential problems that any proposed study is expected to adequately address. The major principles that both associations and institutional boards typically focus upon include: informed consent, preventing harm to subjects, and the confidential treatment of data. Each is described below.

Informed consent

The first requirement concerns the principle of *informed consent*: potential subjects must be fully appraised of what will occur during the research, what risks they may be exposed to and then asked in writing, explicitly and voluntarily, to agree to participate. If there is any reason to suspect that potential subjects cannot adequately assess the consequences of participation (e.g. young children) or if potential subjects may reasonably fear retribution if they refuse to participate (e.g. prisoners), then they are considered unable to give informed consent, and review boards will not approve the research design. Special protocols may then have to be added in order to overcome the limitation. For example, the presence of parents may be required if young children are the subjects.[14]

For informed consent protocols to be fully implemented, the investigator must be clearly identified as an investigator. In most types of social science research, that condition is met. Subjects are explicitly introduced to an investigator conducting an experiment or taking a survey when data collection begins; but that does not typically occur when someone begins a covert field study. In covert field work, investigators often deliberately hide their true identities initially as they try to pass themselves off as someone who shares qualities central to the group being studied. To observe recovering addicts, for example, the investigator may pose as a recovering addict. A covert approach is chosen when investigators believe that disclosing themselves to be investigators, especially at the onset of a field study, would fundamentally alter how subjects behave. The activities of most interest to the research would be hidden from view.

Covert field studies that yielded valuable findings have focused upon how inmates were being treated by attendants in mental hospitals, how juvenile gangs formed in urban areas and how the police interacted with them, and so on. If the subjects of these studies – inmates, attendants, gang members, etc. – were initially and immediately told by an investigator that they were going to be studied, would their subsequent behavior have been unaffected by the presence of the investigator? Could the results of a study conducted in this way still be of any value?

A second requirement for the complete assessment of informed consent requires that an investigator is able to forecast, with reasonable accuracy, what risks (if any) subjects might be exposed to over the entire course of a study. Such information is typically available to investigators that are working deductively. For example, they derive, from a theory, some predictions about what will happen if subjects are exposed to a specific condition: not permitted to interact with others, placed in a room with strangers, etc. The theory, in other words, gives the investigators a basis for forecasting subject risk.

In most field studies, by contrast, the investigator is usually working inductively, and therefore is not certain what direction the people being observed might take and into what role this might place any of them. To illustrate, in Manchester, England, Sociologist David Calvey covertly studied bouncers: the men who were paid to guard the entrances to nightclubs. He passed himself off as one of them rather than as a professor doing research, his true identity, and he experienced a number of problems involving informed consent that he could never have anticipated (see Box 1.3).

In sum, there may be research projects where there cannot be full compliance with the principle of informed consent if the research is to be conducted. Many researchers who rely upon field work, and covert field work in particular, believe that institutional review committees and professional codes of ethics have not been sufficiently sympathetic to their special problems. They believe it has often been more difficult for them than for investigators conducting other types of research to obtain approval from institutional research boards.[16]

If an investigator receives special dispensation to begin collecting data without informed consent protocols in place, investigators are still obligated, as soon as it is feasible, to disclose their true identity and to explain the purposes of the research project to the people they

Box 1.3 Guarding nightclub doors in Manchester, England

Having been a regular customer at clubs and pubs, Calvey found himself fascinated with the role of the bouncers, and decided to covertly study them. He completed a brief training course and then contacted the agency that provided door staff for clubs in the center of Manchester. He had followed a strenuous physical regimen for years, so he looked the part, and was soon hired. He put on his bouncer's jacket and went to work, assuming the role of a bouncer. He had little idea, at this point, who would wind up being subjects in his research, let alone who might be at risk.[15]

One set of problems arose when, at work, he encountered students, or former students, who recognized him standing at the door. In order to maintain his relationship with the other bouncers who he was studying, Calvey had to deny that he was who the students said he was. In one case, for example, he insisted that one young woman – a former student – must be drunk. From what he could observe, it caused her public confusion and distress. Obviously, she had never consented to any of this. She did not even know that she had inadvertently stepped into a research project.

While working at a club or pub, he also faced a variety of other types of unforeseen ethical dilemmas. For example, he was often a witness to, or centrally involved in, bouncers beating up patrons and lying to the police, taking bribes, illicit drug sales, stealing from admissions payments, and so on. In these situations he had to act like one of the doormen or he would have lost their acceptance and been unable to complete the study. When he accidentally encountered doormen outside of work, he also had to continue to lie about where he lived, where he was working, even his phone number.

have been studying. They are expected, in other words, to provide a de-briefing to as many of the study's subjects as they are able to contact. With respect to openness and candor in relations with subjects, late is better than never.

Preventing harm

Unlike medical experiments, where the physical well-being of subjects may be at risk, social science research is more likely to cause stress, humiliation, or other forms of psychological discomfort. A field study of a community, for example, may disclose information about a local business that is embarrassing to its owners. The obligation of the researcher is to examine how any of the ways in which subjects might be harmed, either during or after the research, can be eliminated, or at least minimized.

To illustrate further, suppose an investigator wants to learn how local residents would feel about stores selling pornographic videos, sex toys and related merchandise in their neighborhood. A central part of the study could involve selecting people on the street and showing them pictures of what these facilities typically advertise in their front windows. Might this approach cause some of the selected people to be embarrassed or to feel uncomfortable? If so, the investigator's obligation is to figure out how their reactions could be elicited in ways that would minimize respondents' embarrassment or discomfort. The following alternatives might be considered:

- Present written descriptions of the front windows of the stores rather than explicit pictures.
- Permit residents to view the descriptions or pictures at home rather than on the street.
- Assign interviewers of the same sex as selected residents.

An ethical researcher is expected to design research alternatives that create the least distress for subjects while still permitting the objectives of the research to be accomplished. It is not always easy, of course, to decide whether the goals of the research can still be met with alternatives that may cause less discomfort. In some cases, it may be necessary to conduct a small pilot test that examines specific alternatives prior to the actual study.

Maintaining confidentiality

In some special cases, subjects are completely anonymous, that is, nameless and not identifiable. For example, an investigator might observe locations at which people are more or less likely to jaywalk, and record how many people cross a street against the light. Under this condition, maintaining confidentiality is a moot point. No information linked to a person could be disclosed. However, in most research projects, subjects may be identifiable even if their names were never noted, or were removed from any information they provided, because investigators may have their addresses, student IDs, telephone numbers, or the like.

Investigators often explicitly assure subjects that all information will be treated confidentially, but even when they do not, subjects typically assume that the information they provide to a researcher, or personal information that they permit a researcher to obtain from observations, will be protected from disclosures in which they could be personally identified. *Confidentiality* means that it will never be possible for anyone (outside of the research team) to link a subject's identity with any information obtained from or about any subject.

Maintaining confidentiality is obviously of particular importance when the behavior being studied could potentially create legal problems for the people who cooperated in the study; if they have been asked, for example, about substance abuse, selling illegal products or services, etc.[17] However, virtually any type of personal information that was not safeguarded could potentially be embarrassing to a subject or create difficulties in some relationships if others became aware of it. Therefore, strictly maintaining confidentiality is not only about keeping one's promise as a researcher, but is also required by the obligation not to do harm to subjects.

To maintain confidentiality, during the course of an investigation and beyond, the information provided by every subject must be kept in a secure location. Casually leaving questionnaires or observation sheets on a desk in an unlocked office does not qualify as secure. Confidentiality also requires that as soon as feasible an investigator will remove any personal identifiers from observations about a subject or information that a respondent provided. For example, in a telephone survey, a researcher may randomly dial telephone numbers, and interview selected respondents at each number. Even if the investigator does not ask the respondent's name, the respondent may be identifiable from the phone number. Therefore, as soon as possible, telephone numbers should be removed from the forms on which people's responses have been recorded.

Beyond eliminating such obvious identifiers as telephone numbers or addresses, maintaining confidentiality can also require that, in publications, an investigator does not fully describe a subject with unique personal characteristics with respect to age, race/ethnicity or the like. If the specific location in which the study was conducted is reported, descriptions of individuals with unique characteristics could make it possible for others to identify them.

Neutrality

The consequences of a research design for the well-being of subjects are usually more or less there to be seen, though people can disagree in their evaluations of the seriousness of the risks. Outside pressures on an investigator to alter a research design, by contrast, tend to be less visible. Within universities, for example, academic researchers may want to please the sponsors of the research, that is, the organizations that provided the funding, in order to remain in their good graces for future grants. Or they may be concerned with how a city agency with which their program is involved will react to certain findings. If the results entail implicit criticism of the agency, will it continue to take students from the academic program as interns? Similarly, if investigators are employees of a city or county agency, they may fear that certain results will upset the mayor or town manager, or their department head, and jeopardize their job security. Will a researcher allow these outside concerns to affect how the study is conducted or how its results are reported?

Absolute neutrality may be a hypothetical ideal because investigators are people, after all, and people almost always have values and attitudes that can exert subtle pressures on how they approach a study. Nevertheless, anyone conducting what purports to be scientific research is expected to be committed to the principle of maximum possible neutrality. That means, first, that an investigator prepares a research design according to what are currently considered to be best practices; and second, the investigator does not allow considerations of how any person or group external to the research project may react to alter any aspect of that design or affect the way results are reported.

An interesting case study of a situation with the potential to impose subtle – or not so subtle! – political pressures on a researcher is described in Box 1.4. It presents a very useful example of how an investigator managed to remain neutral, and suffer no adverse consequences, in changing the way his city calculated official poverty rates.

Box 1.4 Changing poverty calculations in New York City

Until 2008, the city of New York utilized federal guidelines to operationally define poverty in assessing the amount of poverty in the city and examining its geographical distribution. Then a new director of poverty research, Mark Levitan, with a Ph.D. and years of research experience, was hired. He believed that the relatively high cost of living in New York required a higher income than in other parts of the US for people to be considered above the poverty line. He also thought it prudent to take into account non-cash benefits, such as food stamps, that some of the city's residents received. Prior to collecting and analyzing any data for the city utilizing his new index, Levitan surmised that the new procedure would be likely to result in an increase in the number of people considered to be in poverty. The increase would be the result of adding to the poverty rolls many low-wage workers making too much to be eligible for most benefits, but not enough to afford the city's high rents and expensive medical and child care costs. The new calculations were also likely, he thought, to provide a less concentrated picture of poverty, that is, not only would more people and families be said to be living in poverty, but the poor would be seen to be spread more widely across the entire city.

Levitan recognized that his possible findings could have obvious political repercussions for the city's current administration, and he discussed the possibilities with city hall staff. When they heard that his findings might be interpreted as indicating that poverty had increased during the current administration because the new index would place more people below the poverty line than the previous index used, aides to the mayor were very concerned. They were even a little reluctant to inform their boss. Some feared that Levitan's research would become "a bludgeon to bash the mayor,"[18] with political opponents claiming that the new figures showed that the mayor's administration was responsible for an increase in poverty across the entire city.

Levitan was, of course, concerned for his job, but as a researcher he felt obligated to be politically neutral, and to examine poverty in the city according to the methods and measures he believed to be most appropriate. At his first meeting with the mayor, Levitan recalled that the mayor was not happy to hear that he would likely be reporting a higher rate of poverty, but the mayor did not try to alter the research. Levitan concluded, with relief, "I had the ability to put the numbers out with integrity."[19]

There is a happy ending to the story that goes beyond Levitan keeping his job. A few years after he implemented the new index in New York City, the US Census Bureau also began to utilize Levitan's model in conjunction with the previous formulas for calculating poverty. And as other cities became aware of the new alternative, it became more widely adopted. We should note, however, that this happy ending for both Levitan and his innovative procedures might not have occurred had he "surprised" the mayor with his new findings. By discussing the likely implications of the methodological change in advance, he was able to alert the mayor and his staff. This provided Levitan with an opportunity to calmly explain and justify the merits of the change from a research perspective before there was any political repercussion that might dominate everyone's attention.

Within most nations, some government agency designates a poverty level, and persons and families whose incomes fall below this cut-off are officially classified as living in poverty. In the UK, for example, individuals whose incomes are less than 60 percent of the national median are deemed to be living in poverty. Households and families are classified as below the poverty level based upon their composition (e.g. number of children) in relation to specific income levels. In the US, federal guidelines similarly examine household income in relation to the number of persons in a household to determine the number of Americans living in poverty. Most cities employ their nation's official classifications to assess the extent of poverty in their city, and they often examine the local poverty population in detail: where it is concentrated, its age, sex and racial composition, etc.

Giving back to the community

In order to successfully conduct almost any type of study in a city or one of its neighborhoods, it is often necessary for a researcher to receive the cooperation of many local groups and institutions. For example, some documents may be available solely at the discretion of the mayor's office or officials at the town hall; the support of neighborhood organizations may be crucial for any investigator hoping to gain access to meetings of community leaders; local leaders may be very helpful in publicizing a survey and getting residents to fill out questionnaires, etc.

While most people consider the support of serious research to be desirable, in its own right, it is probably not the major reason that local officials, organizations and residents cooperate with investigators studying their communities. More to the point is an expectation of some practical benefits; that is, they anticipate that the study will yield information that will lead to improvements in the functioning of the police department, learning in the schools, investments in neighborhood development efforts, or so on. Researchers typically promise such benefits when they approach representatives of a city or community they wish to study, and they are ethically obligated to make good on these commitments. Let us consider what that may entail.

For the city or community to obtain the promised benefits, investigators must make sure that they provide feedback from the study in ways that will enable local residents and officials to utilize the results. Mailing a technically written copy of the study to a representative of the local group is not ordinarily sufficient. City officials, community leaders, and the like may have difficulty fully understanding such a report, and they will almost surely have difficulty figuring out how to apply its findings in a way that will produce beneficial changes. In fact, if the written report is to be useful to the city or community, it may call for a different writing style in which the author becomes more of an advocate than neutral observer.[20]

Ideally, an investigator's feedback will enable the city or community to deal more effectively in the future with issues similar to those addressed in the study. To truly enable people means that that they will be empowered in the future to solve problems, without external assistance. So, if the investigator becomes a consultant to the city or neighborhood after

Introduction

the research is completed – which is not uncommon – the consultant's role should be temporary. The objective is to help people to implement the changes implied by the research findings in a self-sufficient manner.

The principle of giving back to the community is a key element in *social action research*.[21] This is a special type of research that entails a close partnership between an investigator and a community at every step. It typically begins with intense community involvement in the initial design of a research project and later focuses upon integrating the research into community building processes that the local community can maintain. Most urban research does not entail this close a partnership between an investigator and a local community. Action research also places greater emphasis upon empowering disadvantaged groups in the community. However, making sure that one's research contributes in some way to the well-being of the community that made itself available to be studied is an important component of the ethical conduct of most types of urban research, and not just action research.

Notes

1 The problem of popular media's presentation of stories based upon "pseudo-science" is discussed in, Massimo Pigliucci, *Nonsense of Stilts*. University of Chicago, 2010.
2 Thomas E. Kida, *Don't Believe Everything You Think*. Prometheus Books, 2006.
3 Zhan Guo, "Residential Street Parking and Car Ownership." *Journal of the American Planning Association*, 79, 2013.
4 For a review of various measures, see R.C. Weaver and Sharmistha Bagchi-Sen, "Spatial analysis of urban decline." *Applied Geography*, 40, 2013.
5 For a discussion of how people in different positions may have different views of an area's degree of blight, see Jose E.A. Gomez, Jr., "The Billboard-ization of Metro Manila." *International Journal of Urban and Regional Research*, 37, 2013.
6 The classic statement of this interplay, in Sociology, was offered by Merton, and his views have been widely followed in other disciplines as well. See the essays on the bearing of theory and research upon each other in, Robert K. Merton, *On Theoretical Sociology*. Free Press, 1967. For a discussion of this interplay in interdisciplinary research, see Allen F. Repko, *Interdisciplinary Research*. Sage, 2008.
7 What is referred to here as the faithfulness of an operational definition to a concept is technically referred to as the validity of a measure, and it is discussed at length in Chapter 7.
8 For further discussion of bricolage, see Joe L. Kincheloe, Peter McLaren and Shirley R. Steinberg, "Critical Pedagogy and Qualitative Research," in Norman K. Denzin and Yvonna S. Lincoln (Eds), *The Landscape of Qualitative Research*. Sage, 2013.

9 Some of the ways that U.S. investigators can proceed, in the absence of privilege, are discussed by Ted Palys and John Lowman, "Anticipating Law." *Sociological Methodology*, 32, 2002.

10 For a case study of subjects' distress after a classical social psychology experiment, see Philip Zimbardo, *The Lucifer Effect*. Random House, 2008.

11 Will van den Hoonaard, *The Seduction of Ethics*. University of Toronto Press, 2012.

12 The *Statement* is available on-line at: www.britsoc.co.uk.

13 The *Code* is available on-line at: www.apa.org.

14 The ethical and legal background of informed consent is discussed in, Jessica W. Berg and Paul S. Appelbaum, *Informed Consent*. Oxford University Press, 2001.

15 For further discussion of the covert field worker's inability to anticipate what subjects may confront during a field study, see David Calvey, "The Art and Politics of Covert Research." *Sociology*, 42, 2008.

16 See Tina Miller and Mary Boulton, "Changing Constructions of Informed Consent." *Social Science and Medicine*, 65, 2007.

17 See, for example, the discussion of maintaining confidentiality in substance abuse research in, Victor Garcia, "Binational Substance Abuse Research and Internal Review Boards." *Human Organization*, 68, 2009.

18 Rachel L. Swarns, "With New Formula, Unmasking the Face of Poverty in New York." *The New York Times*, December 9, 2013, p. A24.

19 *Ibid.*

20 For further discussion of how such a paper may differ from the conventional academic paper, see Jean McNiff, *Writing and Doing Action Research*. Sage, 2015.

21 Randy R. Stoecker, *Research Methods for Community Change*. Sage, 2012. See also, Ernest T. Stringer, *Action Research*. Sage, 2014.

Glossary

Bricolage: Methods and techniques are selected during the course of a research project as opportunities present themselves.

Concepts: Abstract ideas, or mental images.

Confidentiality: Requires that any information about subjects is completely separated from anything which could personally identify them.

Confirmation Bias: People tend to jump to conclusions as soon as they observe any evidence that seems to be consistent with their initial assumption.

Deduction: Working "down" from an abstract concept or theory to a specific observation or event.

Index: A measure which combines two or more separate indicators.

Induction: Reasoning from the specific, or concrete, to the general or abstract.

Informal Sampling: Characteristic of everyday life, where observations are not selected with deliberate care.

Informed Consent: Requires that subjects be fully appraised of any risks they may confront as part of the research project, and explicitly agree to participate, in advance.

Operational Definition: Specifies the procedures to be followed in order to measure a concept or variable.

Reliability: The consistency of a measure's results over time.

Role Constraints: People's perceptions and experiences are shaped by the role(s) they are in at the time.

Social Action Research: Community and investigator form a partnership in designing a study and translating its findings into practices that can be maintained without external assistance.

Validity: The degree to which a measure is congruent with the concept it is intended to measure.

Variable: Concepts expressed in ways that are capable of assuming different values.

Ethnographic field studies

Outline

- Terminating a field study
  - Disengaging

- Assessing data quality
  - Reliability
  - Validity

- Analyzing ethnographic data
  - Content analysis
  - Geographical Information Analysis
  - Conclusion: Reflexivity again

- Notes
- Glossary

PART ONE: HISTORICAL AND THEORETICAL BACKGROUND

The classic field study can be more or less equated with *ethnography*: the study of a group or society that focuses upon the point of view of the people being studied. This type of research typically tries to present a complete description of the people's attitudes and relationships, in their own words, to the maximum degree possible. Because most field researchers try to gain a sympathetic understanding of the viewpoint of their subjects, they have usually relied more upon rich descriptions than upon a quantitative (e.g. statistical) analysis. As a result, field study methodology is also closely intertwined with qualitative analysis, and much of the literature on field study methodology can be found in books and journals focusing upon qualitative analysis.

Field studies have also been very briefly described as "going native." That expression is inspired by the tendency for investigators conducting field studies to become part of the group they are studying, which entails adopting the attitudes and values of the group members. An interesting, though extreme, example is provided by Sociologist Alice Goffman's dissertation study of a poor, black, inner-city neighborhood in Philadelphia. She spent six years doing field work, many of those years living with "Mike," a local man who was a part-time crack dealer with a lengthy arrest record. When one of his friends was killed by a member of a rival gang, Mike wanted revenge, and went looking for the man he believed to be the killer, she drove him to a suspected location, then waited in the car for him while he hid in an alley with a gun in his jeans. She went with him, she later wrote, because she too desperately wanted revenge. And as she thought about that, she realized that she had become fully caught up in the inner city's culture of violence.[1]

Blending into the group being studied is important to field workers so that their presence will not substantially alter the everyday routines of members of the group. That lack of investigator-effect is not possible as long as group members remain conscious of the fact that an outside observer is in their midst. Any change in people's behavior that occurs because they are self-conscious about being studied is a methodological problem that is typically referred to as the problem of *reactivity*. In field studies, reactivity is largely equated with observer effects. In other types of research, where subjects are studied outside of their routine habitats, reactivity can occur due to any aspect of the research that leads subjects to modify their behavior because they are conscious of the fact they are being studied.[2]

Historical field studies

It is very difficult to identify where the first ethnographic, or classic field, studies were conducted. There are possible candidates in ancient Greece, for example, where philosophers examined the way their fellow citizens viewed spatial arrangements in their cities. In effect, they were combining Geography and ethnography, though both types of analyses were quite limited by contemporary standards.[3] Centuries later, reports that somewhat more closely resemble contemporary field studies could be found in the journals of explorers and missionaries who traveled to tribes living on islands and in jungles that were relatively unknown to outsiders. It was rudimentary ethnography due to the outsiders' very superficial knowledge of the natives they described. Understanding these people and their way of life was secondary to the visitors' other goals, such as looting their jewels or converting them to another religion.

During the middle and late nineteenth century, there were several attempts by journalists, ministers, novelists and others who would today be considered amateur Anthropologists or Sociologists, to understand some distinct group that was typically out of the mainstream of their society: people who were poorer or sicker, who were working in unusual occupations, or so on. These analysts self-consciously immersed themselves in their selected group's everyday life. To understand and describe key features of the group's life, from the perspective of group members, was one of their major objectives, though they only partially appreciated what that would require from a methodological perspective. Harriet Martineau's study was among the very first of these studies, and perhaps the best in terms of following a self-conscious methodology. A native of the UK, she spent several years traveling across the US in the mid-1830s. She examined America's social classes, gender roles, marriage and child rearing practices. Then she reflected upon how anyone ought to observe and make inferences when studying people whose customs were different from one's own. Here she emphasized the importance of investigators not letting their own values influence how they interpreted the behavior of their subjects, and to make sure one was not rushing to conclusions based upon preconceived notions.[4] Both of these principles are emphasized in contemporary field studies.

Of even more direct relevance to us, during the 1890s there were a number of ethnographic studies that focused specifically upon behavior and activities in an explicitly urban context. In the following paragraphs we will briefly describe the contributions of two of the more notable pioneers: Stephen Crane and Paul Gohre. They are a small sample from a large number of scholars not specifically trained as social scientists or as field workers who undertook detailed ethnographic projects in (then) contemporary cities and contributed further to the development of this form of inquiry.[5]

Stephen Crane, best known today as the author of the *Red Badge of Courage*, began his career as a freelance writer for daily newspapers in New York and New Jersey. One of his first lengthy projects was a study of people in New York City's Bowery, then an area that was dominated by homeless alcoholics, prostitutes, bars and cheap hotels. His objective was to discover the viewpoint of the city's marginal residents. Rather than pity or condemn them, Crane wanted to feel what they felt, and see things as they saw them. He hoped his writings would pull the newspapers' readers away from their comfortable distance from these Bowery residents and push them into the world of the down and outers.[6] He provided his readers with rich descriptions of their fighting, drinking and sexual behavior and captured many of their distinctive expressions and speech patterns. However, while Crane provided the detailed descriptions now expected of a field worker, and the objective of his inquiry – acquiring an insider's perspective – holds up well by contemporary field work standards, he apparently paid little attention to how he actually conducted the study. Correspondingly, he provided readers with few methodological details from which to evaluate the adequacy of his research methods.

At the same time that Crane was studying the Bowery, Paul Gohre was completing his theological studies in Germany, and reading popular accounts of the difficult conditions being experienced by the men who worked in German factories. What he read failed to adequately convey to him a feeling for what their lives were like and he decided to discover it for himself, so he took a position in a machine shop in his native Saxony. Gohre spent three months with the workers "as one of themselves," working next to them, going out to clubs to drink beer with them, joining them in their homes, etc. Like Crane, he provided readers with a rich description of the working-class circumstances of his subjects and how they viewed their lives.[7] He was more sensitive than Crane to the limitations of his sample and the (inadequate) amount of time he spent with them, but his publications also indicate that he was substantially less concerned with methodological details than would be expected today.

One of the many people in Germany who were influenced by Gohre's study was his good friend, the notable Sociologist, Max Weber. He and Gohre were not only close friends, but colleagues who together conducted studies of agricultural workers, and co-authored papers analyzing political and religious issues of the day. Central to their joint undertakings was their shared emphasis upon the importance of grasping people's subjective viewpoints, that is, of understanding their intentions and meanings. For Weber, this subjective understanding was the core of *Interpretive Sociology*: putting oneself in the place of others, and trying to fully empathize with the choices they are considering and the values that they are employing to evaluate those choices.[8] Interpretive sociology, as described by Weber and others, became an important theoretical framework for a later generation of field workers.

The Chicago School of Sociology

Between roughly 1915 and 1935, the Sociology department at the University of Chicago was the dominant center of Sociology in the world. That department trained more Ph.D.s in Sociology than the rest of the world combined, and its faculty published what was then the world's leading Sociology journal, *The American Journal of Sociology*, though it also contained writings by leading scholars from across the social sciences. The department's over-riding emphasis was upon the study of cities, and the faculty innovated and emphasized two research agendas in the study of cities: human ecology and field studies.

Human Ecology, as described by the Chicago School, involved an emphasis upon how the spatial location of people, groups or institutions affected their relationships with each other, and the principles that described how cities or communities grow. A similar emphasis upon the spatial distribution of human activities was shared by Chicago's Geography department. To illustrate, in his 1922 presidential address to the Association of American Geographers, Harlan Barrows – a University of Chicago Geography professor – claimed that Geography *was* the study of human ecology.[9] Although the Geographers attached more significance to the role of the natural environment than the Sociologists did, their

Ethnographic field studies

shared emphasis upon human ecology was the beginning of an enduring interconnection between Urban Sociology and Urban Geography.

The Chicago Sociologists' emphasis upon field studies led to quite an array of fascinating inquiries as faculty and graduate students maneuvered themselves into every imaginable social setting in the city. For example:

- Nels Anderson spent some years living in areas with concentrated numbers of hobos: men who continuously traveled and periodically joined up with others in areas called "hobohemia". Anderson dutifully recorded, in detail, their health practices, their songs, political views, and so on, and he lived with them so that he could carefully describe the cheap hotels they sometimes stayed in and the bars and missions that they visited.[10]
- Paul Cressey spent several years studying what was then a common urban enterprise: the taxi-dance hall. This was a ballroom whose patrons were men who typically lacked social connections because they were physically challenged or isolated strangers, or were members of low-status minority groups. These men would purchase ten cent tickets, each of which they exchanged for one dance with a young woman (called a taxi dancer). Often passing himself off as a patron, Cressey had extensive conversations with both dancers and their patrons, trying to understand what brought them to the dance hall, and what they believed they got from it.[11]

In Urban Sociology, field studies that built upon the pioneering research of the early Chicago School subsequently became a widely followed method; but that was less so in Urban Geography, or in Human Geography more generally. For example, at the turn of the twenty-first century, a review of leading journals in Human Geography indicated that fewer than 5 percent of the published articles relied upon ethnographic field data.[12] From a casual inspection, however, the number of field studies being conducted by Geographers during the past two decades or so appears to be increasing. For example, field studies seem to be more preferred by a recently growing number of feminist urban scholars in Geography, and there also appear to be a growing number of methods courses in Geography that emphasize fieldwork.[13]

The Chicago School's link with Social Psychology, by contrast, was strong from the beginning of the Chicago School and has continued to be so. The linchpin in this link was George Herbert Mead because he straddled both fields. Mead was a professor of Psychology and Philosophy at the University of Chicago where he taught between 1891 and 1931. His most popular offering was a graduate course in Social Psychology that was taken by students from many social science departments, resulting in

Mead's subsequently very broad influence across the social sciences. However, his course was explicitly required to be taken by Sociology graduate students, and it was in Sociology that Mead's intellectual legacy has had the most profound influence.

Mead's theoretical framework came to be known as *Symbolic Interaction*. This approach emphasizes the centrality of people's *social* selves, and how these selves are a product of social interaction, the social self being largely the internalization of the responses of others. Mead's colleague, Charles Horton Cooley, summarized this aspect of symbolic interaction with the notion of a "looking looking-glass self:" each person, like a mirror, provides a reflection back to the other. So, if others laugh at her jokes, a person thinks of herself as funny; if others quickly move away when he approaches, a person thinks of himself as unattractive, and so on. Symbolic interaction has provided a theoretical framework for a good deal of ethnography because the theory and the method are congruent in emphasizing how people's behavior is a product of the way they subjectively interpret social situations, and their place in these situations.[14]

British Social Anthropology

At the same time that Chicago Sociologists were studying hobos and taxi dancers, Social Anthropologists from universities in the UK were traveling to remote islands to study native social life, and were developing a parallel (though not identical) ethnographic methodology. The most important figure in these developments was Bronislaw Malinowski because of the way his own field work became a model for later Anthropologists and the fact that he was instrumental in personally training a sizeable group of young scholars who became the core of British Social Anthropology.[15]

Around 1915 Malinowski traveled from London to several Western Pacific Islands where over the next several years he honed his ethnographic skills. Of particularly lasting importance was his study of native reciprocity and exchange rituals. He described how only certain items went to people in specific kinship relations to the donor, and how they in turn reciprocated with only certain items. He concluded that no one gained in an economic sense from these exchanges, but from living with them, sharing their meals and engaging in extensive discussions and observations, Malinowski kept trying to grasp the meaning of these exchanges from the natives' point of view. (He described this method as participatory observation.) Malinowski ultimately decided that the natives regarded these exchanges as important obligations and that meeting these obligations was rewarding because it made one honorable in everyone's eyes.

When Malinowski viewed the rituals as a detached observer, he inferred that the rituals may have functioned to reinforce kinship bonds,

Ethnographic field studies

which were very important to these people's social organization; but the native participants did not typically recognize this more abstract function.[16] Malinowski went to some length to separate his own interpretation of the inferred functions of the rituals from the natives' own understandings, and this separation became one of the characteristic features of Social Anthropology and, to a lesser extent, Sociology. In both disciplines the detached, observer's viewpoint came to predominate briefly in the middle of the twentieth century, and the emphasis upon empathetic field work correspondingly declined. In more recent decades, however, the view of participants has again been accorded more significance, and it has encouraged more field studies because they are ideally suited to this objective.

The substantial influence of Malinowski, his students and followers was not limited to British Social Anthropology. It has had a continuing impact across the social sciences, particularly in establishing ethnographic principles that have become part of everyone's field work methodology. This influence was also not confined to the UK. It spread across the former British empire, and was notably strong in the US, which is where Malinowski spent the latter part of his teaching career in several American universities.

Illustrative of the many studies whose methodology continues to be influenced by Malinowski and his disciples is an ethnographic description of a contemporary scientific laboratory. Social scientists Latour and Woolgar spent a lengthy period observing and talking with biological scientists and engineers about their everyday lives in a research laboratory. At the end of the field work, when they published their findings, the researchers described themselves as having written an "anthropology of science," and referred to themselves as resembling "intrepid explorers" who had been observing "indigenous people."[17]

Historical summation

By the middle of the twentieth century, a number of approaches and strategies developed in different disciplines and at different times were combined into a set of more or less agreed upon steps for conducting field studies. The principles and best practices have continued to evolve, and have sometimes taken specialized directions in different social science disciplines, but the core was established. Its principal components included consensus about the importance of:

1) Studying groups of people in their natural setting, unaffected by the investigator to the maximum degree possible (i.e. minimize reactivity).
2) Interacting with and observing people over a prolonged period of time to provide an opportunity for a full range of events and activities to be observed.

3) Understanding and empathizing with the viewpoint of the people being studied; that is, developing an insider's perspective.

The place of theory

Some field research is designed, explicitly, to test some aspect of a theory; however, such theory-driven field work is relatively uncommon. Field work is not ordinarily employed to test hypotheses deduced from a theory. In that sense, it differs from a classic scientific model's view of the relationship between research and theory. Ethnographers are more inclined to work inductively, that is, to try to let theoretical perspectives emerge from their observations. Collect data first, theorize later. Within this inductive framework, however, field workers take a variety of different positions with respect to the role of theory.[18]

At one extreme, some researchers think it is important, prior to beginning a study, to deliberately avoid considering any theoretical perspectives that could influence how they proceed. Some even extend this ban to the previously published research literature as well. Their objective is to assure that they begin their study without any preconceptions, to the maximum degree possible. They want their findings to emerge, ground up, unfiltered by expectations, and for theories to build upon their detailed observations.

However, for field researchers working inductively there are some theoretical perspectives that frequently guide how they interpret their findings. The most influential theories of this type are probably symbolic interaction (associated with Mead) and Interpretive Sociology (associated with Weber). In addition, there are several other theoretical perspectives that address how research ought to be conducted. They are, in other words, theories about method. In the following pages we will describe the two most important ones: *grounded theory* and *ethnomethodology*.

Grounded theory

The approach to building theory that is probably most frequently followed by field researchers entails some variant of grounded theory. While it advocates for a highly inductive approach at the onset of a study, later in the course of a research project it involves a combination of inductive and deductive steps. The logic behind the grounded theory approach, and guidelines for following it in conducting research, were initially presented by Sociologists Barney Glaser and Anselm Strauss in the late 1960s. In the following decades, each published somewhat different revisions, and current adherents of the approach continue to suggest modifications.[19] We will try here to identify its key features.

Grounded theory prescribes that one begin a research project without any guiding theoretical framework. The development of an abstract perspective is, in fact, considered very important, but the assumption is that it has to be created later, directly from the "data" that are being generated. These data pertain to the researcher's observations about people and settings. Taking thorough notes or making extensive recordings while in the field is very important so that at the end of an investigation it will be possible to describe people's attitudes and behaviors in rich detail; and these notes are the raw data for analysis and theory building. If abstract perspectives were selected first, according to grounded theory, there would necessarily be a discrepancy between researchers' findings and their later generalizations about those findings.

Following Glaser and Strauss, the grounded theory researcher is encouraged to develop theoretical perspectives (i.e. concepts) by focusing upon how "incidents" that occur in the field setting are resolved. For example, in a hospital this could involve an unpleasant exchange between a nurse and a patient. Focusing upon this incident, the field worker tries to understand: the background, how both parties view their behavior, the actual interaction and the emotional responses of all participants. The researcher is also advised to note how the matter was resolved.

While the daily field work continues, the grounded theory researcher continues to analyze a wide range of incidents, while also trying to compare them, seeking to classify similar incidents into more abstract categories. (In a grounded theory approach, this is the core of theory building.) New data continuously are expected to lead the researcher to make changes in the conceptual classifications, however, and that process continues until such time that additional data no longer seem to warrant changes in the conceptual categories. Then the repetitive interplay between data and concepts ends, and the field work can be concluded.

It should also be noted that any study that begins without theoretically derived hypotheses and works inductively to formulate hypotheses and then deductively to test them – while data collection continues – is also considered consistent with a grounded theory approach. Therefore, a grounded theory approach is not confined to field studies. To illustrate, Patrick Jobes and associates were interested in seeing how the transition to capitalism affected the routine lives of ordinary people in a former Soviet-controlled nation, Romania. They decided to conduct interviews focusing upon changes in how people in Romanian cities handled the tasks of shopping for everyday products.

The researchers started by asking people what kinds of shopping trips they had recently undertaken, and how they had experienced them. From these initial interviews, they began to see differences among groups of people: the problems experienced by housewives in food stores, for example, seemed different from those experienced by students in book-stores. This led the researchers to broaden the range of people they interviewed, and then to formulate hypotheses about different groups. The researchers also began to notice what appeared to be similarities in shopping problems that cut across different groups; not having enough money, for example, seemed to be a common difficulty Romanians faced. In sum, while the study was ongoing, the researchers identified key issues as expressed by the people they were questioning, refined their data collection accordingly, formulated hypotheses, and eventually used the data derived from their interviews to test hypotheses.[20] Thus, while field studies typically follow a grounded theory approach, this approach is not confined to ethnographic field studies.

Ethnomethodology

The most fundamental assumption of ethnomethodology is that there are widely shared rules and procedures which people utilize to make sense of everyday situations. Although widely shared, these rules and procedures are not quite consciously held and as such are rarely verbalized. So, even though people utilize them in their everyday lives, they cannot readily describe or explain them.

The orderliness and repetitive patterns of social relationships, according to ethnomethodologists, are not primarily due to formal role requirements, codified laws or norms, or other attributes of a social setting that are external to the people involved. Rather, orderliness is actually created by the participants themselves, following tacitly understood rules and procedures. The task of the ethnomethodologist in any social setting is to discover how the participants construct these orderly patterns of social interaction. To illustrate, at some busy intersections near his campus, Kenneth Liberman watched how pedestrians, cyclists and drivers "negotiated" an order of crossing. He concluded that their informal arrangement worked more efficiently than formal constraints, such as stop signs at other similar intersections. Generalizing more broadly, he noted how in some Indian cities people would appear to swarm around a service gate rather than form a queue, but their unspoken arrangement worked just as efficiently as forming a line, or systematically taking turns.[21] Thus, in each instance, people in everyday social situations were seen routinely to collaborate in order to coordinate unscripted activities and create order, with little wasted effort.

To decipher how people routinely interpret ordinary circumstances and figure out how to act, ethnomethodologists have designed *breaching experiments* in which tacit social norms are intentionally violated. The founding figure in ethnomethodology is Harold Garfinkel, and he provided both the initial description of the approach and devised the first breaching experiments. To illustrate, Garfinkel instructed his students to go home and behave as though they were paying boarders: be polite, but impersonal. At the dinner table, for example, they would say things like, "Excuse me, would you please pass the salt?" This excessive formality at first astonished family members, then provoked them. They devised explanations for the strange behavior, such as: "You must be ill," or "You must have had a fight with your fiancé." In other words, family members responded to the student's violation of established family norms by trying to reconstruct the situation in a way that enabled them to put the disruption behind them.[22] Ethnomethodologists report that people tend to engage in this type of active reconstruction in highly diverse settings in which norms have been breached: in department stores when clerks are offered less than the marked price of an item, in public buses when young men who are standing ask older women who are seated for their seats, etc. In response to the breaching, people create "accounts" (i.e. descriptions or explanations) of the situation that enable them to surmount the disruption.

Although breaching experiments have produced insights, they can – as they are intended to do – cause disruptions. These can be very minor. Others are temporarily confused, for example. However, the disruptions can cause more consequential problems that are not always easy to anticipate. Thought and planning are therefore strongly recommended before one attempts to conduct such an experiment.[23]

PART TWO: CONDUCTING FIELD STUDIES

The first step in conducting a field study is, of course, to select a social setting that one wishes to study, then carefully to consider whether it is a practical choice. If there are legal barriers that limit access to the site (as in schools, prisons, etc.), can they be surmounted? In the absence of such barriers, is there a reasonable possibility that the people in that setting would be receptive to an outside investigator? One would like to know the answer to that question before investing too much time preparing a study. However, if would-be researchers make such inquiries before having given sufficient thought to the project, they may find themselves unable to answer questions about the project; and the premature inquiry may doom access.

In addition, the researcher should initially try to inventory the resources available in terms of time, money, etc. Do they seem adequate to conduct the study? And what about research skills that would likely be required to conduct the proposed study? Answering these questions may be difficult, and time consuming, but it is important to address them initially, or one risks wasting a lot more time later in a failed effort.

Reflexivity

If the preliminary questions can be answered in a way that makes the project seem potentially viable, then the next step that is typically recommended is a careful self-analysis. The objective is for the researcher to try to understand what she or he would be bringing to the people and the social setting to be studied. *Reflexivity* requires looking inward to become aware of, and sensitive to, the possible effects of one's own values, biases, past experiences, etc.[24] The contemplative researcher asks, "Why did I select this group or setting to study? How do I really feel about these people? Can I keep these feelings from distorting my observations and descriptions?" It is not certain that one can completely prevent these inner feelings from influencing what one sees and how one interprets it. However, failure to come to grips with these potential biases virtually guarantees that they will have an adverse effect upon the research project.

In contrast, during the middle of the twentieth century, as previously noted, many of the dominant theories in the social sciences assumed a "detached" view with respect to the people and societies they studied. They held that no direct contact with people was necessary in order to draw inferences about their motives and actions. In fact, the viewpoint of outsiders was often privileged, that is, given more weight than that of the people being studied. Correspondingly, many of the major research techniques that were employed – such as mailed questionnaires and the analysis of census documents – were highly congruent with a detached viewpoint. And typically associated with this viewpoint was the assumption that any biases the investigator might bring to a study could relatively easily be contained.

During the last third of the twentieth century, and continuing to the present, there has been a growing concern with the validity of detached researchers' conclusions. One of the most influential proponents of placing more focus upon the relationship between investigator and the people being studied was Clifford Geertz. Although trained as an Anthropologist, Geertz was strongly influenced by Max Weber's Interpretive Sociology, and viewed the relationship between investigator and "subjects" through this lens. He summed up the major problem with the conclusions of detached researchers by noting that there appeared to be a disjunction between the participants' experiences, as they lived them, and the written reports produced by detached experts that purported to capture those experiences.[25]

Being informed by ethnomethodology and Interpretive Sociology led many social scientists to emphasize field studies and reflexivity; with reflexivity not only entailing an inward-directed sensitivity, but seeing oneself and one's interactions with others as important components of the research process. This leads to a blurring of the distinction between the views of insiders and outsiders. To illustrate, in discussing relationships between Anthropologists and the Native Americans they studied, Edward Bruner noted that they are the same as people in every other relationship in that both parties "are co-conspirators who construct their ethnography together. . ."[26]

It is important to recognize that becoming a reflexive researcher does not just occur naturally once one is in the field. One must learn how, and some of the pedagogical exercises that can help to foster reflexivity are discussed in Box 2.1. This case study involves Geography students, but the same experiences would be helpful in fostering reflexivity regardless of students' majors.

Box 2.1 Learning to be reflexive in the field

Prof. Michael Glass teaches Urban Geography in the Urban Studies Program at the University of Pittsburgh. Part of his course includes a study abroad segment in which he brings a small group of undergraduates to places like Singapore and Malaysia. A major objective of the study abroad unit is for the students to become more reflexive, which he defines as understanding what they personally bring to the research sites and how what they take from these sites is constructed and shaped by their positions as researchers.[27]

Glass found a number of research exercises that seemed to be helpful to the neophyte researchers who would be working in a society whose customs and values were different from those of the society in which they were raised. In Singapore, two of the exercises were conducted during field trips:

1) The National Museum of Singapore presents the colonial and post-colonial heritage of the city in a series of walking paths that take visitors through different events. Each visitor must choose which paths to take and which exhibits to visit, so thinking later about the choices they made provided the students with a reflexive experience. The students were asked to carefully consider how what they brought to the museum shaped their choices and their subsequent emotional experiences.

2) The students were brought to two very different shopping areas: the first contained large malls carrying familiar brands and the second was an older retail site whose small stores offered fewer global brands. Both areas had a mix of tourists and natives. In each area, the students' assignment included practicing participant observation, focusing upon the composition of shoppers and how they utilized space. Then the students were asked to consider what routes they

had selected in navigating through each area, and why; and what they may have missed as a result. The instructor was particularly interested in having students grapple with what made them feel uncomfortable in either setting.

In addition to the field studies, there were two other assignments that were designed to encourage students to engage in critical self-reflections, and these exercises also appeared to be successful in this regard:

3) Research diaries: Unlike conventional field notebooks, these diaries described the process of research rather than providing a catalog of gathered data. Of special significance in these diaries were student reflections upon the situations they encountered in the field and how their positions as researchers could be affecting their observations.
4) The students collectively authored a blog that enabled them to share their reflections on Singapore and their research experiences with family and friends. This forum enabled them to consider their research experience in a more informal and more public mode. The collaborative nature of the blog also acknowledged the fact that the students were negotiating through the research exercises and related tasks in a collective way.

These exercises and assignments helped students to become better field researchers in the future, according to Glass. In addition, he believed that they also enhanced the students' understanding and appreciation of Singapore: the reflexivity-encouraging tasks enabled the students to go beyond a mere visual sense to engage with the very texture of the city.

Even if one is going to conduct field work in a more familiar setting, it is still important to engage in exercises that increase awareness and sensitivity because it is very easy in a familiar setting for old habits to lead one to overlook the potential importance of situations and events, or to misinterpret them by applying labels that do not fit. The objective is to work at looking beyond overt trappings and taken-for-granted meanings, and that is not easy to do. One exercise that helped a group of undergraduates in a setting which had been part of their routine and to which they had become accustomed, entailed the professors instructing them to visit the Student Union and other sites on their campus and to imagine themselves as visitors, seeing the sites for the first time. The students reported that the experience initially felt weird. Once they became accustomed to the newcomer-tourist-stranger role they were playing, however, they reported feeling less awkward, and that deliberately and self-consciously assuming the role helped them to concentrate on really looking at these familiar campus sites, and they then saw them differently than they had in the past.[28]

The participant-observer continuum

When doing field work, every researcher is to some degree both a participant and an observer. The balance between them can vary greatly, though. In some cases, the field worker is preparing primarily to be an observer who will not continuously interact with the people being studied. The assumption is that the researcher's prolonged presence will lessen people's self-consciousness about being observed, and that reactivity will therefore not be a problem. To illustrate, two British Geographers were interested in finding out more about Street-Pastors, Christian volunteers who go on patrols through public areas in large British cities overnight. They greet people, hand out bottles of water, try to help the people they encounter if they are drunk or ill, and convene prayer groups. The researchers went along with small groups of Street-Pastors, and observed their interactions. The researchers did not formally play any roles in these interactions. As they walked along with the Street-Pastors, the researchers would ask them about their reactions to the people they met, and at the end of a shift they would take a break together and discuss how the Street-Pastors experienced the events of the night.[29] The researchers were clearly doing field work, but primarily as observers rather than participants.

At the opposite end of the participant-observer continuum is a study by Asad and Bell. These two Sociologists wanted to learn more about how high school debate judges evaluated the formal debate competition between student teams. The competition occurs in rounds after which judges assign points, and explain their decisions. However, the judges are volunteers who receive relatively little training. To understand how the judges evaluated the debates, the ethnographers volunteered to serve as judges, and made themselves available for tournaments and league events. This enabled them to build rapport with league staff and volunteer judges. The researchers also attended league banquets, and met with league officials, all to get a better sense of the mission and role of the judges. From their participation with fellow judges, the researchers reached some conclusions about how the judges viewed the debates and the debate styles that judges valued. The judges knew that the Sociologists were conducting a study, but they also fit comfortably into the judges' routines as participants.[30]

Gaining access

Gaining access to study any particular group is almost never easy. Exactly how this will be accomplished depends upon whether the proposed research site is part of a formal organization. If it is not, then physically gaining access is not typically a problem. For example, Julie Kleinman spent hundreds of hours observing and conversing with West African migrants who regularly congregated in a large train station in Paris. She was interested in understanding how they created and maintained a social network in this large, busy and anonymous social setting.[31] She just entered the train station like everyone else. However, while anyone is free to enter a train station, or approach a group hanging around a street corner, that does not mean that the group will be amenable to being observed, especially by a person they (initially at least) consider to be an outsider.

If the group to be studied is part of a formal organization, such as a school, hospital or prison, the would-be investigator will typically have to begin the process of negotiating access with *gatekeepers*, that is, people who have the power to control who gets the right to enter. Their authority may lie in a formal title, such as principal of a school, or it may be more informal, such as the person most admired by a group that hangs around a street corner. In any case, the field researcher should expect to have to negotiate with the gatekeeper. The researcher may have to agree to put certain issues out-of-bounds, and not pursue them. There may also be limitations on what information can later be publicly presented.[32] If gatekeepers have control over a researcher's ability to enter a site and their demands are too great, the researcher may simply have to seek a different site.

The above discussion presumes that the researcher discloses his or her identity in advance, as is typically required in informed consent protocols (see Chapter 1). If the study is to be conducted in a formal organization, such as a school or prison, immediate disclosure is likely to be necessary in negotiating with a gatekeeper. When the research site involves public space in a neighborhood, people's private homes, a public bar, or the like, then there is the possibility of covert access, or at least, of delaying disclosure until after initial contacts are made informally. (The ethical issues involved are also discussed in Chapter 1.)

Investigators may also have access to a group based upon their past experiences or past group memberships. For example, Derek Roberts was interested in studying people who voluntarily modify their bodies with tattoos or piercings. He had been, for some years, a member of an on-line community accessible only to registered users who, as a prerequisite, must have modified their bodies. He had an insider's perspective before he began to observe and interview members of this on-line community. Roberts described his methodology as "virtual ethnography," and as an insider he could employ it without any barriers to accessing the body modification subculture.[33]

More typically, ethnographers are interested in studying groups with which they were not previously affiliated, and if the background and/or

Ethnographic field studies

personal attributes of the investigator differ from those of the group to be studied, access can be difficult. An illustrative experience is provided by the graduate student research conducted by the now prominent Urban Sociologist, Loic Wacquant. He was born and raised in France, then came to the University of Chicago to pursue a graduate degree. Living near the edge of the black ghetto that surrounded the university, and working with faculty members who had written extensively about ghetto life, Wacquant decided to study it first-hand. His middle-class upbringing, French background and white skin set him far apart from the people he wanted to study, but nevertheless he began to search for "an observation point from which to scrutinize . . . up-close the everyday life of the black American ghetto."[34]

He spent months looking for this point of entry, until a friend took him to a local gym where young black men were training to be boxers. Although he had never boxed before, he joined them in training, working hard every day to learn this new set of skills. For the first months he absorbed a lot of physical beatings in the ring, but he learned the ropes and eventually could hold his own, even with the best local boxers. This earned him their trust and friendship both inside and outside of the gym, and he eventually spent the next couple of years accompanying his new friends on shopping trips and picnics, to church services, pool halls, taverns, funerals, weddings, etc. He became one of them: "Brother Louie."

The researcher's personal attributes – age, gender, race, etc. – can always influence ease of access. The attitudes or lifestyles implied by a researcher's demeanor, type of clothing, jewelry, or the like can also either create or lift barriers. Typically, the greater the difference between the researcher and members of the group to be studied, in ways that group members consider significant, the more barriers to access a researcher is likely to encounter, regardless of whether there is a formal gatekeeper.

To illustrate, Jaime Waters was interested in studying "older" adults (over age 40) who were "hidden" users of illegal drugs, meaning they had no contact with the criminal justice system or treatment agencies. He suspected there might be a large number of them in British cities, but prior research had largely ignored them in favor of studying younger drug users. Waters spent two years trying to locate and then talk to people who fit his criteria, but managed to interview only nine of them, despite his impression that their numbers were sizeable. He wondered why. Of course, potential respondents were interested in keeping their drug use hidden, and worried about how disclosure might affect their jobs, friends and families. However, he also concluded that differences between his overt personal characteristics and those of potential participants probably also played an important role. Waters was a foreign national; most of them were not. He was also about one-half of the age of many of the people he wanted to study. These differences, he concluded, likely made them suspicious, interfering with his ability to establish trusting relationships with them.[35]

Personal attributes, such as age, gender or race, are not ordinarily subject to much alteration. If these attributes separate investigators from groups they wish to study, there may not be a lot that can be done. However, attributes that reflect attitudes, values and lifestyles also matter, and they are usually much more mutable. Field researchers must, therefore, consider how they might prepare and rehearse a presentation of self that will be attractive to the group they wish to study. They also need to be attentive to, and ready to pick up on, clues when they first meet members of the group to be studied. Harrington describes this process as "informed improvisation."[36] Note, this is not advising field workers to try to fake an identity to gain access, but to be ready to share genuine experiences that can emphasize commonalities between them and people in the group they wish to study.

Obtaining access is obviously an important practical problem for the field researcher. However, when multiple sites are involved, differences in ease of access can also provide researchers with potential information about the groups or communities they wish to study. How one field researcher turned these differences in ease of access into a useful source of data is described in Box 2.2.

Box 2.2 Accessing sexuality-based women's enclaves

Japonica Brown-Saracino wanted to do field work among, and interview, women in lesbian, bisexual or queer (LBQ) enclaves. She also wanted to conduct this study in three small cities, in different regions of the US When she encountered substantial differences in ease of access in the three cities, she later examined potential reasons for the differences, and found they shed further light on LBQ enclaves.[37]

In the first community she visited, Brown-Saracino tried to locate women who considered themselves LBQ in a lesbian bar, at private parties, and so on, but none of her initial attempts were very successful. She did finally find two women who were willing to talk with her, but they would not refer her to other possible informants. Slowly, with much effort, she found a few additional women, but even then most were not willing to have her interview them in their own homes and many were unwilling to talk to her at any length unless their partners (who did not participate) were also present. Given the reluctance and cautiousness of the women she initially encountered, Brown-Saracino was worried about whether her project was going to be feasible as she moved on to the second research site.

Brown-Saracino's access to LBQ women in the next city turned out to be dramatically easier, though. She found women to interview in a number of social groups, and they readily referred her to their friends. She was soon invited to a number of lesbian organized activities, such as gay bingo, potluck suppers and dance parties, and in each of these events she continued to find additional women willing to be included in the study.

Site three also turned out better than expected, based upon her experience in the first city. Her first interview at this site led to an invitation to attend a party whose guests included a number of LBQ women who were eager to be helpful. One of them even posted a notice about the research project on Facebook, and that led to a large and enthusiastic response from potential local subjects.

To try to explain the differences, Brown-Saracino began by examining the socio-demographic characteristics of the LBQ women in each city's sample. She found that their educational levels, ages, race, and so on did not appear to vary substantially across the three cities. However, when she looked at the identities that informants revealed and the corresponding characteristics of their networks, then consistent differences appeared to emerge. Most strikingly, in the first city – where access was by far the most difficult – Brown-Saracino's findings indicated that most of the women in the sample did not regard their sexual preferences as critical to their social identities. They viewed themselves in more eclectic ways. As one woman put it, I am a lesbian, but I am also Asian, a musician, and so on. In the latter two sites where access was easier, by contrast, women's sexualities tended to be more central to their identities, and this probably was what made them more comfortable about participating. Correspondingly, women in these latter two cities were also more likely to belong to LBQ groups and organizations, so news about the new researcher in town spread quickly; and the LBQ networks in these cities were more receptive and welcoming of newcomers.

Sampling

There are a variety of strategies that field researchers can employ in building a sample of people to be interviewed, places to be observed, or the like. Relying solely upon what is convenient – for example, who happens to come by – is not a valid alternative if one hopes to generalize to any population beyond the specific individuals studied. One may be able to devise a sampling strategy before beginning the study, or it may have to wait until the investigator is more familiar with the people and setting being studied. Whenever it is devised, however, it is important to make sure that the strategy will throw a sufficiently broad net over the potential sample.

Day and time sampling

Researchers, where possible, should systematically vary the days and times in which they observe and/or interview. During some weeks, this could mean the researcher is in the field on Monday and Thursday mornings, Tuesday and Saturday afternoons, Wednesday, Friday and Sunday evenings. In other weeks, the researcher might be in the field on Monday and Wednesday evenings, Tuesday, Friday and Sunday mornings, and so on. This can be varied from week to week until all combinations of days and times are systematically included.

On the other hand, there may be no need to be in the field on certain days and times; for example, if one is doing fieldwork in churches or bars. And the routine rhythms of the people or events being studied may suggest a special mode of sampling days or times. In a field study of a hospital or police department, for example, the sample units might correspond with personnel shifts. However, the precise days and times to be sampled might depend upon natural rhythms that occur at the research site, and then a sampling strategy might have to wait until the investigator is more familiar with the site.

Spatial sampling

In some cases, the field researcher might want to set up a systematic way to sample by spatial location, in addition to days and times. That can be important if certain activities or patterns of interaction correspond with particular places in the study area. In some cases, it is possible for the researcher, prior to entering the field, to obtain an overall map of the study area; for example, if the study area is a demarcated neighborhood, a college campus, or the like. If no map is available, the fieldworker may be able to create one by walking through and around the area, and this is a recommended activity in any case. After obtaining or preparing a map, one simple way of creating geographical subareas to be sampled is to superimpose a grid of regularly spaced horizontal and vertical lines completely across the study area. Each subarea can be labeled or numbered, and checked off once the researcher has visited it.[38]

An interesting alternative is to utilize the participants to create their own maps of the study area. This has the advantage of producing spatial configurations that correspond with subjects' mental images of a place. To illustrate, in a study of young homeless people in London, Emma Jackson asked them to "draw your London." Many of the young

Ethnographic field studies

people meticulously drew in the places that were most important to them, such as bus stops, welfare agencies and youth hostels. She also found that most of their maps divided the city, and the places of importance to them, into a series of bounded areas.[39] With information of this type, a researcher could set up a plan for systematically observing or interviewing homeless people within these bounded areas.

There are some field studies in which a spatial referent would not facilitate the collection of cases; for example, the physical area being examined may be too small for spatial sampling to be meaningful as in Wacquant's study of a boxing gym. Systematically varying one's field work activity by time of day and day of the week, however, is almost always practical and worthwhile in field studies.

Snowball / Respondent-driven sampling

In field studies, one commonly employed means of creating a sample is referred to as *snowball* sampling. It usually begins when the field worker makes an initial contact with a member of the group to be studied, or a non-member who has access to the group. An example would be the neighborhood man that Wacquant met who took him to the local boxing gym. From such initial contacts, the field worker looks for referrals to others who are in the targeted group, piggy-backing from one to the next. The circle grows wider as the field worker meets the friend's friends and then the friends of the friend's friends, etc. The sample accumulates rather like a snowball being rolled in the snow, hence its name. Creating a snowball sample heavily depends upon the ingenuity of the researcher, and it can be very time consuming.

Note that this mode of acquiring a sample presupposes that members of the targeted group have ongoing social relationships with each other or that they are, at least at certain times, in close proximity to each other. Otherwise, it will not be possible for the field worker's referrals or contacts to accumulate. It also means that someone who shows the characteristics of interest to the researcher, but who happens to be an isolate, is not likely to be included in the sample.

While many field work samples are most likely to be of the snowball variety, snowball samples are not confined to this mode of gathering data. They are sometimes used in sample surveys when the targeted group has very few members or its members are very difficult to locate. Examples could include members of very small religious organizations, undocumented workers, members of racist hate groups, or so on. When snowballing is used in sample surveys, however, at some point the relations among members of the target group are often statistically examined in order to assess the representativeness of the final sample.[40] When the adequacy of the sample is formally tested in this way, the procedure is more likely to be referred to as respondent-driven sampling (RDS) than as snowball sampling. (RDS is discussed, in detail, in Chapter 4.) In most field studies, by contrast, the adequacy of the snowball sample is not statistically assessed, though that does not mean that it is of no concern as we note below.

Consequences of point of access

The point at which a fieldworker gains access to a group can be very consequential because it can strongly influence who within a large group the investigator gets to know best. Viewed from afar, a group of people different from oneself can initially appear homogeneous. A male investigator may not initially recognize the variations within a group of women; a researcher who is straight may not be sensitive to the cleavages within a gay community, and so on. Outsiders may, therefore, erroneously conclude that who they first get to know does not matter very much. In fact, however, any point of entry can lead a researcher to one particular segment of a group or organization, and getting close to it may limit contacts with other segments.

To illustrate, Wacquant's acquaintance with a man who boxed in the local gym led him to a sample that did not include many women from the local community. If he would have relied upon this fieldwork as his access into the entire community, as he initially intended, it would have ultimately provided a distorted picture. Would anyone want to assume that the women's perspective on everyday life in their community was the same as that of the men's? Or that all groups of local men shared the outlook and experiences of those who trained in the boxing gym? (In fact, his later field work accessed ghettos from diverse points of entry.)

Mitchell Duneier proposes that after investigators conduct field studies they should imagine themselves standing trial for "ethnographic malpractice." In this hypothetical trial, witnesses who represent "inconvenient truths" would be called to testify. These are representatives of segments of the group the fieldworker overlooked or gave short notice to, and at this trial they would present the information about themselves that the investigator failed to note. To illustrate, Duneier described a classical anthropological analysis of Balinese cockfights. The Anthropologist's access to the Balinese community began in a meeting with the village chief and his wife, and this couple introduced him to their circle of friends and acquaintances. Duneier would be willing to wager that the final sample of people the Anthropologists studied did not include many poor villagers without important connections.[41]

To avoid being guilty of ethnographic malpractice, Duneier recommends that, while still conducting the field work, the investigator ask: Are there people in the community I studied who, if brought before this imaginary court, would claim to be overlooked? If so, then the investigator's task is to select an "inconvenience sample," that is, a group of people whose perspective may run counter to that of the group whose viewpoints and experiences provided the core of the investigator's conclusions.

Following the principles advocated by Duneier also suggests that ethnographers systematically look for evidence of activities that run counter to their thesis. To illustrate, Marco Garrido spent one year in Manila studying the ways that residents of villages and slums in the metropolitan area maintained social distance based upon social class differences. His interest and emphasis was upon segregation, so he deliberately also asked informants if there were times when people of different social standing were sometimes incorporated in social activities. Garrido did this, he wrote, to correct for the possibility that his fieldwork was overemphasizing segregating practices at the expense of integrating practices.[42]

Writing field notes

While doing field work in most settings, a great deal of activity is occurring around the researcher. It is very difficult for field workers, even if they are highly experienced, to capture everything as it unfolds, and remembering fully what they saw and felt can be extremely difficult. That can create serious problems because good ethnography requires full information about social situations and rich, nuanced descriptions that convey people's moods and motives. Such descriptions sometimes require capturing people's exact words or phrases. However, few ethnographers employ any type of recording equipment and they usually avoid any conspicuous note-taking. They refrain from calling attention to the fact that they are studying the people they are with in order to minimize reactivity. In addition, and equally important, the "natural" face-to-face encounters between the field worker and the people being studied are an important part of the ethnographic experience. As Emerson and associates write, to fully understand and appreciate behavior from the participants' perspective, one must be intimately involved in their everyday activities.[43] From engagement in social interactions, the reflexive field worker gains insight into people's daily lives. Such engagement is impossible if the field worker is putting a microphone in people's faces or halting conversations in order to take notes.

Experienced field workers are often able to re-create, even many hours later, detailed descriptions of interactions as well as their sequences and conditions. After spending a day in the field they are able to return home and write lengthy and accurate notes on the day's events. This is a skill that usually takes a good deal of time to cultivate, though. For newcomers, it may be important periodically to inconspicuously withdraw from the field to seek a private place in which they can take some brief notes – often referred to as *jottings* – about conversations and events they have witnessed, and their personal reactions. Later that day, elaborating upon these jottings will produce a fuller set of field notes. Trusting one's memory and waiting until the next day to prepare these notes is almost never a wise option. Too much forgetting is likely to occur, and potentially important observed details as well as the field worker's impressions are lost.

Many field workers, especially if they are following a grounded theory approach (introduced earlier in this chapter), also try diligently to develop codes: words or phrases that summarize field notes or other information they have acquired, such as documents or photographs. The codes represent concepts the researcher initially thinks are important in summarizing the data. To illustrate, Saldana gives the following example from the field notes prepared by a researcher walking through a city's run-down neighborhood:

> . . . The great majority of homes here have chain link fences . . . There are many dogs with signs on fences that say, 'Beware of Dog.'

The descriptive code the researcher assigned to this set of notes was "concern with security."[44]

From past experience, field workers have typically found it helpful to separate their field notes into four specific categories, as described in Table 2.1.

The four categories described in Table 2.1 are useful because they remind field workers to make sure that their reflections and notes cover

Table 2.1 Field note categories

Category	Description of contents
Direct observations	Who the researcher saw, what they did, who else was there, what did each say, how were they dressed, etc.
Inferences	What seemed to be the moods of the people, did they seem different today, what actions did others appear to respond to, etc.
Concepts or codes	How can the behavior of people best be summarized, what abstractions seem to fit an event, an interaction, an incident, etc.
Personal notations	How did you, the fieldworker, feel today, how did you feel about your interactions with people and about situations you witnessed, etc.

Ethnographic field studies

all four of these areas, and that they try to maintain clear distinctions among the categories; for example, not confusing observations with inferences or personal feelings.

As the field work continues and the field notes are accumulating, researchers typically continue to regularly read and think about their prior jottings and notes. How do the most recent events cast a different light on earlier events? How do the codes developed at different times compare to each other? By immersing themselves in these notes and codes, field researchers continuously try to refine their theoretical insights by juxtaposing concepts and data. Remember: the congruence between concepts and data should be as close as possible.

Supplemental information

Along with their personal field notes, ethnographers typically seek other types of information pertaining to members of the group they are studying, the group's relation to larger entities and the setting(s) in which the group's activities occur. This can include materials provided by members of the target group, such as diaries, journals or e-mail correspondence; or it can include documents not created for the study, but nevertheless helpful, such as maps of the area or census-type reports. To illustrate, in the previously discussed study of homeless youths in London, Jackson kept the "draw your London" maps she asked the young people to prepare, and many of them also volunteered photographs of themselves with their friends and other personal artifacts. In Brown-Saracino's study of the LBQ groups in three cities, to illustrate further, she supplemented her ethnographic descriptions of the groups with socio-economic and demographic profiles of each of their cities. These data can provide depth or context that is very helpful in writing an ethnographic profile, and field researchers should always be on the lookout for such data that can either be integrated into field notes or kept as supplements.

Terminating a field study

There are a great many different types of triggers that can signal the end of the field work phase of a study. Many of them are external, outside of the control of an investigator. For example, funding for the researcher's fellowship may end and, for better or worse, the researcher cannot afford to continue the study without it. Or the researcher may be a student whose thesis advisor insists that it is time to get out of the field and to start writing. Or the study may require a research team, and if so, then staff have to be hired. That involves agreements containing end dates of employment, after which staff members move on to other jobs.

In addition, some field work is part of an action research project,[1] and external events may make its continuation impossible. To illustrate, John Lofland was involved both as a participant and an ethnographer when a group of local citizens tried to prevent the demolition of an historic hotel in a small California town. Like the people he was studying, Lofland wanted to preserve the old building; but unlike the others, he was also doing field work, observing the protesters, talking with them, taking photographs to add to his field notes. However, their efforts failed and one day when the protesters came to the site, they found that the old hotel had been taken down, and its former space was being paved for a parking lot. Then there was no longer a protest group to study.[45]

There may also be internal triggers that are within the control of the investigator. At some point, researchers find that adding observations and inferences to their field notes no longer leads to changes in their coding or conceptualizations. Their data and their theories seem both congruent with each other and unchanging. They could continue to do field work, but it seems apparent they will experience diminishing returns from any future efforts.

Disengaging

After an extended period of very frequent contact, field researchers typically form attachments to the individuals they are studying, to the site, and sometimes to the way of life associated with the people and the site. To illustrate, consider Wacquant's feelings after he had spent years immersed in the daily lives of people that revolved around boxing and the gym near the University of Chicago. He was so fully involved that when he finally finished his graduate studies and was otherwise ready to move from Chicago to pursue his academic career, he felt anguish at leaving his friends and the local gym. He described himself as having been totally "seduced" by that life.[46] At that moment, a conventional academic career, by contrast, seemed meaningless and depressing. Of course, the people who were the objects of study may also feel strongly attached to the researcher who has become their friend and confidant, and they may continue to reach out to the investigator to continue the relationship.

Given the strong bonds that can form in a field study – and that are frequently considered a necessary part of good ethnography – an abrupt termination, even if anticipated from the onset, can be exceptionally difficult. As a result, extended disengagements are not unusual, and field researchers and members of the group that was studied sometimes remain in contact for a prolonged period of time, though such extensions are not ordinarily recommended.

Ethnographic field studies

The new field researcher is probably best advised to have an end date in mind at the onset of the study, and stick to it. That means cutting ties with the people and the place at either the previously established time or when the diminishing fruits of the research suggest it is time. The good-byes should be explicit so that no one expects the field worker to show up again, and even though the investigator may remember these people for a long time, he or she still ought not to return. One ethnographer who studied families in St. Louis said she wished she could maintain contact with some of them, but did not in deference to the study design agreed-to at the onset. Several years later she admitted, "I think about the people in the study often, and have thought about contacting them, but then thought the better of it."[47] There is a time to move on.

Assessing data quality

Some of the social scientists who specialize in field research contend that the only meaningful way to evaluate the data generated by a field study is to examine the research experience of the investigator. To grasp the point of view of others, a major objective of any field study, requires that one be immersed in their world. The field researcher's data – observations, inferences, and so on – cannot be considered independently of how the investigator participated in the daily lives of the people who were studied.[48] The quality of the data may therefore be inferred from the quality of the descriptions they enable the field researcher to produce at the end of the study. If those descriptions are rich, reflexive, textured and detailed then it is likely they were based upon good data, generated by the insight and understanding of an ethnographer who had been deeply immersed in the social world of the people described.

Another, and perhaps more direct, way to evaluate a field study's data might entail an analysis of a researcher's field notes and related materials. However, the jottings and theoretical speculations contained in such field notes might not be meaningful to anyone who did not share the in-field experiences of the investigator. So, who is to judge? One way this question has been answered is by turning to the subjects of a study, and asking them to verify the facts and motives attributed to them in the researcher's field notes. To illustrate, in a large ethnographic study, members of a research team studied low-income families in a number of cities. One researcher was assigned to each family, participating in daily activities and routinely conducting informal interviews. At the end of the data collection period, a local researcher shared a written report with each family. Then that researcher and the project director met with each family to discuss both the facts and interpretations contained in the written report. If family members disagreed with any parts of the report, they would present their view to the report's author and the project director, and they would of course respond. From the discussions that followed, family members sometimes came to better recognize aspects of themselves, and endorsed the content of the report. Sometimes a family convinced the researcher to modify some part of their report. By the end of the discussions, relatively few disagreements remained.[49]

How to share the data they have gathered and analyzed with other professional colleagues is an ongoing issue for ethnographers. More specifically, the problem they confront is how to present evidence and communicate insights derived from a field study in a transparent way that will convince readers who may be totally unfamiliar with the groups and settings that were studied. For some ethnographers, the task requires that they follow the model of quantitative social science, and demonstrate the reliability and validity of their measures in an analogous manner. They view reliability and validity as universally required in social science, so ethnographers are obligated to address them like everyone else. Other ethnographers argue that their method of research is an enterprise that is fundamentally different from other social science methods, and therefore its data are not subject to the same assessments.[50]

The argument over where ethnography fits has been around for a long time, and will not be completely resolved any time soon. However, the recent growth of mixed-methods research – which has often conjoined ethnographic data with quantitative surveys, experiments, or the like – has pushed ethnographers to again consider ways in which their method can accommodate the mainstream social science requirements of reliability and validity.

Reliability

As introduced in Chapter 1, reliability refers to the consistency over time of a measure, or measurement procedure. In an ideal situation, a concept of interest (such as blight in a city or group morale) would be measured in the same way, under the same conditions, at two points in time. The two times would be selected so that they were: (1) close enough to each other to prevent change in the phenomena itself from actually occurring, but (2) far enough apart to prevent contamination from the first measure. For example, if people remembered how they responded the first time, they may try to be consistent, and that would artificially increase the apparent reliability of the measure.

The ideal circumstances described above rarely occur in any type of research. They are especially unlikely in a field study because of the assumption that any interaction involving a researcher and subject in the field is a unique product of the moment. It cannot be re-created to permit

Ethnographic field studies

re-examination. As a result, some ethnographers think that reliability, as conventionally defined, is irrelevant to field studies.[51] Others, while recognizing the limitations, nevertheless look for alternative ways to assess reliability in field studies.

The most frequently employed alternative in field studies is probably *inter-rater* or *inter-coder reliability*, especially if multiple researchers are in the field. It entails having two (or more) people who are familiar with the measurement procedure independently assign a category or a numerical value to the same observations. To explain why this procedure is a reasonable alternative to assessing reliability over time, let us back up for a moment. Assuming a phenomenon itself does not change, why would two measurements over time not yield the same, or at least very similar, results? One important reason is because of random errors: These are typically unknown, unpredicted sources of variation. For example, if field workers wake up cranky one morning, they might be more inclined to consider a subject's behavior to be hostile than if they woke up smiling. That day's coding could differ from other day's. The more such random errors occur, the less will the results of two measurements be the same. So, perfect reliability could occur when there was no random error; and correspondingly, there would be no reliability if a measure was solely the result of random error.

Now, let us return to inter-rater reliability. If there is a lot of random error, the measurement will lack over-time reliability, and two coders, doing a rating at the same time, will have a low rate of agreement with each other. Phrased differently, if two raters at the same time cannot agree in assigning a category or numerical value to the same observation, then the error in the measurement will also prevent agreement over time. Inter-rater reliability is therefore necessary (but not sufficient) for reliability over time. So, if sufficient inter-rater agreement is obtained, the investigator at least has a basis for optimistically assuming the measurement will be reliable over time.

An interesting illustration of inter-rater reliability assessment in a field study is provided by the previously discussed study of how judges in inner-city high schools evaluate formal debates.[52] The investigators, a man and woman from different racial and ethnic backgrounds, both worked as volunteer judges, often as part of the same panel of judges. Given their different backgrounds, they were concerned with making sure their coding was congruent. While judges were offering their views on debates once they were concluded, each investigator independently jotted observations of their colleagues. The two investigators later met to share and explain their notes and observations and they continued the discussions until they reached interpretive consensus (i.e. inter-rater reliability).

Depending upon how measures or codes are expressed, there are a number of statistical assessments that can be employed to quantify inter-rater reliability. Chapter 7 contains an extended discussion of inter-rater reliability and describes the statistical assessments that can be employed.

Validity

As introduced in Chapter 1, validity refers to the congruence between a concept and an indicator; it shows the degree to which a phenomenon is "captured" in a particular measurement. To illustrate, the morale of a city's police department (concept = morale) might be manifested in the percentage of times that officers, in discussing the department, state "we" rather than "I" (indicator = we/I ratio). There are a number of procedures that are routinely employed, with some research designs, to assess the validity of such measures. To many ethnographers, however, the conventional means of assessing validity do not apply to field work studies because of their theoretical emphasis upon the field worker developing and sharing a subjective understanding of people's orientations.

The closest approximation to validity assessments in most field studies involves *triangulation*: searching for congruence among streams of data produced by different methods. To illustrate, are the implications derived from following people around and observing them the same as the inferences that follow from interviewing them? And are both of those sources congruent with the implications derived from listening to what others say about them? In the above example, do police officers whose speech involves high ratios of "we" to "I" also act as though they strongly identify with their department, say that is how they feel, and is that how they are viewed by their colleagues? The more different types of pertinent data the better, and of course, the greater the congruence among them the more validity is implied.

In experiments and surveys, a similar procedure involves looking for congruence among different indicators of the same concept, rather than among different data sources. For example, suppose an investigator thought morale was indicated by (1) a we/I ratio and (2) by members' attendance at voluntary police department activities. If they are both reflections of the same concept, then the two indicators ought to correlate well with each other. This type of assessment of measures, in an experiment or survey, is typically referred to as demonstrating criterion validity.[53] Note, though, that the logic underlying triangulation and criterion validity is very similar. Chapter 7 also contains an extended discussion of triangulation, validity and the ways in which validity can be statistically assessed.

Ethnographic field studies

There is also the argument made by some ethnographers that because field researchers directly observe people's behavior, their ability to explain people's behavior is better than that permitted by other types of research that rely entirely upon self-reports, for example, from interviews or questionnaires in a survey. Problems can arise from the fact that people's self-reports and people's attitudes can both be weakly related to their actual behavior. In the view of most ethnographers, people's actions are dependent upon their definitions of a situation, and those definitions are a function of concrete face-to-face encounters rather than people's reflections about how they might react in such situations.[54]

Because of the lack of congruence that often occurs between attitudes and behavior, if it is behavior that social scientists wish to explain – and it frequently is – then field work may be capable of attaining a higher degree of validity than studies based upon methods that do not rely upon direct observation (e.g. telephone interviews, self-report questionnaires, etc.). Box 2.3 describes a study that relied both upon field work and interviews, and shows the apparent superiority of what the investigators termed "naturalistic observations."

Analyzing ethnographic data

For many ethnographers, as we have noted, data analysis is on-going, conducted along with, and simultaneous to, gathering data in the field. And for most of these ethnographers, analysis is exclusively qualitative, consisting of detailed and nuanced descriptions and analysis of the people and settings in which they were immersed. For some field study researchers, however, data collection occurs first and when it is completed then the data – mostly in the form of field notes – are subjected to an analysis which can be either qualitative or quantitative. In this section we will briefly discuss a few of the major analytic techniques that have been employed in conjunction with field studies.

Content analysis

Content analysis is frequently utilized to analyze data generated in field studies. It has historically been used as a technique for analyzing almost any type of text taken from almost any source: field notes, historical documents, the media, communication exchanges of any type, and so on. The basic process entails utilizing a coding scheme by which the text is broken down into categories and sub-categories that can be based upon words, phrases, sentences or themes. The analysis can examine the frequency of the selected words, phrases, etc. or it can show the relationships among the selected words, phrases, etc. The analysis could be conducted by hand,

Box 2.3 Parenting: Attitudes and actions

In order to study social class differences in child rearing within a city, Annette Lareau studied a dozen families from diverse socio-economic and racial backgrounds.[55] She and her research assistants spent hours in each home observing parent-child interaction. She described their role as participant-observers engaged in the rituals of everyday family life. The researchers jotted field notes when they could and in a few households they also videotaped family interactions for later analysis. All of the included families had 9- or 10-year-old children when the study began. About ten years later the families were re-visited, giving the investigators an opportunity to see how the former 9- and 10-year-olds had moved into young adulthood.

With respect to parents' attitudes toward their children, Lareau found almost no class-related differences. For example, in interviews, both working- and middle-class mothers described themselves as engaged in "intensive mothering." Virtually all of the parents expressed deep concern for their children's current and future well-being. However, she found systematic differences in their behavior. Middle-class parents structured more of their children's time in organized activities, and almost never complained about the cost of sports equipment, musical instruments, or the like. They also tended to reason and negotiate with their child, regularly soliciting the child's thoughts and feelings. By contrast, the working-class parents gave their children more free time, but were more likely to impose strict rules, without negotiation. They were also more likely to remind their children of the family's limited resources.

Lareau found some striking differences in the middle- and working-class children which she attributed to the parenting differences she had observed. Most notably, she concluded that the middle-class children seemed to exhibit a sense of entitlement. They seemed both comfortable and assertive in their relationships with teachers, doctors, coaches and other adult authority figures. The working-class children, on the other hand, seemed to exhibit a greater sense of restraint. They worried more about the cost of things, and they shied away from interrupting adults more than the middle-class children did.

In her conclusions, Lareau emphasizes that she was able to infer, from observing everyday family life, class differences in parent-child interaction and how these differences affected their children's later behavior. Had she relied upon what parents told her in interviews, she would have missed these class-related differences. Why did the parents' descriptions of their parenting leave out these crucial items? Lareau's explanation is that they could not articulate these issues to interviewers because they were such taken-for-granted aspects of everyday life that they were not salient in parents' minds. In other words, it simply did not occur to them.

Ethnographic field studies

and until late in the twentieth century it was. However, content analysis is now available in one of a variety of software packages.

A content analysis can be designed to test a theory, in which case the categories and sub-categories to be examined are arrived at deductively, and the coding is determined by theoretical considerations. The alternative is an inductive, or data-driven, coding scheme, and this is how most ethnographic studies employ it.[56] If the field researcher followed a grounded theory approach, the conceptual categories to be examined in the content analysis may have already been ascertained by the time data collection is complete from the interplay between observations and conceptualizations in the on-going analysis of field notes. If that did not occur, then at the end of the field work, the field notes are scrutinized in order to arrive inductively at a set of categories to be employed in the content analysis.

To illustrate the technique, a phrase such as "blighted neighborhoods" – and/or the words associated with it (run-down, deteriorated, etc.) could be analyzed with the text taken from: field notes, daily newspapers, urban journals, etc. A content analysis of blighted neighborhoods would typically measure four qualities of the phrase in whatever text was selected:

1) Frequency: the rate at which the phrase appears
2) Direction: whether it is viewed or presented positively or negatively
3) Intensity: strength in a positive or negative direction
4) Space: amount of time or space allocated to the phrase

Depending upon what the initial findings of the content analysis look like, the investigator might pursue a variety of additional analyses; for example, the categories and sub-categories might be modified and re-analyzed; or blighted neighborhoods might be examined in relation to other key words or phrases, such as age of city, location of neighborhood, racial composition, or so on.

As previously noted, content analysis can also be utilized in dissecting non-textual materials. An interesting example is provided by a study of how Iranian cinema has portrayed urban spaces in the city of Tehran. The investigators began from the premise that movies can be useful tools for examining how a city's spaces and buildings are understood and interpreted because films teach audiences how to see and imagine their city.[57] For this analysis, the investigators selected a number of Iranian films that were set in Tehran and began by categorizing the kinds of urban spaces (alleys, streets, squares, etc.) that were used to establish an urban context for events in the films; then they qualitatively described the characteristics attributed to these spaces.

Ethnographic field studies

Geographical Information Analysis

A Geographic Information System (GIS) is a computer-backed system that both stores and analyzes many types of data, but is designed primarily to include geospatial data. GIS applications enable a user to create and edit maps, analyze and model spatial data. They are also routinely used by city officials and administrators to help resolve a wide range of problems or questions. For example, they may want to utilize a GIS system to identify what, based upon multiple variables (such as local population density, people's age distributions, etc.) would be the best location for a new park or subway entrance.[58] In addition, the system can also handle highly diverse types of qualitative data, including photographs, audio files, texts, etc. This makes GIS useful to an ethnographer who wants to place qualitative information about the target study group (observed in the field) into a detailed spatial context.

To illustrate the potential value of coupling GIS analysis with ethnography, consider a study of low-income families in neighborhoods in three cities conducted by a research team comprised of Sociologists and Geographers. The ethnographic component of the study involved field researchers' observations and interviews that covered: family routines, housing, health care, residential moves, employment history, etc. The field workers also recorded the specific locations of diverse facilities – including daycare centers, libraries, churches and health clinics – that families in the study had visited. The investigators were then able to prepare mapped presentations of the ethnographic field work data and the space-time activities of the families.[59]

To complete their picture of the living conditions of the families in their sample, the investigators used GIS to add neighborhood information from a variety of government documents and reports pertaining to: crime rates, school boundaries, racial and ethnic composition, etc. The result was a rich set of geospatial data that enabled the investigators to place their studied families into neighborhood contexts that contained diverse data in relation to a family's school, work site, public transportation facilities, and so on.

Conclusion: Reflexivity again

When data analysis is complete, it is time to start writing. The final product might be a consultant's report to a city, a presentation at a conference, a journal article, or a term paper for a student's course assignment. At this time it is important again to consider reflexivity. It is of great significance not only while one is in the field collecting data, but at every step of a research project, including the final one when the results are presented. In the last stage, reflexivity refers to the creation of a product that "takes

Ethnographic field studies

into account its own production."[60] In other words, researchers should recognize and be sensitive to the fact that, just like the people they have been studying, they too typically create orderly accounts of social situations. Thus, they may feel that the audience for their report expects them to present an analysis in which the behavior of everyone they observed seems entirely coherent, and there are no loose ends, even though social life often contains inconsistencies and paradoxes.

The ethnographer must guard against succumbing to what he or she perceives as external expectations that the final report will present a narrative that reads smoothly from start to finish. This can result in pressures to retroactively give more emphasis to certain events than seemed warranted at the time or to entirely leave out other events observed along the way that seemed important at the time, but ultimately did not fit with the major conclusions. So, the final task, in preparing a report, is to ask oneself what must be retained for the ethnographic report to remain reflexive?

Notes

1 Alice Goffman, *On the Run*. University of Chicago, 2014.
2 For further discussion, see Lynne E.F. McKechnie, "Reactivity," in Lisa M. Given (Ed), *The SAGE Encyclopedia of Qualitative Research Methods*. Sage, 2008.
3 A number of these very early ethnographies, conducted by scholars who might today be considered Geographers, are included in Kurt A. Raaflaub and Richard J.A. Talbert, *Geography and Ethnography*. Blackwell, 2010.
4 Harriet Martineau, *How to Observe Manners and Morals*. Transaction Publishers, 1989. (Originally published in 1838.)
5 For an overview of field studies focusing upon working- and lower-class urban communities during this period, see Mark Pittinger, *Class Unknown*. New York University, 2012.
6 For a compilation of Crane's fictional and non-fictional writings, see Stephen Crane, *Great Short Works of Stephen Crane*. Harper Perennial, 2004.
7 Paul Gohre, *Three Months in a Workshop*. Cornell University Press, 2009. (Originally published in 1895.)
8 For further discussion, see Stephen Kalberg, *Max Weber's Comparative-Historical Sociology Today*. Ashgate, 2012.
9 Harlan H. Barrows, "Geography as Human Ecology." *ANNALS*, 13, 1923.
10 Nels Anderson, *The Hobo and Homelessness*. University of Chicago Press, 1999. (Originally published in 1923.)
11 Paul Cressey, *The Taxi-Dance Hall*. University of Chicago Press, 2008. (Originally published in 1932.)
12 See Steve Herbert, "For Ethnography." *Progress in Human Geography*, 24, 2000. Herbert notes that although ethnography must be considered a "peripheral" method in geography, there have been some excellent field studies conducted by Geographers.

13 Two journals are particularly relevant to examine here: *Gender, Place and Culture* is a favored site for feminist writings in Urban Geography; and *Journal of Geography in Higher Education* is a major site for discussions of field study courses in Geography.

14 For an introduction to the major concepts of symbolic interaction, see Herbert Blumer, *Symbolic Interaction*. University of California Press, 1986. For a wide range of ethnographic studies utilizing the symbolic interaction perspective, see Norman K. Denzin, *40ᵗʰ Anniversary of Studies in Symbolic Interaction*. Emerald Publishing, 2013.

15 Malinowski's place in British Social Anthropology is discussed in, Adam Kuper, *Anthropology and Anthropologists*. Routledge, 1996.

16 Bronislaw Malinowski, *Argonauts of the Western Pacific*. Waveland Press, 2013. (Published previously, various dates between 1913 and 1922.)

17 Bruno Latour and Steve Woolgar, *Laboratory Life*. Sage, 1979 and Princeton University Press, 1986. For a discussion of their analysis, focusing upon the role of reflexivity, see Jan-Hendrik Passoth and Nicholas J. Rowland, "Beware of Allies." *Qualitative Sociology*, 36, 2013.

18 See the discussion of the various roles field workers/qualitative researchers assign to theory in, Pedro G. Bendassoli, "Theory Building in Qualitative Research." *Forum: Qualitative Social Research*, 14, 2013.

19 The most complete initial statement was, Barney B. Glaser and Anselm L. Strauss, *The Discovery of Grounded Theory*. Aldine, 1967. For a discussion of later modifications, and a guide to implementing this analysis, see Anthony Bryant and Kathy Charmaz, *The SAGE Handbook of Grounded Theory*. Sage, 2010.

20 Patrick C. Jobes, et al., "Using the Constant Comparative Method." *Teaching Sociology*, 25, 1997. For another non-field study example, this one from Psychology, see Ruth E. Fassinger, "Paradigms, Praxis, Problems and Promises." *Journal of Counseling Psychology*, 52, 2005.

21 For a discussion of these, and other, examples, see Kenneth Liberman, *More Studies in Ethnomethodology*. SUNY Press, 2014.

22 Harold Garfinkel, *Studies in Ethnomethodology*. Prentice-Hall, 1967. See also, Harold Garfinkel and Anne W. Rawls, *Ethnomethodology's Program*. Rowman & Littlefield, 2002.

23 See Matthew Braswell, "Once More unto the Breaching Experiment." *Teaching Sociology*, 42, 2014.

24 For further discussion, see Sarah J. Tracy, *Qualitative Research Methods*. Wiley-Blackwell, 2013.

25 Clifford Geertz, *Work and Lives*. Stanford University Press, 1988.

26 Edward M. Bruner, "Experience and Its Expressions," in Victor W. Turner and Edward M. Bruner (Eds), *The Anthropology of Experience*. University of Illinois, 2001, p. 19. (This volume was originally published in 1986.)

27 Michael R. Glass, "Encouraging Reflexivity in Urban Geography Fieldwork." *Journal of Geography in Higher Education*, 38, 2014.

28 Shaul Kelner and George Sanders, "Beyond the Field Trip." *Teaching Sociology*, 37, 2009.

29 Jennie Middleton and Richard Yarwood, "Christians, Out Here?" *Urban Studies*, 50, 2013. (Special issue.)

30 Asad L. Asad and Monica C. Bell, "Winning to Learn, Learning to Win." *Qualitative Sociology*, 37, 2014.

31 Julie Kleinman, "Adventures in Infrastructure." *City & Society*, 26, 2014.

32 For a discussion of gatekeepers and researchers, from a very practical perspective, see David E. Gray, *Doing Research in the Real World*. Sage, 2013.

33 Derek Roberts, "Modified People." *Sociology*, 49, 2015.

34 Loic Wacquant, *Body and Soul*. Oxford University Press, 2004., p. vii.

35 Jaime Waters, "Snowball Sampling." *International Journal of Social Research Methodology*, 17, 2014.

36 Brooke Harrington, "The Social Psychology of Access in Ethnographic Research." *Journal of Contemporary Ethnography*, 32, 2003.

37 Japonica Brown-Saracino, "From Methodological Stumbles to Substantive Insights." *Qualitative Sociology*, 37, 2014.

38 The size of the squares in the grid may not be ideal for the area being studied, but in the absence of additional information, a simple grid may be the best way to make sure no part of the study area is ignored. For some more ambitious alternatives, see Robin Flowerdew and David Martin, *Methods in Human Geography*. Taylor & Francis, 2005.

39 Emma Jackson, "Fixed in Mobility." *International Journal of Urban and Regional Research*, 36, 2012.

40 Douglas D. Heckathorn, "Extensions of Respondent-Driven Sampling." *Sociological Methodology*, 37, 2007. See also the "Comments" by Mark S. Handcock and Krita J. Gile and by Leo A. Goodman, in *Sociological Methodology*, 41, 2011.

41 See Mitchell Duneier, "How Not To Lie With Ethnography." *Sociological Methodology*, 41, 2011.

42 Marco Garrido, "The Sense of Place behind Segregating Practices." *Social Forces*, *91*, 2013.

43 Robert M. Emerson, Rachel I. Fretz and Linda L. Shaw, *Writing Ethnographic Fieldnotes*. University of Chicago Press, 2011.

44 Johnny Saldana, *The Coding Manual for Qualitative Researchers*. Sage 2013.

45 John Lofland, *Davis*. Arcadia Publishing, 2004.

46 Loic Wacquant, *op. cit.*, footnote 3, p. 4.

47 Roberta R. Iverson, "'Getting Out' in Ethnography." *Qualitative Social Work*, 8, 2009, p. 15. See this paper for further discussion of field researchers' difficult disengagements.

48 Emerson, et al., *op. cit.*

49 Remaining disagreements were noted in the final manuscript. See Iverson, *op. cit.*

50 These alternative positions are summarized, and an excellent set of references is provided in, Corey M. Abramson and Daniel Dohan, "Beyond Text." *Sociological Methodology*, 45, 2015.

51 See the discussion of this issue in, Sharan B. Merriam, *Qualitative Research*. Jossey-Bass, 2009.

52 Asad and Bell, *op. cit.*

53 Validity is often divided into two very broad types: internal and external. External refers generally to the ability to generalize from a study while internal involves confidence in interpreting the results. Successful triangulation in

field studies and criterion validity in other types of studies can, therefore, be interpreted as indicative of internal validity.

54 For further analysis of the attitude-behavior connection, see Colin Jerolmack and Shamus Khan, "Talk is Cheap." *Sociological Methods and Research*, 42, 2014.

55 Anette Lareau, *Unequal Childhoods*. University of California Press, 2011.

56 For further discussion of data-driven content analysis and discussion of commercial software packages (in Chapter 12), see Margit Schreier, *Qualitative Content Analysis*. Sage, 2012.

57 Mohsen Habibi, Hamideh Farahmandian and Reza Basiri Mojdehi, "Reflection of Urban Space in Iranian Cinema." *Cities*, 30, 2015.

58 For a thorough overview, see Peter A. Burrough, Rachael A. McDonnell and Christopher D. Lloyd, *Principles of Geographic Information Systems*. Oxford University Press, 2015.

59 Stephen A. Matthews, James E. Detwiler and Linda M. Burton, "Geoethnography." *Cartographica*, 40, 2005.

60 Passoth and Rowland, *op. cit.*, p. 471.

Glossary

Breaching Experiments: Studies in which an investigator deliberately violates an everyday norm in order to observe how people respond.

Ethnography: Field studies in which researchers immersed in a group adopt the point of view of the group being studied.

Ethnomethodology: A theoretical perspective that assumes there are widely shared, but rarely verbalized, rules that people routinely use to maintain orderliness in everyday situations.

Grounded Theory: A perspective that advocates developing and assessing concepts and hypotheses while field work is occurring.

Human Ecology: The study of how spatial location affects relationships among people and institutions, and determines patterns of growth.

Inter-rater, or Inter-coder, Reliability: A comparison of agreement between raters in coding observations; typically utilized as a precondition for reliability across time.

Interpretive Sociology: Associated with Max Weber, it emphasizes empathy in order to understand how people evaluate their choices.

Jottings: Brief notes by researchers while in the field, usually written inconspicuously.

Reactivity: Changes in people's behavior that occur because they are aware of being studied.

Reflexivity: For field researchers, this entails being aware of the possible effects of one's own values and past experiences.

Symbolic Interaction: A theoretical perspective that emphasizes how the self is a product of social interaction.

Snowball Sampling: Building a sample by having people who have been contacted introduce, or refer, the investigator to others in the potential target population.

Triangulation: In field studies, it entails looking for congruence among data that were obtained using different methods. (In experiments and surveys, it involves congruence among indicators.)

chapter 3

Experimental design

Outline

- Experiments introduced
  - Manipulating the independent variable

- Contrasting experiments and ethnographic studies
- Experimentation in social science
  - Urban experiments
  - Helping behavior
  - Climate change

- Causal inference
  - Temporal ordering
  - Association
  - Spuriousness
  - Statistical and experimental control
  - Theoretical congruence
  - Types of causal reasoning

- Experimental designs
  - One group design
  - The classic experiment
    - Pre-test contamination
  - More complex designs
  - Simulating an experimental design

- Assigning subjects to experimental conditions
  - In a natural setting
  - In a laboratory setting
  - Contamination and blinding
  - In Internet-based experiments
- Internal and external validity
  - Internal validity
  - External validity

- Notes
- Glossary

The first thing that comes to many people's minds when they think of an experiment is a laboratory. They imagine a white-coated scientist surrounded by test tubes. There is relatively little about social life in cities that can be examined in a laboratory, so if that was all there was to experimentation we would not be interested. However, the principles of experimental design can be applied outside of laboratories and utilized very effectively with other research methods.

What is valuable about the principles of experimental design is their unmatched ability to enable an investigator to reach a conclusion concerning a causal connection between variables. To illustrate, consider the other everyday meaning in which to experiment typically means to change something, and then note its consequences. For example, a student may try re-writing notes after each lecture, rather than waiting until just before an exam, and see whether test scores improve. If the student was really anxious about grades, then the student might also attend class more often, spend more time reading assignments, participate more in classroom discussion, etc. All of that might combine to produce the desired result, a better grade; however, it would also spoil the experiment because it would then be impossible to know how much any one of the changes contributed to the improved result.

Experiments introduced

A scientific experiment, technically defined, similarly involves changing something and then noting its effects, but to be more precise we have to introduce two types of variables:

- *Independent variable* (IV), is the causal variable, believed to cause, determine, act upon or lead to the dependent variable. (In the above example, it would be when in relation to an exam the student re-wrote lecture notes.)

- *Dependent variable* (DV), is so named because its value is thought to be dependent upon, or the result of, the IV. (In the above example, it would be the student's test grade.)

Note, variables are conceptualized as IVs or DVs only for a given study (or in a particular theory). These are not permanent placements of variables. For example, in a subsequent study, someone could examine the effects, or consequences, of students' grades. This would transform students' grades from a DV in the first study, to an IV in this subsequent study.

Another basic feature of experiments is the existence of experimental and control groups that differ from each other in their subjects' exposure to different values of the IV. In many classical experiments, the IV is present in the experimental group, absent from the *control group*. In an urban transportation study, for example, people in the *experimental group* may be given reduced cost bus tokens that are withheld from the control group, and then the rates at which people in each group subsequently rode the bus (DV) would be compared. Everything else is (hopefully) kept unchanged so if there is a difference in ridership, it is presumably due to the bus tokens.

There are also some experiments in which the IV is simply different in the two groups: high in one, low in the other; positive in one, negative in the other, or so on. These variations are a function of the theory being tested in the experiment, and examples will follow throughout the chapter. In every other respect – i.e. other than the different values of the IV – steps are always taken to ensure that the two groups are the same so that any difference between them in the DV can be attributed to the different values of the IV.

Manipulating the independent variable

According to most definitions, a "true" experiment is one in which an investigator deliberately manipulates an IV, then notes its effect upon the DV. If an investigator merely observes the effects of different values of an IV, but is not responsible for the variations, the study is often referred to as a quasi-experiment.[1] Following this definition, there is a very long tradition of conducting quasi-experiments in cities, much of it designed to answer practical questions of immediate concern. To illustrate, around the year 900, the Iranian physician and philosopher, al-Razi, was assigned the task of deciding where in Baghdad to build a hospital. To answer this question, he designed a simple test. He hung raw meat in various quarters of the city, and proceeded to note the different rates at which the meat decomposed. Then, as the site for the hospital, he selected the location with the slowest decomposition rate, assuming that was the place in Baghdad that patients would suffer the least from illnesses.[2]

Experimental design

Al-Razi did not conduct a true experiment because he did not manipulate the IV. It is not even clear what he thought the IV was. He simply believed there was something in the air (IV) that varied in different parts of Baghdad and he observed its effects upon the DV, the rate at which the meat spoiled. It was about 800 years later that bacterium was discovered, however, so al-Razi must be excused if he failed to specify his IV, let alone manipulate it.

Whether a study will be an experiment or a quasi-experiment often depends upon where it is conducted. In a laboratory for social science experiments, chairs and tables can be arranged to suit the experimenter's interest. There are typically one-way mirrors and recording devices, and during the experiment the facilities enable an investigator to maintain control over the actions and interactions of subjects. Therefore, in laboratory experiments, it is usually possible to deliberately create variations in the IV.

Experiments conducted utilizing the Internet similarly provide opportunities for investigators to manipulate their IVs. To illustrate, in order to assess whether people's moods were only affected by others with whom they were in direct interaction, as in face-to-face groups or crowds, a team of researchers systematically exposed thousands of people on Facebook to News Feed content that was either positive or negative (IV). The investigators hypothesized that people's subsequent postings would similarly be either positive or negative (DV).[3] The hypothesis was confirmed, suggesting that emotional contagion could occur without face-to-face interaction. However, while the results were theoretically interesting, the investigators' manipulation of the IV was criticized on ethical grounds for exposing subjects to potentially unpleasant experiences without their informed consent. Obtaining such consent, especially without spoiling the experiment, poses a difficult to resolve problem that limits Internet experiments (see Chapter 1 for more discussion of this issue).

Research conducted in a natural setting, like al-Razi's, is less likely to afford the possibility of deliberately manipulating an IV. Investigators in the field often have to accept conditions (such as Baghdad's air) as they find them, leading their studies to be considered quasi-experiments. In some cases, however, investigators are able to find or create a natural setting they can alter in some ways to produce variations in an IV.

Some true experiments, as defined here, have been conducted to test hypotheses directly related to cities. For example, studies have attempted to simulate city-like conditions in laboratory settings and complete "artificial" communities have been created. However, the size and scale of cities very much limits experimentation in laboratory-type conditions, meaning that experimental studies of cities and city life are more often conducted in natural settings which do not permit an investigator to manipulate an IV, and hence are quasi-experiments.

While experiments and quasi-experiments can be distinguished from each other, the assumptions that underlie them are essentially the same: try to hold everything except an IV constant, and see if variations in the IV produce consistent differences in the DV. This model for assessing causal relationships is extremely important to understand because it always informs investigators' thinking about causality, regardless of how closely their research methods emulate a true experiment.

Contrasting experiments and ethnographic studies

We turn now to a discussion of the assumptions that underlie experimentation, focusing upon how they differ from the underpinnings of ethnographic field studies, as discussed in the preceding chapter. To begin, experiments are almost always part of a deductive design; that is, the research is driven by a theory that specifies precisely what variables are to be studied, and hypothesizes a relationship between those variables. Ethnographic field studies, on the other hand, were seen to be primarily inductive in design, the variables to be emphasized discovered (or at least developed) during the field work.

In addition, field studies tend to place a good deal of stress upon a sympathetic understanding of people's subjective states, including their: perceptions, motives, values, etc. In most experimental studies, however, the primary objective is to isolate causes in order to predict one very specific behavior: helpfulness to a stranger, willingness to trust a partner, etc. Experimenters will typically make suppositions about people's subjective states only in so far as these suppositions enhance predictions of the behavior, or provide a theoretical explanation for why the prediction holds. Further, if the subjective states they have inferred facilitate predictions or theoretical explanations, then many experimenters would not be concerned if the study's subjects disavowed or failed to recognize the qualities attributed to them. Subjects are not usually regarded as an experimenter's "collaborators," and the status difference between subjects and experimenter is unambiguous.

An example should help to clarify the above issue. A long series of experiments have reported that when conventional norms are violated – people cut in a line, litter in the park – if others respond at all, their signs of displeasure are muted (e.g. a disapproving look). These findings led a group of experimenters to conclude that the conventional norms that sustain collective life are maintained in very subtle, rather than overt, ways and that because people are typically concerned with social exclusion, they are sensitive to these faint cues. Building upon this theoretical position, a group of investigators wanted to see how people, in a highly controlled experiment, would be affected by varying lengths of silence as the only response after they expressed an opinion. The researchers found that a few seconds of others' silence (IV) led to a change in the subsequently expressed attitude (DV) of the person who offered the opinion. It appeared to the experimenters that others' silence acted like subtle disapproval, and people's wanting to belong was responsible for their shift in attitudes. Therefore, they concluded that another's silence led to changes in expressed attitudes.[4]

However, note that the experimenters did not seek any direct evidence that subjects in the experiment were sensitive to how the silence affected their behavior, or that the subjects were even aware of the silence. Consider, by contrast, the interpretive approach of Max Weber which was seen (in Chapter 2) to guide many ethnographic studies. Even highly predictive patterns of behavior should not be of interest, according to Weber, unless the investigator possesses an understanding of people's corresponding subjective states. In other words, an investigator must always, according to an interpretive approach, sympathetically understand the sentiments and outlooks that underpin a person's behavior. By contrast, experiments usually consider being able to predict an attitude or behavior to be sufficient.

When the objective is prediction, a premium is placed upon a research design that permits an investigator to control a setting, and experiments – as we will describe – provide the greatest degree of control. In an unfettered natural setting, where ethnographic studies typically occur, many interactions and events are happening simultaneously, and it can be extremely difficult to infer exactly what may have led to something else. Isolating causes in order to make a prediction is not the typical ethnographer's objective, though.

With our current description of experiments in mind, let us reconsider the "breaching experiments" described in the preceding chapter. Are they aptly termed as experiments? From our current perspective, the answer is no, primarily because while an investigator who intentionally violated some everyday norm was manipulating something, that something was not an IV because it did not assume different values. (By definition, a variable must assume different values or it is a constant.) There is only one condition in these studies: violation of a norm. Had investigators systematically varied whether they did or did not violate norms (i.e. manipulated values of the IV) and followed that by observing the effect on some DV, then the breaching studies would qualify as experiments. However, the fact that, by our definition, they do not qualify does not make the breaching studies invalid or un-interesting; just not true experiments.

Experimentation in social science

While experimentation has been a dominant method in the natural sciences, that has not been true in the social and behavioral sciences, with the exception of Psychology and Social Psychology. However, there are reasons to believe that experimentation is likely to increase in the social sciences, and that would also be expected to impact Urban Studies research. One indicator of an upward trend in experimentation comes from a review of studies published in the leading American journals in Economics, Political Science and Sociology. It shows that over the past few decades, the number of studies in these leading journals that relied upon experimentation has increased.[5] While it remained less than 10 percent of the total, the experimental studies enjoyed disproportionately high visibility and influence, reflected by the fact that they were more frequently cited than studies in these journals that relied upon any other method. In the UK, to illustrate further, there has recently been a substantial increase in expenditures for building and equipping laboratories necessary to conduct many types of experimental research across the social sciences. Impressive facilities opened in the last decade at the Centre for Behavioural and Experimental Social Science at the University of East Anglia, the ESSEXLab in the Social Science Research Centre at the University of Essex, and elsewhere. Investigators are using these facilities to conduct experiments of relevance to Urban Studies, and the availability of these facilities is likely to promote more experimental studies in the future.

Urban experiments

As in other specialty areas within the social sciences, experimentation has not been a dominant method of conducting research on cities and city life. There are, however, several specialized issues, or subareas, in Urban Studies that have been extensively studied utilizing experimental research designs. In this section we will discuss two of these special areas: helping behavior and climate change.

Helping behavior

The 1964 murder of Kitty Genovese provided a major impetus to experimentation on when people, in urban settings, would help strangers, and related questions. The basic facts were that around 3 am on a cold March night, Kitty was returning to her apartment in New York. As she walked toward the apartment building, a man approached her. Frightened, she started to run, but he caught up to her and stabbed her twice in the back. She screamed for help, which attracted the attention of a neighbor, and her attacker fled. Seriously injured, she staggered to the back of her apartment building and collapsed. Her attacker came back, stabbed her repeatedly, then raped her and took the money out of her purse. Another neighbor heard the commotion, called the police and an ambulance was summoned, but she died on the way to the hospital. The New York Times story, and a subsequent book, claimed that 38 neighbors living in the building heard her screams, but ignored them. Everyone asked the question: How could so many people fail to come to the aid of a person in such dire need of help? Many years later, a re-examination disclosed that few neighbors actually heard anything. It was after 3 am, people were sleeping and windows were closed on a cold night. Further, those who did hear anything took the noise to be a drunken brawl or a lover's quarrel that did not require them to respond.[6] However, Kitty Genovese's callous neighbors had already become part of the pool of urban legends.

In Psychology, Social Psychology and Sociology, the response to the immediately popular version of the Genovese murder was a rash of experiments designed to study the conditions under which people would come to the aid of a stranger. The studies, conducted in laboratories and in carefully controlled natural settings, focused upon such DVs as whether people would try to help an apparently injured person lying on the ground, and whether they would give directions to a stranger who claimed to be lost. The studies also examined diverse IVs, including the personal qualities of subjects, such as their religiosity; situational effects, such as the presence or absence of bystanders; and macro effects, such as the size of the city in which the study was conducted.[7]

Helping behavior, broadly defined, was also studied extensively not only in US cities, such as New York, where the infamous murder occurred, but also in: Ankara, Athens, London, Paris, Sydney, and elsewhere. A natural experiment that is representative of this line of research is described in Box 3.1.

Box 3.1 Helpfulness in different cities

In the decades immediately following Kitty Genovese's murder, a number of studies reported that helping strangers declined as the size of a city increased. This inverse relationship was particularly pronounced among cities with populations over 300,000. Perhaps the willingness to help declines because larger cities promote more impersonal relationships or perhaps it is because their pace of life is so fast that it keeps people from really noticing each other. In any case, a group of Social Psychologists reviewed these studies, and wondered what about cities, other than their size, might be related to differences in helping. In order to find out, they confined themselves to a sample of 23 of the largest cities of the world, and manipulated three measures of helping in the centers of these cities:

1) When the experimenter was 10 to 15 feet from a pedestrian, the experimenter "accidentally" dropped a pen and continued walking.

(Helping was indicated if the pedestrian actually retrieved the pen, or at least told the experimenter about it.)

2) Limping and wearing a leg brace, the experimenter dropped a pile of magazines in front of a passing pedestrian, and then struggled to pick them up. (Helping occurred if the stranger offered to help, or began picking up the magazines without asking.)

3) Wearing dark glasses, the experimenter stopped at an intersection as the stop light turned red, held out a white cane and stood there for one minute. (Helping involved any stranger alerting the experimenter to the red light, or otherwise trying to restrain the experimenter from trying to cross against the light.)

The percentage of people who offered help in the above situations provided each city with a score on the three DVs. The experimenter found that within each city, the proportion of people who provided help tended to be much the same, regardless of how help was measured. This congruence enabled the investigators to combine the three DVs into a single helping score for each city.[8]

The IVs were taken from previously developed measures of the economic and cultural life of the cities (or their nations). Included were measures of: the cultural emphasis upon individualism versus collectivism, economic productivity, the degree to which amiability and friendliness (*simpatia* in Spanish) were traditionally emphasized, and so on.

In sum, the 23 cities were the subjects, each given scores on IVs as described above, and on the DVs (i.e. helping). Note, the IVs were not manipulated by the experimenters; only the DV, measures of helping, involved manipulation. The study might, therefore, best be described as a quasi-experiment, as previously defined.

Overall helping scores (the DV) were found to vary greatly among the cities, from a high of 93 percent (in Rio de Janeiro) to a low of 40 percent (in Kuala Lampur). The two IVs found to be most strongly related to the DV were: economic productivity and the tradition of amiable friendliness (*simpatia*) associated with Spanish and Portugese cities. The economic productivity of the city-nation, the other IV, was found to be negatively related to the DV; people in city-nations that were higher in productivity were less helpful. (Positive and negative relationships are further discussed later in this chapter.)

The research that focused upon helping also expanded into additional lines of inquiry, such as bystander effects upon a wide range of behaviors other than helping. And much of this research was experimental or quasi-experimental in design, conducted either in laboratories or carefully selected natural settings. The net result was a substantial increase in experimental research focusing upon cities and urban life.

Experimental design

Climate change

As previously noted, climate change is a second area within Urban Studies in which a good deal of research has been experimental in design. Compared to helping behavior research, climate change experiments are more recent, beginning very late in the twentieth century, and accelerating after the Kyoto climate agreement in 2005. Included in this specialty area are hundreds of urban experiments conducted by Geographers, atmospheric scientists, and others.

Some of the climate change research has been very ambitious in scope while some has been highly focused and limited. These differences have probably been due to the marked variations in what provided the impetus to the research. Urban experiments have been undertaken in response to natural disasters, such as floods, the availability of funds for infrastructure renewal programs, and frustration with delays in national and international responses to what is perceived in many cities as an imminent ecological crisis.[9]

To illustrate the nature of many of the experiments, we may note that a number of cities have tried to encourage the use of public, or mass, transit in order to reduce private automobile emissions. In Tallinn, Estonia, for example, a city of nearly half a million residents, the city agreed to manipulate the cost of public transportation (IV). In fact, the city eventually eliminated the fare to ride on the city's buses and trolleys. When the cost was reduced to zero, the results showed a disappointingly small increase in the use of public transportation (DV). It only rose about 1 percent, so the reduction in emissions from private automobiles was negligible. Being able to ride for free was also found unexpectedly to decrease the amount that people walked in the city, but that was not a DV of interest to the investigators. It was just more disappointing news.[10]

On the other hand, researchers and activists have networked corporations and municipal governments to fund programs to provide cities with LED lighting, which was expected to markedly reduce greenhouse gas emissions compared to conventional lighting. In those urban areas that installed LED lighting (IV), greenhouse gas emissions (DV) were found to decline by 10 percent or more (compared to conventional lighting.) Findings of this magnitude of reduction have been reported in experiments in a number of major cities, including New York and London.[11]

Causal inference

As we have noted, experimentation is the method most ideally suited to testing a hypothesis that specifies a causal link between an IV and DV. This quality intrinsically connects experimentation and causal analysis. We will begin this section with a discussion of how one demonstrates a causal relationship between an IV and a DV. Then we will turn to a more philosophical consideration of the meanings of causality.

To show that a relationship between an IV and DV is causal, at least four requirements have to be met. Each is essential: if it is absent, the relationship cannot be causal; but none of the necessary conditions, by itself, is sufficient to enable one to infer a causal relationship with any degree of confidence. The four required conditions are: temporal ordering, association, non-spuriousness, and theoretical congruence. Each will be discussed in turn.

Temporal ordering

If an IV is to be considered a cause, or part of the cause, of a DV then it follows that the IV must precede the DV in time; that is, it must occur first. Data from most surveys and public documents are often difficult to interpret in this respect because all the variables pertaining to people's attitudes and experiences are collected or measured at the same time. It can be difficult, therefore, to infer with certainty which variables may have preceded others. However, in experiments, the ambiguity with respect to temporal ordering is removed because any potential causal variable (i.e. IV) is made to precede its presumed consequence (i.e. DV) as part of the experimental design – if the experimenter is manipulating the IV.

If an experiment is conducted outside of a laboratory, and the IV is not manipulated by the experimenter, then the natural setting selected must be one in which there is little doubt about the temporal ordering of the variables. In the previously discussed experiment on the cost of public transportation in Tallinn, for example, the cost could be presumed to antecede people's usage. In a well-designed experiment, the only question should concern whether the temporal ordering of the variables in the experiment corresponds closely with the ordering between them that would be observed in a natural setting, not contrived for an experiment. This correspondence is an aspect of the external validity of an experiment, an issue only to be noted here, and discussed later in this chapter's section on the internal and external validity of experiments.

Association

If an IV is a cause of a DV, there must be an association between them. This means that they vary together in a consistent manner: as one increases in value, the other also increases (a *positive relationship*) or as one increases in value, the other decreases (a *negative relationship*). To illustrate a positive relationship, the more people in a city were willing to help a stranger pick up dropped magazines, the more they were willing to help a blind person cross the street. They co-varied in the same direction

Experimental design

so that as one increased so did the other. To illustrate a negative relationship, the larger the size of a city, the less people were willing to help a stranger in any way. The more of one, the less of the other.

For theoretical purposes, the direction of a relationship is obviously very important. However, for purposes of prediction or for meeting the causal requirement of an association, the direction of a relationship is irrelevant. All that matters is the size, or strength, of the relationship. The greater it is, the more closely connected are the IV and DV, and therefore, the greater the ability to predict values of the DV from the IV.

If there is an observed association between an IV and a DV, and the IV is observed to precede the DV, people are inclined immediately to infer that the relationship between the IV and the DV must be causal. However, even when the IV is seen to precede the DV, and the IV and DV are observed to be related, there are still formidable hurdles to cross before one can infer the relationship is causal, and the first one is the possibility that the relationship is spurious.[12]

Spuriousness

The association between an IV and a DV is *spurious* if it is due to their shared relationship with a third variable (TV). An association that is spurious is not, technically, an illusion: it could be repeatedly observed. However, spuriousness and causality are mutually exclusive; hence a relationship shown to be spurious would not be interpreted as causal.

To illustrate, suppose there were a city in which all post-primary education was private, and that it became increasingly expensive at higher levels: high schools cost more than elementary schools, colleges more than high schools, and post-graduate schooling was even more expensive. Further suppose that the wealth of parents was the major determinant of how much schooling their offspring obtained because admission standards were low and there were few scholarships. Finally, suppose that in this city most employment was in a family business, and most youngsters upon completing their education went into the family business.

If an analysis of data from this city showed a strong, positive association between the level of education of offspring (hypothesized as the IV) and the wealth of offspring (the hypothesized DV), would a causal interpretation be warranted? Arguing in favor, we know that the IV (education) typically precedes the DV (wealth), and the data did show an association between IV and DV. The first two conditions are met; but one TV should come immediately to mind: parent's wealth. The offspring of wealthier parents would typically attain higher levels of education and they would then go into more successful businesses. The apparent connection between offspring's education and offspring's wealth is probably due,

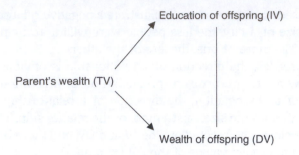

Figure 3.1 Illustration of spuriousness.

therefore, to the shared relationship of both variables with parent's wealth. This pattern is illustrated in Figure 3.1.

In other words, in the example illustrated in Figure 3.1, the TV is the cause of both IV and DV, and the association between IV and DV is spurious.

Statistical and experimental control

With data from a survey, public document, or the like, spuriousness is assessed statistically, after the fact. The analyst attempts to statistically hold constant all the variation associated with the TV(s), thereby also removing the variation the TV(s) shared with the IV and DV. In the above illustration, variation in parent's wealth would be held constant, statistically creating a set of data in which all parents were the same with respect to wealth. If shared variation with a TV fully accounts for the relationship between the IV and the DV, then the relationship between them will disappear under this statistical condition, and be considered spurious – hence, not causal. It is also possible that holding constant the TV(s) reduces the apparent relationship between IV and DV, but it does not completely disappear. The reduction can be equated with a *degree* of spuriousness, and the remaining portion of the relationship between IV and DV may be considered causal, if the other necessary conditions are met.

In some instances, however, spuriousness cannot be adequately assessed statistically because the data do not permit all the potential TVs to be held constant. For example, some statistical analyses can require a larger number of cases (i.e. subjects) than the investigator possesses, or the investigator may lack an adequate measure of some potential TV. Therefore, full statistical control can sometimes only be approximated.

In an experiment, by contrast, control over TV(s) is built into the experimental design, and thereby, before the fact. For example, if people's gender was considered a potential TV, an experimenter would have several ways of controlling for its effects. A study could be conducted including

Experimental design

only males or only females, or the sex of subjects being placed into experimental and control groups could be matched. Either procedure would prevent any variability that might be associated with gender from affecting the relationship between the IV and the DV. As is usually the case, prevention is better than searching for a cure: experimental control is typically more efficacious than statistical control.

Before concluding this discussion of spuriousness, we must note that one can never be absolutely certain that all potential TVs have been controlled, statistically or experimentally. There is always the possibility that some TV will be discovered in the future and that its inclusion in a study would show the causal connection between an IV and DV to be spurious. Therefore, when we conclude that a relationship is causal, because every TV we thought relevant at the time was controlled, we must always acknowledge that the relationship seems to be causal – for now.

This element of uncertainty explains why, many years ago when government hearings on the possibly harmful health effects of tobacco first began, scientists called to testify were asked by representatives of the cigarette manufacturers if they could be absolutely certain of the causal link between smoking and cancer. The scientists "hedged" in their conclusions, out of concern with the possibility that the association might someday be shown to be spurious. Lawmakers who poorly understood the nature of causal inference were confused by the scientists' caution, and this contributed to the delay in legislation controlling tobacco products.[13] Eventually, however, the weight of numerous studies reporting a causal connection, with adequate statistical controls in place, led almost everyone to feel virtually certain of the causal link between smoking and cancer.

Theoretical congruence

As a final criterion for inferring causality, most analysts insist that there ought to be a theoretical perspective that could account for the connection between IV and DV. In most instances, this entails identification of a mechanism that provides the causal bond. A *mechanism* has been defined as a "how-possible explanation."[14] It clarifies how the DV could, in principle, be produced by the IV by describing a causal process that identifies the variables involved and their properties that make a difference. For example, experiments indicate that when one voter in a two-voter household receives a get-out-the-vote message in person, that voter is more likely to vote *and* another person in the household is also much more likely to vote. Note, the time order of the IV and DV are clear, and the relationship between them persists when the obvious TVs are held constant. This brings us to the final criterion: What might be the mechanism that ties the voting of cohabitants to each other? One analyst proposed that it might be social pressure, because such pressure expressed in a variety of ways seemed to have increased turnout in other election experiments.[15] There was no direct evidence that cohabitants felt social pressure or that they responded to it, and no such evidence was necessary for an analyst to posit it as the possible mechanism. This is not meant to imply that mechanisms typically cannot be observed or measured, only that they need not be in order for an investigator to infer them, if the research is following a well-defined theoretical tradition.

In sum, even if IV and DV are associated, IV is seen or known to occur first, and the relationship between them is apparently not spurious, unless the mechanism that links IV and DV can also be identified and placed into a cogent theoretical framework, a causal inference with respect to IV and DV is not warranted.

Types of causal reasoning

Further insight into the ways various experts think about causation comes from a comparison of science and law. A small group of professors, with backgrounds in both law and science, recently provided some detailed contrasts between these realms and their thoughts are helpful in thinking about causality. To begin, they point out that science typically studies individual subjects with the objective of making statements about a larger population. In trying to generalize a causal connection to a population, scientific inquiry focuses upon the *effect of causes*. Will the IV lead to the DV?

The law, however, examines data about populations in order to reach conclusions about individuals.[16] In the courtroom, juries or judges are usually obligated to try to discern the *causes of effects*. For example, a person goes to court seeking damages for an illness (the presumed DV) which is alleged to have been due to an environmental toxin (the putative IV). The question before the court is, did a condition, such as an illness, result from a specific cause, such as exposure to a toxin?

The distinction between the legal emphasis upon causes of effects and the scientific emphasis upon effect of causes has its counterpart in the philosophy of science's historic distinction between ideographic and nomothetic explanations. *Ideographic* explanations provide a complete, or exhaustive, description of how one particular instance occurred. This form of causal reasoning is most strongly associated with the study of history, which tries to explain unique and non-repetitive events. To illustrate, one might want to know all of the variables that led to a city having to declare bankruptcy, even including those variables that may have made a small contribution. Completeness is important. Not being able to generalize to the causes of any other city's financial collapse would not be important. An ideographic explanation would also be characteristic of: the humanities in general, the judge trying to decide a specific case, and clinicians trying to understand what led to one particular person's distinctive symptoms.

The alternative type of causal explanation is labeled *nomothetic* and it attempts to provide a probabilistic explanation for a class of events. It is associated with the natural sciences, and it stresses parsimony over completeness. The objective is to include the minimum number of variables necessary to explain events, and in addition, being able to generalize to similar types of events would be very important in a nomothetic explanation.

The social sciences, including most Urban Studies, are intermediate to the humanities and natural sciences, and can focus upon either type of causal explanation. Associated with the specific research methods that they favor, however, social scientists (including those who specialize in Urban Studies) tend to tilt in one or the other direction. To be specific, nomothetic explanations are more strongly associated with experimentation (and its emphasis upon causal effects that can be generalized) while ideographic explanations would more frequently characterize ethnographic studies (with their emphasis upon sympathetic understanding).[17]

Experimental designs

In the most simple, but very common, experiment there is a single IV and a single DV. The research hypothesis is that the IV leads to the DV, and values of the IV to which subjects are exposed determine who is in the experimental (E) and who is in the control group (C). The objective is to design an experiment which eliminates the possibility that the DV is affected by any variable other than the IV, and a design is judged by its ability to accomplish that objective. It is also usually assumed, nomothetically, that the hypothesized effect being studied in the experiment would occur in any group, or subgroup, of the population. In this section we will examine a number of forms that experiments can take, differing from each other in their degree of complexity.

One group design

The one group design, sometimes also referred to as a before-and-after design, is the least complex arrangement that can qualify as an experiment. It contains one group of people who begin as members of a control group (IV absent), then are exposed to the IV and thereby become the experimental group, and then the IV is removed, and they end up as they started, in the control group setting. For example, the IV might be how much time is devoted to student discussion in a class. The DV might be class attendance. At time one – control situation – baseline measures of the DV are obtained in a non-discussion setting. At time two the IV (time for discussion) is present, and the DV is again measured, this time under the experimental group condition. At time three the IV is withdrawn (sometimes referred to as a reversal) and the group is returned to the control group situation. The DV is again measured.

It would probably be hypothesized that class attendance would increase from time one to time two, then decrease from time two to three; and that in time three, attendance would approximate its time one level. This one group design, and its corresponding hypotheses, is summarized in Figure 3.2.

The problem with this one-group-serves-as-both design is that it may not eliminate all extraneous factors – anything other than IV leading to DV – from producing the results, and lacking a control group, this design may fail to detect these extraneous influences. The hypothesis could, therefore, be confirmed or rejected for the wrong reasons. For example, suppose all or most of the subjects who were included in the experiment happened to share something unique in their past experience, outlooks, or the like, and that something else they happened to share (that was not measured in the study) predisposed them to respond as they did in the experiment; in other words, that something else was responsible for the results. Generalizing the findings that attributed the observed effects to the IV (providing a nomothetic explanation) would then not be warranted.

In addition, changes in the DV might be the result of unmeasured changes occurring among all or most of the subjects. Referred to as *maturation effects*, this could entail any experiences common to all or most of the subjects as they go through an experiment; for example, by the end of the classroom discussion experiment all of the subjects will be older, have taken more courses, etc. and these maturation effects may be responsible for any observed changes in class attendance. Similarly, there might also be the influence of events occurring outside of the experiment that impinge upon subjects, for example, changes occurring in the college or department in which the course being studied is located. Finally, if the subjects are aware that they are part of an experiment (reactivity, as previously defined) that might also lead to changes in their behavior that could impact the DV.

	Time One	Time Two	Time Three
Hypothesis: DV2 > DV1 or DV3	C	E	C
Other expectation: DV1 = DV3	DV1	DV2	DV3

Figure 3.2 The one group design.

Experimental design

In sum, a wide range of extraneous events can lead to changes in a DV that are not properly attributable to the IV, but these changes can pass undetected in a one group experimental design because of the absence of a control group. Many of these problems plagued a famous study conducted at the Hawthorne Works factory of Western Electric outside of Chicago, and the Hawthorne Effect has come to stand for the problems of a one group design. That study is described in Box 3.2.

Box 3.2 The Hawthorne Effect

During the 1920s and 1930s, a group of Psychologists and Sociologists conducted a series of experiments at the Western Electric factory in suburban Chicago. It involved a number of separate studies conducted by different investigators in different sections of the factory. What tied all of the studies together was their common focus upon worker productivity as the DV, though differences in the type of work being performed necessitated that the investigators use different operational measures of productivity. The IVs also varied, and included variations in the length of breaks, payment incentives, lighting and other working conditions. However, one group designs were utilized in almost all of the experiments, meaning that the same group of people sequentially went through the experimental and control situations.

The findings of all the experiments conducted in the factory were not the same, though for the most part they failed to confirm their hypotheses. The measured IVs were either unrelated to the DVs or the direction of the relationship between them was opposite to the one expected. For example, increased financial incentives did not consistently lead to productivity gains. A later overview of the puzzling findings by two of the main researchers simply summarized them as "screwy."[18]

To understand why investigators would offer such a summary, consider the most often cited of the Western Electric experiments, the illumination studies. Over a period of years, workers who were assembling and inspecting parts for telephone relays were observed under lighting conditions (the IV) that were manipulated by the experimenters. Specifically, the investigators increased illumination in the room and initially found that productivity (the DV) increased: more wire coils were wound, more parts inspected, etc. So far so good. There appeared to be a positive relationship between IV and DV, as hypothesized. Then the investigators slowly reduced levels of illumination, expecting that workers' output would correspondingly decline. However, productivity tended either to remain the same or, contrary to all expectations, actually to increase – even when illumination was set at its lowest level (classified as "moonlight").

Later analyses of the data concluded that most of the findings of the various experiments were largely the result of variables that were not controlled by the investigators. In the telephone relay room, for example, the workers apparently responded favorably to the fact that someone was finally paying attention to them, and asking them how they felt about working conditions, such as lighting. The one group design of the studies did not disclose these unanticipated and unmeasured influences, which are now referred to as maturation effects and/or reactivity effects; but what later came to be termed the Hawthorne Effect subsumes them both.

In order to identify any of the above Hawthorne Effect problems, it would be necessary to assign separate groups of people to experimental and control groups. If any extraneous-to-the experiment factors were operating, such as workers' appreciation of being asked their opinions, the same trends in the DV would be noted in both the experimental and control groups. From this observation, an experimenter could correctly conclude that values of the DV were not dependent upon values of the IV. The one group design, by definition, could fail to disclose such effects not properly attributed to the IV, and hence it is not a recommended design except in situations in which there is no alternative.

The classic experiment

In the classic experiment there are: separate experimental (E) and control (C) groups comprised of different people; the DV is measured in both groups in a pre-test; E is exposed to the IV, C is not; then the DV is measured at the end of the experiment in a post-test. The form of this design is summarized in Box 3.3.

Box 3.3 The classic experiment

- Pre-test: Measure DV in E and C. There should be no significant difference, which shows that subjects did not initially differ from each other on DV.
- Experiment: IV is present in E, absent in C.
- Post-test: Measure DV in E and C.
- Hypothesis: In the post-test, DV in E will differ from DV in C (in a predicted direction).
- In addition, DV in C in the post-test should not differ from DV in C in the pre-test or it would indicate that DV was not solely dependent upon IV.

Experimental design

The main features of a classic experimental design, as outlined above, can be illustrated in the previously introduced study of the effects of silence upon people's attitudes. The hypothesis was that others' silence, in response to a person's expressed opinion, was tantamount to a subtle rebuke, and that it would lead people to alter their views.[19] In the pre-test, subjects were given a questionnaire asking their attitudes toward a number of different topics. Only one attitude was of interest to the experimenters, but they utilized a longer than necessary questionnaire so subjects would not be tipped off as to their true interest. They did not want to increase the salience of the one attitude of interest, which was whether subjects thought that heavy smoking should lower someone's eligibility for an organ donation. From a pilot study, the investigators knew that most people in the subject pool were in favor of discriminating against heavy smokers. However, the sample included 29 participants who, in the pre-test, said they were opposed to discriminating against heavy smokers. The investigators were particularly interested in how these subjects would respond to the experimental conditions.

In each session, one naive student subject, taken without coaching from the subject pool, was placed in a room with two other students. Both of the latter were *confederates* of the experimenter, which whenever used in an experiment means that they appear to be subjects, but unbeknown to naive subjects are trained to play a pre-determined role. On the surface, though, they look and act just like naive subjects, giving the naive subjects no reason to assume they differ in any way. In these sessions, when the one naive subject was asked to express an opinion on the discrimination against smokers issue, the two confederates were instructed either to:

1) Smoothly continue the conversation (C – no silence condition) or
2) Remain silent for four seconds (E) before resuming the conversation.

The two above conditions represented the experimenter's manipulation of the IV. The sessions were also videotaped, and a trained coder later viewed them, classifying each session as corresponding with the silent or non-silent condition, thereby providing a measure of inter-rater reliability (introduced in Chapter 2) for the measure of IV.

In the post-test, each (naive) subject's attitude toward heavy smokers was again measured in order to assess the hypothesis that the DV in E will be lower (i.e. less favorable to heavy smokers) than the DV in C. Among the subjects who wanted to remain in the group, and especially among those who initially were opposed to discrimination against smokers, the silent response condition (E) was associated with larger attitude changes than non-silence (C), as predicted; and the changes that occurred in subjects' attitudes typically moved them closer to the pro-discrimination views shared by the other members of the group.

Pre-test contamination

The pre- and post-tests in the classic experimental design are sometimes a matter of concern. Perhaps subjects' exposure to the DV in the pre-test will somehow influence how they score on the post-test. They might, for example, remember how they answered a question the first time, and then try to be consistent when they answer it a second time. There are a number of possible ways to prevent this problem. Sometimes an investigator is able to devise two separate, but equivalent, measures of the DV, and use one in the pre-test and one in the post-test. Sometimes an investigator tries to utilize a pre-test measure of the DV that will (hopefully) not attract much of the subjects' attention. For example, in the effects of silence pre-test, experimenters asked a brief question about discrimination against smokers, and embedded it in a long list of questions on other topics in order to make it less conspicuous.

When an investigator cannot utilize any of the above methods for preventing a pre-test from potentially increasing the salience of the DV, experiments are sometimes conducted without a pre-test. To illustrate, three Psychologists in Palermo, Italy, devised a laboratory study of helping behavior. The IV was subjects' exposure to lists of words that differed in their pro-social content. In E, many of the words were pro-social (e.g. "to gift") while none of the words were pro-social in C. After each subject completed an assigned task with the different groups of words, he or she was dismissed and walked along a corridor where a woman (a confederate of the experimenter) was carrying 20 books. When she was five meters from the subject, she dropped all of the books. The DV: Would the subject help her to pick them up?[20] The hypothesis was confirmed, though weakly. Subjects in the experimental condition were more likely to help than subjects in the control condition, as expected, but most subjects in both groups refused to help pick up the books.

Left unanswered in this helping study is the possibility that, prior to the experiment, there were relevant differences between subjects assigned to C and E. That loophole can be closed by randomly assigning subjects to C and E, described in a subsequent section of this chapter focusing upon subject assignments. For now we simply note that if the experimental design does not include a pre-test, assessment of the hypothesis is obviously limited to a comparison of E and C on a post-test measure of the DV. However, a post-test measure, by itself, does not permit an investigator to demonstrate explicitly that the DV changed more in E than in C; it can only be inferred.

Experimental design

More complex designs

When a pre-test is considered desirable, but an experimenter is not certain whether the overall research design to be employed will prevent the pre-test from potentially contaminating the post-test, a Solomon four group design can be employed. It involves two E and two C groups, as conventionally defined, but only one of each is given the pre-test. See the illustration in Table 3.1.

If the pre-test does not contaminate the post-test, then groups one and two will score the same on the post-test as will groups three and four. If that pattern occurs, then the hypothesis is tested by comparing changes in the DV in group one to group three. Note, groups one and three are the same as E and C in the classic experiment. On the other hand, if there is contamination, it can be estimated by the differences between groups one and two, and between groups three and four.

A similar design can be employed when an investigator is testing a causal theory in which there is more than one IV. This could entail a theory that specifies the dependence of a DV on the joint (i.e. additive or multiplicative) effects of two or more IVs, or a theory that specifies IV leads to DV, but only when some other specific variable is either present or absent. All of these theories are similar with respect to their implications for the design of an experiment. Described in Box 3.4 is an experiment that was designed to test a theory that focused upon the way IVs, either separately or in conjunction with each other, affected a DV.

Simulating an experimental design

We conclude this section by considering studies in which an experimental design, resembling one of the previously discussed types, is employed to analyze data that were not obtained in a study that meets the criteria by which experiments are defined. These are situations in which investigators cannot conduct an experiment or a quasi-experiment, and must rely for data upon a survey, observations in a natural setting, or a document prepared for another purpose (e.g. a census report). If the investigators

Table 3.1 The Solomon design

Group	Pre-test	IV	Post-test
One (E)	Present	Present	Present
Two (E)	Absent	Present	Present
Three (C)	Present	Absent	Present
Four (C)	Absent	Absent	Present

Box 3.4 Intervening in a city's high poverty area

Illustrating a complex experimental design, a group of investigators wanted to study the effects of a two-year-long intervention by a community health worker who taught parenting skills to mothers in a city's high-poverty area. During 1986–87, the investigators selected a sample of poor families in Kingston, Jamaica, all of whom had 9 to 24-month-old infants who were growth stunted. The intervention (IV) involved teaching mothers how to interact with their infants in a way that would help to develop the infants' cognitive and emotional skills. The DV was the future earnings of the then grown up children, which were measured 20 years later.[21]

The investigators also introduced another variable, nutritional supplements, which were given to some of the infants. The investigators wondered whether the psycho-social intervention would be of long-term economic value to the children if nutritional supplements were not part of the protocol. The research team also wanted to consider the possibility that nutritional supplements, by themselves, would have an effect on later earnings. Therefore, their experimental design involved four groups, as displayed in Table 3.2.

When earnings 20 years later were measured (the DV), the investigators found them to be highest for the now adult subjects who, as infants, were in groups one and two; and people in these groups were not significantly different from each other. In addition, average incomes in groups three and four, which were lower than in groups one and two, were also roughly equal to each other. These findings enabled the investigators to conclude that the psycho-social intervention, by itself, had a long-term (and presumably causal) effect upon later earnings; but that nutritional supplements, by themselves or in conjunction with the special training of their mothers, did not have any effect.

Table 3.2 Experimental conditions in the Kingston study

	IV1 (Psycho-social intervention)	IV2 (Nutritional supplements)
Group One	Present	Absent
Group Two	Present	Present
Group Three	Absent	Present
Group Four	Absent	Absent

Experimental design

utilizing such data are interested in trying to establish a causal connection between an IV and DV, they often try to superimpose an experimental design over the analysis because of the advantages associated with such designs in inferring whether relationships between variables are causal.

Included here are studies in which investigators have not directly manipulated any of the variables and their control over the conditions under which data were generated was substantially less than that typically associated with an experiment. However, the researcher arranges the data in a way that creates an approximation to experimental and control groups. This enables a causal analysis that resembles that followed in a conventional experiment. An interesting example of this type of research is described in Box 3.5.

Box 3.5 Neighborhood effects on student performance

Specialists in urban education often assume that if a family lives in a middle-class neighborhood, the children will perform better in a local school than if the same family lived in a high-poverty neighborhood. This assumption, of course, provides one of the major justifications for school busing. However, in prior studies, almost all of which have been non-experimental, it has been extremely difficult to demonstrate a causal link between the socio-economic status of the neighborhood (the IV) and children's educational performance (the DV) because the effects of a host of other, potentially confounding, variables could not be ruled out. Of particular concern is the lingering question of whether the poor families that seek middle-class neighborhoods to benefit their children's education are different from the poor families that do not try to move out of an impoverished area, and it has been difficult to eliminate the effects of such differences, either statistically or experimentally.

In an effort to isolate a causal connection, Casciano and Massey designed what they termed a quasi-experimental study. Their data came from local schools and from records kept in a subsidized housing development in a middle-class suburb of Camden, New Jersey. Between 2003 and 2010 approximately 100 families with school-age children who were living in high-poverty neighborhoods applied for housing in the middle-class development. About one-half of these families were accepted and moved in; the other half, for one reason or another, had not moved in when the study was conducted. The investigators assumed that these two groups of families approximated experimental and control groups.[22]

To test their principal hypothesis, the investigators obtained diverse measures of all the children's school and school-related performance, the DV. They then compared the children whose families lived in the suburban development to the children whose families continued to live in high-poverty neighborhoods. The investigators found that children living in the development, compared to those who remained outside, had higher grades in school, as expected; and that their superior grades were largely due to the fact that school-aged youngsters in the development spent more time reading at home than their counterparts in high-poverty neighborhoods.

Note that the values of the IV, attending school in a middle-class or in a high-poverty neighborhood, varied: the children whose families moved to the development lived in a middle-class community while the children whose families did not move remained in a high-poverty neighborhood. The researchers did not manipulate the IV; it was mostly determined by the admission decisions of the housing development office. Nevertheless, these variations in the IV, and the ability of the investigators to also obtain measures of a DV (children's school performance) that was theoretically linked to the IV, enabled them to make causal inferences resembling those that would result from conducting an experiment.

To some methodologists, studies such as the one described in Box 3.4 merely mimic an experimental design, with groups created for analysis that only superficially approximate experimental and control groups. For example, to deal with the many potential differences between families in the two groups, the investigators had to rely upon statistical rather than experimental control. This entailed trying to hold constant whatever differences between families they could obtain, and they were entirely dependent upon the data the housing development office or the schools could provide. Included were such relevant variables as families' criminal histories and their economic problems; but despite the investigators' creative efforts to statistically hold constant other variables that could potentially have confounded their analysis, one cannot rule out the possibility that some unmeasured differences persisted, with unknown effects. And no pre-test was possible to see if there were differences between the experimental and control groups at the onset of the study. Finally, the investigators had to utilize students' and parents' questionnaires to obtain information about students' school (and school-related) performance; and although they very carefully scrutinized these measures of the DV, they clearly had less control over the measurement of their variables than would be typical in most experiments.

Other methodologists, recognizing the practical limitations to utilizing a true experimental design to study urban social problems, would include studies of this type under a broad "quasi-experiment" category.[23] They may be the closest things to experiments that are possible. Even though their status as quasi-experiments remains ambiguous, we have included studies of this type here because (1) they are clearly inspired by experimental designs, and therefore are methodologically instructive, and (2) despite their design limitations from an experimental perspective, they make important contributions in advancing the causal analysis of many relevant issues.

Assigning subjects to experimental conditions

All of the elements of an experimental design, as we have described them, are intended to permit an investigator to reach a conclusion concerning a causal connection between IV and DV. This presupposes that subjects in the experimental and control groups do not differ from each other prior to the onset of the study. If there is a pre-test, then E and C can be compared on the DV, and the IV is under the experimenter's control; but how can an investigator know whether subjects in C and E are the same with respect to other variables that might affect DV? The answer lies in the way subjects are placed into E and C, and how that is best done differs somewhat according to the type of setting in which the experiment occurs. In this section we will examine the assignment of subjects to experimental conditions in: natural field settings, laboratories, and Internet-based experiments.

In a natural setting

In a natural setting, the operational definition of the IV establishes when or where the experimental and control situations are operating. For example, in a classic, award-winning experiment, Murray Melbin studied how people's helpfulness (DV) varied by time of day (IV) in the middle of a city, and he chose downtown Boston as the research site. He hypothesized that people would be more likely to help a stranger in the middle of the night because people who he described as "inhabiting the night" feel a bond to each other that is unmatched by people whose lives are spent in daylight; and at night there are fewer others around to whom people might – at least in their minds – delegate the responsibility for helping.[24]

Melbin could not, of course, control or change time; but by approaching people with the same requests for assistance during the day and at night, the IV was manipulated. Specifically, 12:15 am to 7:29 am was defined as night; 9:30 am to 4:14 pm was defined as day. One test of helpfulness involved approaching strangers and asking for directions to a well-known Boston site. When the request occurred – in relation to day and night as defined above – determined whether the subject who was approached would be considered part of the experimental (i.e. night) or control (i.e. day) group condition.

In a natural setting, the experimenter has relatively little control over who happens to be in the field when the experiment is conducted. However, that does not mean that one should passively accept whoever shows up at a given time. In Melbin's study, during both day and night tests, subjects were systematically selected from among all the potential people on the street. Specifically, for a five-minute period, the experimenters counted the number of passers-by, and the larger their number, the greater the sampling rate. For example, if the investigators in the field counted 3 or 4 people going by, they selected the second person to pass; if they counted 5 to 25 people, they selected the third person to pass, and so on. This mode of selection was intended to minimize *selection bias*. This bias can operate whenever researchers fail to follow any rules for selecting subjects because then they may, consciously or unconsciously, overlook unappealing passers-by, disproportionately choose members of the opposite sex or the same sex, etc. If a selection bias is not prevented, the sample of people selected may systematically differ from all those who are out at night or during the day.

Making sure other people passed between the people who were selected as subjects also addressed another potential problem associated with the selection of subjects and their assignment to experimental or control groups: *contamination*. It occurs in natural experiments when subjects see other subjects selected. They may then infer they are part of an experiment (the reactivity problem, again), or at least conclude that something strange is occurring. In either case, their behavior may be altered. Not selecting continuous passers-by was one of the ways that Melbin's study avoided this type of contamination. It is always important in a natural experiment to allow sufficient time between subject selection, or to vary the locations of subject selection, to minimize the possibility that any potential subject sees other subjects being selected for the experiment.

In a laboratory setting

In a laboratory setting, an experimenter typically begins with a pool of potential subjects. Very often they are students at an experimenter's college: undergraduates in an introductory course, students with a specific major, etc. In some cases advertisements attract potential subjects within a particular geographical area and induce them to participate with promises of some form of payment (cash, free treatment, etc.). Or the subjects may be volunteers, recruited from local organizations. Whether the pool of subjects is appropriate for the experiment and whether the generalizabiltiy

Experimental design

of findings is impaired by the subject pool are important questions – to be discussed later in this chapter's section on internal and external validity. For now, we will take the pool as given, and turn to issues surrounding how they are best assigned to experimental and control groups.

Careful assignment is critical in order to assure that personal qualities that subjects bring to the experiment will not be responsible for any observed differences in the DV. That places a premium on making sure these personal qualities share the same distributions in the experimental and control groups. There are two ways this task can be accomplished: matching and randomization.

As its name implies, *matching* entails measuring relevant qualities of potential subjects, using those measurements to create matched pairs of subjects, then assigning one from each pair to each experimental condition. For example, if gender were considered relevant, then the experimental and control groups would be created with each having the same distribution of males and females. Typically, however, it is some combination of attributes that is potentially important to match; for example, it might be both gender and age. In that case, pairs might be comprised of: females and males over age 60, females and males aged 50–59, and so on. Explicit matching of subjects assigned to each experimental condition has the advantage of guaranteeing that the attributes matched will be held constant, and therefore, will not affect values of the DV.

Relying upon matching becomes problematic when large combinations of attributes are of concern to the experimenter because that requires a large subject pool. For example, if it is important to the experiment to control for the effects of gender, age, race and educational level, then – depending upon the degree of specificity with which each of these attributes is to be measured – one might need a sample of thousands to create all the necessary matched pairs. And a subject pool that large is not often available.

There is a second problem with matching, regardless of the combination of attributes involved or the size of the subject pool. This problem arises because matching obviously requires an investigator to identify in advance, and measure, all of the potentially important attributes to be controlled. However, an investigator may not be aware of all the relevant variables, especially in advance.

Because of the above noted problems, the typically preferred method is to treat the pool of potential subjects as though they were a population and then randomly assign people from that pool to serve as subjects in either the experimental or control group. Random samples are fully discussed in the following chapter. For now, we can state that to randomly place subjects into each experimental group requires a mechanical procedure for determining each subject's assignment in which each subject has the same chance of being placed in either group. For example, if the subject pool is very small, one could improvise and put everyone's name in a hat and assign them to E or C by blindly selecting names from the hat. However, when the subject pool is large, such improvised procedures become very cumbersome. There are a number of straightforward and manageable ways of mechanically selecting a random sample, discussed in detail in Chapter 4.

In principle, samples that are randomly selected from the same population have a very low probability of differing from each other in any respect. One can therefore conclude, with a known degree of certainty, that randomly assigned members of E and C will not significantly differ from each other. It is not necessary to identify specific variables to be controlled by matching, and that is one reason for the general superiority of randomization over matching. In addition, the statistical analyses that are usually employed to test whether the difference between E and C is due to chance presuppose random assignments. On the other hand, to have confidence that the laws of probability will apply requires a large sample. If an experiment is to involve only a small number of subjects in E and C, then matching may be preferable, especially if there is a single TV to be controlled.

To many experts in experimental design, the advantages of randomization are so great as to make it required except under the very limited conditions described above. Rose McDermott, for example, presents randomization as a commandment, "thou shalt randomize," arguing that it is, "the crux of the experimental method upon which all analysis of results depends. . ." because it permits "the reasonable exclusion of alternative explanations for observed findings."[25]

Contamination and blinding

Contamination was seen to be a potential problem in field studies if people selected as subjects became aware they were part of an experiment because they saw others being selected. In laboratory experiments, everyone is usually well aware that they are subjects in an experiment. Contamination arises in this setting if subjects can deduce whether they are in E or C, or think they can deduce it. They may feel rivalry (us against them), superiority if they suspect they are in E, demoralized if they believe themselves to be in C. To minimize contamination of this type, it is important to keep subjects assigned to E and C far apart from each other. This parallels the objective of selecting subjects who do not see each other being selected in a natural setting.

It is also critically important that subjects do not know whether they are in E or C because such information could affect their expectations, and their expectations may be sufficient to produce the effect the investigator would like to be able to attribute to IV. Subjects who are ignorant of whether they are in E or C are referred to as *blind*. It is correspondingly important that whoever evaluates or assigns scores on the DV does not know the experimental condition to which subjects were assigned. This creates a situation referred to as *double blind*. Then neither the subjects' nor the experimenters' expectations are likely to distort the values of the DV. In any experiment, it is important to follow the double blind principle as much as possible.

In Internet-based experiments

The IV in Internet-based experiments typically involves the manipulation of a fictitious set of people or events, placing an online subject into E or C. The responses of actual people who believe they are in contact with the fictitious people or who are exposed to the unreal event become the DV. Despite the fakery that is involved, however, the assignment of subjects to E or C presents investigators with the same choices as in any other type of experiment.

To illustrate the assignment issue in an Internet-based experiment, consider a well-established line of inquiry that focuses upon racial, ethnic or gender discrimination in on-line recruitment for jobs. These studies, often conducted simultaneously in one or more cities, typically rely upon creating job applicants who (appear to) submit resumes to be considered for posted vacancies, and then investigators note how potential employers respond to variations in candidates that were created by the investigator. Except for the IV – which may be their race, ethnicity or gender, or some combination of these attributes – the fictitious applicants have to be the same on a potentially very lengthy list of other known-to-be-relevant personal characteristics: age, education, work experience, etc.

As we have previously seen, attempting to use matching to control large combinations of attributes is at best very cumbersome. In addition, there is always the danger that still other not considered (and therefore not matched) attributes will make a difference to potential employers, and will therefore exert an extraneous influence on the DV. As a result, randomization remains the recommended choice even if subjects are invented for the experiment.

Representative of these online studies is an experiment reported by Blommaert, Coenders and van Tubergen. They studied the degree of ethnic-based discrimination faced by Arabic-named applicants, compared to Dutch-named applicants, applying via the Internet for jobs in cities in the Netherlands. The investigators created fictitious resumes based upon the portfolios of actual job seekers, but then randomly assigned either a typically Arabic or typically native Dutch name to the resume.

This provided the experimenters with two pools of candidates who were comparable to each other except with respect to their apparent ethnicity, enabling the experimenters to isolate the effect of the IV (ethnicity) upon employers' decisions (the DV). They found evidence of discrimination against Arabic-named applicants at every stage of the selection process.[26]

Internal and external validity

In previous chapters we discussed validity in reference to specific measures, and it involved the congruence of these measures with the concepts they were supposed to reflect. This referent will be further examined in detail in the discussion of types of validity in Chapter 7. However, with respect to experiments, the term has two distinctive meanings: internal and external validity.

Internal validity

Internal validity refers to the overall adequacy of an experiment's design in enabling an investigator to reach a conclusion concerning a causal connection between IV and DV. The primary objective of most experiments, as we have noted, is to test a hypothesis that posits a causal relationship. The assessment of the design, therefore, focuses upon how well it makes that causal inference possible. We have previously discussed most of the issues that potentially threaten the internal reliability of an experiment. They include: selection bias, contamination, maturation effects, measurement error, reactivity and subjects' and evaluators' expectations.

The one threat to internal validity not yet considered is statistical, and it involves a frequently observed phenomenon known as *regression to the mean* (rtm). First recognized in the nineteenth century, rtm describes the tendency for extreme scores on any variable to be followed by less extreme scores, that is, for scores to revert toward the mean, or average. For example, very tall parents have been found to have children who are taller than average, but less tall than themselves. Very short parents also tend to have children who are shorter than average, but taller than themselves. Illustrating rtm, both sets of offspring are closer to the mean than their parents. Similarly, people who score very high on a test will often score less high when re-taking the test. Of course, if they score high enough the first time, the only way they could change would be to score lower at a later time. Very low scores would be subject to the same rtm.

If at the beginning of an experiment, subjects in the experimental or control group happen to have extreme scores with respect to the DV, their pre-test score may differ from their post-test score as a result of rtm. Depending upon the experimental design, the change could be erroneously attributed to the IV (rather than rtm). The risk of this happening would be most pronounced in a one group design with a pre-and post-test. A classic design, with random assignment of subjects to experimental and control groups, is the best defense against incorrectly interpreting rtm effects. Especially when that is not possible, it is important for an investigator to examine the subjects' range of scores to see whether rtm is likely to occur.[27]

External validity

External validity focuses upon the generalizability of the findings of an experiment. It most typically refers to whether the experimental conditions sufficiently resemble un-manipulated situations to permit one reasonably to expect the same outcomes in "real life" as those that are observed in the experiment.[28] The answer to this question depends, in part, upon where the experiment was conducted. All else equal, the external validity of a natural or Internet experiment is likely to be higher than one conducted in a laboratory where the setting may be artificial, or unrealistic, and reactivity is more likely to be a problem.

Comparing laboratory and natural experiments is difficult because they tend to differ from each other in numerous respects. The laboratory setting offers more control, a greater ability to standardize measurement procedures, and a more condensed time between subjects in E's exposure to the IV and measurement of the E–C differences in DV. In a laboratory experiment, elapsed time is typically very limited, comprising hours or even minutes. In a natural setting, by contrast, the time period between exposure to IV and measurement of DV may extend over weeks or even months. The differences in control, measurement and time may all lead to larger observed effects in laboratory settings, and there is little empirical evidence bearing on the issue. Fortunately, one recent study has reported highly suggestive results.

One of very few studies to address the above questions was reported by Jerit, Barabas and Clifford. They recruited thousands of students and randomly assigned them to serve as subjects in either a laboratory (a computer lab at their university) or natural setting (the subjects' homes). The subjects were also randomly assigned either to an experimental group – that read particular stories from a local newspaper – or to a control group that was not exposed to the stories. The DV – their attitude toward the issues covered in the local stories – was measured by surveys, taken either in the computer lab or at home.[29]

In this experiment on experiments, the investigators found that differences between E and C on the DV were almost always significantly greater in the laboratory than natural setting. However, they also found that much of the difference was apparently due to the more truncated time period in the laboratory: subjects read the articles, then almost immediately took the surveys. At home, more time typically elapsed between subjects' reading of the articles and filling out the survey. To demonstrate time effects, the investigators divided the subjects who took the survey at home into two groups: early and late finishers. (The earlier finishers filled out the questionnaire closer to the time they read the articles.) They found that E–C differences between the subjects who finished the survey early were significantly greater than between those who finished the survey later. In other words, temporal proximity between IV and DV increased the effect of IV regardless of setting, but brief proximity was imposed in the laboratory so it was shortened for all laboratory subjects, and that was an important part of the overall difference between the observed effects in the laboratory and field settings.

Notes

1 For further discussion of the distinction between true and quasi experiments, see Michelle Jackson and D.R. Cox, "The Principles of Experimental Design and Their Application in Sociology." *Annual Review of Sociology*, 39, 2013.

2 For more information about al-Razi, see Peter E. Portmann and Emilie Savage-Smith, *Medieval Islamic Medicine*. Georgetown University Press, 2007.

3 Adam D. Kramer, Jamie E. Guillory, and Jeffrey T. Hancock, "Experimental Evidence of Massive-scale Emotional Contagion through Social Networks." *Proceedings of the National Academy of Sciences*, 111, 2014.

4 Namkje Koudenburg, Tom Postmes and Ernestine H. Gordijn, "Resounding Silences." *Social Psychology Quarterly*, 76, 2013.

5 See Jackson and Cox, *op. cit.*

6 For a discussion of the original reporting and subsequent re-analyses, see Kevin Cook, *Kitty Genovese*. W.W. Norton, 2014.

7 A number of these studies are reviewed in, Susan T. Fiske, *Social Beings*. Wiley, 2009.

8 Robert V. Levine, Ara Norenzayan and Karen Philbrick, "Cross-Cultural Differences in Helping Strangers." *Journal of Cross-Cultural Psychology*, 32, 2001.

9 For an overview of the different types of urban experiments on climate change, and a way of classifying them in relation to urban governance issues, see Harriet Bulkeley and Vanese C. Broto, "Government by Experiment?" *Transactions of the Institute of British Geographers*, 38, 2013.

10 Oded Cats, Triin Reimal and Yusak Susilo, "Public Transportation Pricing Policy." *93rd Annual Meeting of the Transportation Research Board*, Washington, D.C., January, 2014.

11 These findings are reported by The Climate Group. For more information and lists of publications, see: www.theclimategroup.org.

12 For a discussion of the differences between statistically demonstrating association and causation, see Judea Pearl, "The Foundations of Causal Inference." *Sociological Methodology*, 40, 2010.

Experimental design

13 For further discussion of this general problem, see Dennis Meredith, *Explaining Research*. Oxford University Press, 2010.

14 Peter Hedstrom and Petri Ylikoski, "Causal Mechanisms in the Social Sciences." *Annual Review of Sociology*, 36, 2010.

15 D.W. Nickerson, "Is Voting Contagious?" *American Political Science Review*, 102, 2008.

16 A. Philip Daid, David L. Faigman and Stephen E. Fienberg, "Fitting Science into Legal Contexts." *Sociological Methods and Research*, 23, 2013.

17 For further discussion, see Michael Karson, "Nomothetic Versus Idiographic." In Neil J. Salkind (Ed), *Encyclopedia of Measurement and Statistics*. Sage, 2006.

18 William J. Dickson and F.J. Roethlisberger, *Counseling in Organizations*. Harvard University Press, 1966.

19 Koudenburg, et al., *op. cit.*

20 Constanza S. Abbate, Stefano Ruggieri and Stefano Boca, "The Effects of Pro-social Priming in the Presence of Bystanders." *Journal of Social Psychology*, 153, 2013.

21 Paul Gertler, et al., "Labor Market Returns to an Early Childhood Stimulation Intervention in Jamaica." *Science*, 30 May, 2014.

22 Rebecca Casciano and Douglas S. Massey, "School Context and Educational Outcomes." *Urban Affairs Review*, 48, 2012.

23 See, for example, the discussion in, Macartan Humphreys and Jeremy M. Weinstein, "Field Experiments and the Political Economy of Development." *Annual Review of Political Science*, 12, 2009.

24 Murray Melbin, *Night as Frontier*. Free Press, 1987.

25 Rose McDermott, "The Ten Commandments of Experiments." *PS: Political Science & Politics*, 46, 2013.

26 Lieselotte Blommaert, Marcel Coenders and Frank van Tubergen, "Discrimination of Arabic-named Applicants in the Netherlands." *Social Forces*, 92, 2014.

27 For further discussion, see Donald T. Campbell and David A. Kenny, *A Primer on Regression Artifacts*. Guilford, 1999.

28 There is a second referent to external validity, namely whether experimental conditions provide a sufficiently faithful rendering of the conditions specified in a theory to enable the experiment to be viewed as a test of the theory.

29 Jennifer Jerit, Jason Barabas and Scott Clifford, "Comparing Contemporaneous Laboratory and Field Experiments on Media Effects." *Public Opinion Quarterly*, 77, 2013.

Glossary

Blind: When subjects do not know if they are in the experimental or control group.

Confederates: Allies of the experimenter who try to appear like other subjects, but carry out roles pre-arranged by the experimenter.

Contamination: In a natural experiment, when subjects see other subjects selected; in a laboratory experiment, when subjects are aware of their place in the experimental design.

Control Group (C):   The group of subjects that is usually not exposed to, or does not receive the treatment associated with, the independent varaible.

Dependent Variable (DV):   The variable thought to be dependent upon, or determined by, the independent variable.

Double Blind: Neither the subjects nor the investigator rating the subjects knows who is the experimental or control group.

Experimental Group (E):   The group of subjects that is typically exposed to the independent variable or receives the treatment associated with the independent variable.

Ideographic: A complete explanation of a singular event or specific person.

Independent Variable (IV):   The variable believed to cause, or produce, the dependent variable.

Matching: Measure relevant attributes of subjects and assign them to experimental and control groups in matched pairs.

Maturation Effects: Changes occurring in subjects during the experiment that have nothing to do with the experiment.

Mechanism: The process, or means, by which an IV and DV are causally connected.

Negative Relationship: As one variable increases in magnitude, the other variable declines.

Nomothetic: A parsimonious and probabilistic explanation for a class of events or people.

Positive Relationship: As one variable increases in magnitude, the other does also.

Random Assignment: Subjects are mechanically assigned to E or C, with each having an equal probability.

Regression to the Mean (rtm):   When scores are extreme at time one, they are likely to move toward the average at time two.

Selection Bias: An unrepresentative sample of subjects is chosen, usually because an experimenter did not follow mechanical rules in selecting the sample of subjects.

Spuriousness: An association between an independent and dependent variable that is due to their shared relationship with a third variable.

chapter 4

Sample surveys

Outline
- History of urban sampling studies
- Sampling: Basic terms
- Sample accuracy
- Determining sample size
- Types of samples
  - Probability and non-probability samples
  - Cross-sectional and longitudinal studies
  - Probability samples
    - Simple random samples (SRS)
      - Random digit dialing (RDD)
        - Refusal rates
    - Systematic samples
      - Multi-stage sampling
      - Stratified sampling
      - Cluster sampling
    - Final step: Selecting a respondent
    - Panel studies
      - Recruiting a sample
      - Attrition
  - Non-probability samples
    - Quota samples
    - Snowball/RDS sampling

- Reaching respondents
  - In-person
  - Telephone
  - Mail
  - On-line
  - Mixed mode

- Nonresponse bias
  - Adjusting for nonresponse bias

- Notes
- Glossary

Among the first issues most investigators confront in preparing to conduct a study concerns who or what to sample, and how that sample will be selected. That is true regardless of whether the investigator is planning to study individuals, organizations, metropolitan areas, or any other entity. In this chapter, we will examine the assumptions that underlie the selection of a sample, and discuss the diverse ways that samples are designed and executed. This chapter will also review the modes by which members of a sample, once selected, are questioned or observed: in person, by phone, mechanically, by mail, or via the Internet.

The major methods of obtaining information from sampled respondents – questionnaires and interviews – are discussed in detail in the following chapter. Treatment of these methods in a separate chapter is recommended by the fact that the principles of conducting interviews or of constructing questionnaires are essentially the same within any overall research design. A questionnaire, for example, would be judged by much the same criteria whether it was employed in a sample survey or an experiment.

History of urban sampling studies

The first studies of cities and city life to rely upon sophisticated sampling procedures – as opposed to a haphazard selection of people or places – were probably those conducted by the British economist and statistician, A.L. Browley. His pioneering research involved five UK towns that he studied around the turn of the twentieth century. To understand his contributions in a larger context, however, it is helpful to view Browley's research in relation to, and as part of, the Social Survey Movement.

The *Social Survey Movement (SSM)* refers to a large collection of studies conducted during the second half of the nineteenth century, and the first decades of the twentieth century. The studies were carried out in England and the US by religious leaders, social reformers and pioneering social researchers who were trying to document the extent of poverty and its effects upon family life in early industrial cities. They examined British cities, including London and Manchester, and US cities, including New York and Pittsburgh.[1] A couple of decades after the first studies were conducted in England and the US, similar studies were undertaken in larger Canadian cities.[2] Despite variations in time and place, all of these studies shared the objective of arousing the middle class and stimulating progressive reforms. And several of the projects that were parts of the SSM were successful in leading to minimum wage legislation, improved food and medical care for school children, and so on.

These early studies were very ambitious attempts to canvass every household in an entire city, or in very large sections of a city. The researchers believed that such completeness was necessary in order to provide documentary evidence of the prevalence of poverty and its effects upon family life in communities that were dominated by factory employment. The studies were conducted by well-meaning, civic-minded people who typically had little formal training in either research methods or data analysis. Their staffs were small, containing a mix of volunteers and paid workers who also tended to have little prior research experience, but they nevertheless made exhaustive efforts to obtain information about every individual or household. It was in this context that Browley entered the picture. He wondered whether, to answer the questions that inspired the SSM research, it was really necessary for these researchers to try to conduct complete enumerations. Given that efforts to include every person or household in any large area are inevitably incomplete and prone to biases, might well-drawn samples be as good (or better) to ascertain the extent of poverty?

Shortly after the turn of the twentieth century, Browley published a series of papers proposing that the application of probability theory would produce samples that were representative of the larger entities from which they were drawn, regardless of whether one was studying people, business firms, cities, or anything else. He greatly admired the time and effort that went into producing the previously published SSM studies, but insisted that trying to obtain complete enumerations, following the model of the census, was more expensive and time consuming than was necessary. He wrote:

> "We can obtain as good results . . . by sampling, and very often small samples are enough; the only difficulty is to ensure that every person . . . has the same chance of inclusion . . ."[3]

To prove his contention, he conducted a series of small experiments, repeatedly taking samples of cases from such diverse sources as listings of business firms' profits, people's death rates, and so on. In each instance he was able to demonstrate that carefully taking a sample of cases from the list and then analyzing them enabled an investigator to infer an average for the entire collection of cases that was extremely close to the average that was obtained when every case was included in the analysis.

A few years later, Browley applied sampling theory to actual studies of working-class households in Reading, Northampton, and other British towns. To conduct these studies, he obtained lists of streets and buildings, and then selected households from every twentieth building in each street. From this sample, he projected figures for the entire towns. He then meticulously calculated the "probable error" that could arise from "estimating the whole by measuring a part."[4] (Such calculations later became standard features of almost every sample survey.)

During the 1930s, the work of Browley and others became building blocks in contemporary sample survey research. It was during this decade that sampling and surveys moved from the realm of the social reformers into academic settings. Professional researchers from across the social sciences, journalism, marketing, and so on were brought together in newly formed survey research centers at leading universities, such as Princeton and Columbia. These scholars began a journal devoted to studies of sampling and surveys (*The Public Opinion Quarterly*), and formed related professional associations. One result was a growing body of empirical studies and theories about sampling and sample surveys, and by the 1950s sample surveys had become one of the major methods used to study urban life as well as public opinion, voting, etc.

In every modern society, sample surveys are now ubiquitous parts of everyday life. From very small samples of adults, pollsters predict elections and provide measures of consumer confidence; from price fluctuations in the stocks of a small number of companies, analysts construct an overall picture of stock market activity, such as the Dow Jones Average, and so on. In virtually every realm, citizens, corporations and cities rely upon estimates derived from samples rather than attempt complete enumerations.

Sampling: Basic terms

In this section, we will define and discuss the basic terms and procedures that are involved in the selection of any sample. To begin, the first consideration is a population. In everyday terminology, a population usually refers to all of the individuals who reside in a particular place. However, recall that one can sample almost anything: people, business firms, cities, etc, so a population must, for this purpose, be viewed more abstractly to be able to subsume diverse collections. Thus, a *population* is defined by the characteristic(s) that distinguish all of the included elements, or as the sum of all the elements that share the defining characteristic. The population is the larger entity to which the sample is intended to generalize. For example, it could be defined as all automobiles registered in a city or all students enrolled in a city college.

No matter how well-known the parameters of any population appear to be, the formal definition of a population, by a researcher, always requires some careful consideration. For example, if the population is defined as all students at a city college, does that include both full- and part-time students? Graduates and undergraduates? All students regardless of whether they are in degree-granting programs? From a sampling perspective, there are no intrinsically right or wrong answers to such questions. How they should be answered depends upon the interests/ purposes of the research. So, if the objective of a study is to determine how many parking spaces might be needed in a new student parking lot, it might make sense to define the population broadly, to include as many potential student drivers as possible. On the other hand, if one wanted to know how large a venue would be needed to hold an undergraduate commencement ceremony, and a sample was to be taken from a student population to estimate how many guests graduates would like to invite, then the population would likely be more narrowly defined as students in degree-granting programs.

At the end of a sample survey, an investigator wants to make an inference to a particular population. At the onset of the study, therefore, the investigator must decide what that population ought to entail, and define it accordingly. If the population is initially misconstrued, the value of the entire study will be diminished, regardless of how well a sample is ultimately drawn from that (misconstrued) population.

The next term to be considered is an *element* and it refers to each individual case included in a population. The defining qualities of an element follow directly from the definition of a population. Thus, if a population is defined as all registered automobiles, then each of these automobiles would be an element of the population.

A sample could be defined simply as any group of elements from a given population; that is, a part of a larger whole. However, that is not a very helpful definition because it fails to include the technical criterion of most importance in evaluating any sample, *representativeness*: the degree to which a sample is a microscopic reflection of a population in every respect. That, in turn, means that the distribution of characteristics in the sample is essentially the same as the distribution of those characteristics in the population. A sample of students would, therefore, be representative of a population of students if the sample contained the same proportion of older and younger students as were found in the population, both had essentially the same grade point average, the same distribution of majors, and so on. If there is a difference between a population and a sample drawn from it, the sample is said to have a *bias*. In other words, a non-representative sample is referred to as a biased sample.

In some cases, the parameters of a population are known, and the representativeness of any sample drawn from it can be directly assessed. More often, though, the population's exact qualities are not known, and in fact, the population is known only through the sample. To predict a national election, no one asks every registered voter (a population) how they intend to vote. Only a sample is taken, and from that sample an investigator infers how party preference will influence voting, how men and women will differ, and so on. Estimates for the population are inferred from the sample, which leads to an emphasis upon procedures: that is, *how* the sample is selected. Remember, there are often no independently derived figures for a population to which a sample could be compared. The representativeness of a sample is therefore assumed if its selection followed procedures that have been demonstrated to produce samples that are representative of the population from which they are drawn. Much more on this later.

The final term we will introduce here is a *sampling frame*: an actual listing of the elements of a population from which a sample is drawn. In many instances, a population can be defined conceptually, but there may not be an adequate sampling frame for the population, as conceptualized. For example, there may be no sampling frame to correspond with all households in the north end of London or the west side of Chicago. Possibilities, such as utility company records, school and voting lists, may all be incomplete and contain errors. If so, the errors in a sampling frame are likely to result in a sample that is biased with respect to the population.

The most (in)famous example of sample bias due to an inaccurate sampling frame is the *Literary Digest* poll taken prior to the 1936 election in the US. The magazine primarily utilized two sampling frames: automobile registrations and telephone directories. They selected about 10 million potential voters from these lists, and mailed post cards to them containing questions about their voting intentions. Almost two and a half million post cards were returned. Despite obtaining this huge sample, the magazine erroneously predicted a large victory for the Republican candidate – but the Democrat candidate won.

The prediction was wrong because the sampling frames did not accurately represent the voting population. In 1936, wealthier people in the US were more likely than poorer people to own both automobiles and telephones, and hence be on either or both lists; and wealthier people were also more likely to vote Republican. The size of the magazine's sample could not make up for the over-representation of Republican-leaning voters in the sampling frames.[5]

Because many, though not all, ways of taking a sample require the prior existence of a sampling frame – and a sampling frame that is incomplete or otherwise presents a distorted picture of a population can ruin a sample survey – a premium is placed upon locating an adequate sampling frame. An investigator may be aware of numerous possibilities, but it would be risky to utilize any without some analysis of their completeness. Assessing the usability of a potential sampling frame frequently entails comparing it to a previously used frame to see whether the new alternative would represent an improvement. An example of such an assessment is presented in Box 4.1.

Box 4.1 Using administrative records as sampling frames in the UK

In many countries, government agencies at local and national levels collect a great deal of administrative data pertaining to residents' employment, income, taxes paid, and so on. In most cities and nations, researchers have made only limited use of these records in constructing sampling frames. The hesitation is due to fear that the government lists would not be complete, and that systematic omissions would result in sampling frames that did not represent the populations of interest to the researchers. Focusing upon the UK, Antonia Simon questioned whether government administrative records could provide an inexpensive way to create sampling frames from which representative samples might be drawn.[6]

As a case in point, Simon examined how well the administrative data held by the Department of Work and Pensions could be used to construct a sampling frame for a study of household income. Such studies in the UK had typically relied upon samples taken from the Postcode Address File (PAF). It provides a list of all addresses receiving less than 50 items of post daily, hence excluding all businesses except for small ones. It has provided the most widely used sampling frame for sampling the general population in the UK.

The PAF contains only addresses, and no information about who resides at any address. Researchers cannot, therefore, prepare in advance for what they will find at a selected address, or design a sample to focus upon particular types of households. However, Simon's main consideration was whether the government's administrative records might provide a more complete enumeration than the PAF of the population to employ as a sampling frame. Completeness is an important criterion because the list with fewer omissions is less likely to suffer from systematic exclusions or over-representations of particular groups of elements.

In this study, Simon compared two sampling frames, one compiled from the PAF and one compiled from a government-held administrative data set. She found that 98 percent of the postcodes, or addresses, on the PAF list were also included in the administrative databases. Thus, the government records seemed very complete when compared to the PAF listing. However, only 81 percent of the postcodes in the administrative databases could be identified in the PAF. Further investigation showed that almost all of the addresses in the administrative lists that were absent from the PAF were valid addresses, indicating that the incompleteness in the PAF reflected erroneous omissions.

From the matching of cases, it was possible to conclude that the administrative records probably provided a better sampling frame than the postcode file. In addition, the administrative records provided information about household composition and income, thereby permitting investigators who wished to focus upon specific sub-groups to tailor their samples accordingly, in advance. Based upon these advantages, Simon concluded that government records, at least in the UK, should be more widely used to create sampling frames.

Sample accuracy

Even in theory, it is not assumed that the estimates obtained for a sample, regardless of how perfectly the sampling process was designed, will be absolutely identical to those of the population from which it was drawn. The sample results may, for example, indicate that 52 percent of a city's population will vote for the incumbent mayor in the next election or that the average (mean) years of schooling completed by adult residents of a city's west end is 12.5 years. If the samples from which these figures were derived followed an appropriate probability model, then the sample's figures will likely be very close to those that would be obtained if the entire population was canvassed; very close, but not identical. This principle can be illustrated by a simple coin toss experiment. If a coin is tossed 100 times, would exactly 50 heads and 50 tails always occur? The answer is, only sometimes. One would also expect a lot of 51–49 results, some 52–48 results, and so on. The further the outcome was from 50–50 – the true population figure – the less often it would be expected to occur.

The size of the discrepancy between the characteristics of a sample and population is largely a function of the variability, or dispersal, of the variable in question. Thus, if in the west end of a city, people's educational levels differed greatly from each other, then the 12.5 mean would be in the middle of a highly dispersed distribution. By contrast, if most people in the area completed either 12 or 13 years of education, then 12.5 would be in the middle of a highly compact distribution. How close the sample figure is (likely to be) to that of the population depends upon this degree of variability. The more highly dispersed the sample distribution, the more likely is a greater difference between the figures that describe the sample and the population.

To grasp the impact of dispersion upon the closeness between a sample and population, consider people's noses. A silly example, but it clarifies the point. Suppose one took a sample of people in order to count the number of noses on their faces. On rare occasions a person with no nose or with two noses might be encountered. (Neither occurs often, but both do exist.) Because of the vast preponderance of one nose per face, the sample mean would be one and virtually every element in the sample would also have a score of one. Hence, there would be extremely little dispersion around the mean, implying that there was also little dispersion around the population mean, and so the sample mean would almost certainly be very close to that of the population. On the other hand, if the length of people's hair or their height was studied, there would be a good deal more variation around the sample mean, implying more dispersion around the population mean as well, and therefore, a greater possibility of a large difference between the means of the sample and the population.

The dispersal of elements' scores above and below the mean of a sample is statistically summarized by the *standard deviation*. It basically sums the magnitude of difference between the score of each element and the mean of the sample, regardless of whether the score is above or below the mean. It is only the magnitude of difference that matters, and the sum of these differences is summarized by the standard deviation.

Neither the actual population mean nor the dispersal of cases around that mean are typically known. They could be known only by canvassing the entire population, or by repeatedly taking samples from the population. Each such sample would produce results that differed somewhat from every other (unless one was measuring a variable with almost no dispersal). The mean of all the samples would be the mean of the population, and the dispersal among sample means would resemble the standard deviation, but because it pertains to the population it is referred to as *Standard Error* (S.E). The S.E. of a population is estimated from the standard deviation of the sample, adjusted for sample size. The logic behind this assumption is that the greater the variability within a sample, the greater the likely variability among samples.

A *Confidence Interval* (C.I.) refers to a range of values above and below the sample mean (or other sample figure) which contains a known likelihood of encompassing the corresponding population value. The C.I. is typically referred to as the margin of error in the popular reporting of survey and poll results. The specific terms included in the calculation of the C.I. vary, depending upon the way the variable in question is being measured. If it is percentage, such as the percentage of a sample who favor candidate X in the mayoral election, then the percentage split is included in the formula; for example, 50–50, 60–40, etc. If it is an average, or mean, then the C.I. formula usually includes S.E.

The size of a C.I. is determined, first, by variability or dispersion, and can be measured by S.E. The more homogeneous the variable in the sample, the smaller will be the C.I. Another variable determining the size of a C.I. is sample size (n). The larger the sample, the smaller the C.I., but diminishing returns usually sets in. Thus, as the sample size initially increases, there are substantial declines in the C.I. However, as n continues to increase beyond some point, the C.I. ceases to decline proportionately. These diminishing returns from increases in n can be seen in Table 4.1.

Finally, the size of a C.I. is determined by a *confidence level* (C.L.): a probability corresponding with the confidence interval that is set by the investigator. The level is typically set at 0.95 (95 percent), which means there is a 95 percent probability that the population characteristic lies within plus or minus the C.I. around the sample mean. For example, if the mean educational level of a sample was 12.5 years, and the C.I. was 1.5 years when the C.L. was set at 95 percent, then one could conclude the following: There is a 95 percent likelihood that the population mean was between 11 (12.5 − 1.5) and 14 (12.5 + 1.5) years of schooling. If the probability level is lowered, to 0.90 (90 percent), then the C.I. will be reduced, but at the price of less certainty. Raising the C.L. to 0.99 (99 percent) increases certainty, but it results in an enlarged C.I. Thus, there is a trade-off between precision and certainty, which is also illustrated in Table 4.1. It shows the size of the sample that would be necessary given different values of C.I. and C.L.

Table 4.1 presents the figures that would be obtained in a typical election study, for example, when a 50–50 split is assumed. (In the absence of

Table 4.1 Confidence Level, Confidence Interval and sample size

C.I.	Sample size required if C.L. = 0.95	Sample size required if C.L. = 0.99
2.0	2401	4160
2.5	1537	2663
3.0	1067	1849
3.5	784	1358
4.0	600	1040

information to the contrary, most investigators simply assume a 50–50 split for purposes of these calculations.) If the C.L. is set at 0.95, for example, and the C.I. is 2.0, then a sample of 2,401 elements (e.g. registered voters) would be required. Note, however, that if the C.L. is raised to 0.99 (last column) then the same C.I. (2.0) would require a sample of 4,160 cases.

The diminishing returns of increased sample size can be seen by looking up either of the last two columns. For example, when C.I. = 4.0 and C.L. = 0.95, to reduce C.I. by 0.5 (to 3.5), it would be necessary to increase the sample size by only 184 elements (i.e. 784 − 600). However, with the same C.L., when the sample size is 1,537, then to reduce the C.I. by 0.5 (from 2.5 to 2.0), the sample size would have to be increased by 864 elements (i.e. 2,401 − 1,537). Diminishing returns from increases in sample size are similarly illustrated by moving up or down in the last column. In sum, we see that a reduction in the C.I. of a larger sample requires a much larger addition of elements than when the sample is smaller.

Determining sample size

The formula for calculating C.I. includes three terms: C.L., a measure of variability or dispersion (such as S.E.), and sample size. It is conventionally calculated at the end of a study. However, a C.L. can be set in advance and if one can estimate variability or dispersion then the only initially unknown term in the equation is sample size. By inserting various sample sizes into the equation, a range of C.I.s can be viewed. Selecting a specific C.I. then establishes what the sample size will be. In other words, by working backward, an investigator can determine sample size based upon the degree of precision and certainty that is desired. There are also on-line "calculators" that compute C.I., C.L. or sample size, when the other two terms are plugged in.[7]

Types of samples

Probability and non-probability samples

Samples can generally be classified as falling into one of two types based upon the ways in which they were selected. The first, probability samples, are defined by the fact that every element of the population has a known probability of inclusion, and it is greater than zero. To illustrate, if 100 names (the population) were placed in a hat and a blindfolded person selected ten of them (the sample), then each of the names (the elements) would have a one in ten (10/100) chance of being included. Because the probability of each element being included is known and is greater than zero, this means of selection would result in a probability sample. In addition, probability samples rely upon *mechanical* means of selection, meaning that the investigator does not decide which specific elements to include. Picking names out of a hat, as above, or writing a program to randomly select phone numbers are examples of mechanical selection.

Probability samples are generally expensive to conduct, but they offer invaluable advantages to compensate for their cost. Most importantly, they are very likely to be representative of the population from which they are drawn; and that likelihood can be precisely calculated, and expressed in terms of C.I.s and C.L.s.

With non-probability samples, by contrast, the chance of any element's inclusion cannot be calculated, and some elements typically have no chance of being included. In addition, non-probability samples tend to provide investigators with a great deal of latitude in deciding which elements to include. For example, a reporter on a street corner questioning passers-by at will to find out how people in a city feel about a new sports arena, is selecting a non-probability sample. The chance of anyone in the city being on that street corner at the time of the survey is not known, and for those not at the street corner at the time of the interviews, the chance of being included is zero. Finally, the reporter explicitly decides which of the people who happen to be there to include, hence the selection is not mechanical. As a result, it is not known if the reporter, consciously or unconsciously, favored males over females, attractive people over homely ones, young over old, or the like.

The representativeness of non-probability samples is questionable. They can contain large biases, but at other times be very accurate. And they do not permit the calculation of most of the statistics used to assess the likely closeness between a sample and a population. For these reasons, non-probability samples are typically employed in pre-tests, in special situations in which no probability sample seems feasible, or when cost constraints are overwhelming because non-probability samples almost always cost less per element included.

Cross-sectional and longitudinal studies

A second basic distinction between types of samples concerns whether elements are observed or questioned only at one point in time – a *cross-sectional study*; or whether the same elements are observed or questioned over an extended period of time – a *longitudinal study*.

The typical sample survey takes a stop action picture of a cross-section of a population at one point in time. It is analogous to a photograph. With a cross-sectional survey it is important to complete the data collection as quickly as possible because the longer the time period involved, the greater the possibility that changes will occur in the population, and that will increase variability, which we have previously seen to increase the size of C.I.s. To pursue the analogy, lengthening the time frame of data collection in a cross-sectional sample survey can be likened to over-exposing a photograph by leaving the shutter of the camera open too long. In the following discussion of probability samples, cross-sectional designs are assumed unless stated to the contrary.

In order to analyze change when relying upon cross-sectional studies, it is necessary to examine a series of such studies, arranged chronologically. Because such trend analyses typically involve analyzing previously collected data, trend studies are discussed in Chapter 6, with other types of secondary data analysis. The only type of longitudinal study that always involves primary data collection is a panel study, and it is discussed later in this chapter.

Probability samples

The model for all probability samples is the simple random sample (SRS). It is the model that is most congruent with the mathematical principles that underlie sampling theory. Therefore, estimating population characteristics is most straightforward when the estimates are derived from a SRS. This type of sample is also unsurpassed in its simplicity of design.

Simple random samples (SRS)

Let us begin by offering a technical definition of random. In everyday conversation, the term is used interchangeably with haphazard. However, technically defined, the terms have very different referents. *Random* only means that all elements have an equal probability of inclusion. Pulling names from a hat would constitute a random sample because every element had the same chance of being selected. The disorderly, chaotic selection of passers-by on a street corner would qualify as haphazard, but there would be no reason to assume that it was random. For example, the street corner interviewer could not usually include two successive passers-by. While the first was being interviewed, the second (and maybe third) would pass unnoticed. The inclusion of some elements would, with haphazard selection, preclude the selection of other elements. Hence, all elements would not have the same chance of being included as every other element.

To grasp the difference between haphazard and random in this respect, consider a random selection process based upon a coin toss in which if a head (h) turns up, the element is selected, if a tails (t) turns up, the element is not selected. The results of the first coin toss would have no effect on the second, the second would have no effect on the third, etc. Any t or h would be followed by another t or an h with the same likelihood. Thus, the equal probability feature of random selection means there are no sequences that are more likely than any other.

The first step in conducting an SRS usually entails obtaining or constructing a sampling frame, previously defined as a complete listing of all elements in the population. And as previously noted, it is often difficult to obtain a complete, or unbiased, sampling frame, which is why, despite its advantages, an SRS is often not feasible. A discussion of alternatives that can be employed follows later in this chapter, but first let us consider situations in which an SRS is feasible.

One way to select an SRS from a sampling frame would be to utilize a table of random numbers that is available in the appendix of many statistics texts. Table 4.2 includes a very small section of the random numbers included in the rows and columns of such a table.

To begin sampling, each element in a sampling frame is numbered consecutively. The basis of the ordering is irrelevant; it could be alphabetical, based upon age, or the like. The total number of elements in the frame determines the number of digits to be used in selecting random numbers. Thus, if there were 500 elements in the sampling frame, a three-digit random number would be used; if there were 8,500 elements, it would entail using a four-digit number, and so on.

To illustrate, suppose one wished to select a SRS from a sampling frame comprised of the 427 persons on a city's sex offender registry. (Let us assume it has no systematic exclusions.) One could start selecting three-digit numbers anywhere on the page of random numbers. By definition, there is no pattern; and one could move up or down the columns or across the rows. Starting at Row 1, the number in the first three columns is 375. The registered offender who was assigned number 375 on the sampling frame would be the first one selected for the sample. Moving down to Row 2, Columns 1 to 3, the next element selected would be number 84 on

Table 4.2 Section of a table of random numbers

Row number	Column number		
	1–5	*6–10*	*7–11* . . .
1	37542	04805	
2	08422	68953	
3	99019	02529	
4	:	:	:
5	:	:	:

the sampling frame. Continuing in the same way, the next number selected would be 990, but it exceeds any number in the sampling frame so it would be ignored, and the selection process would continue.

If one were selecting a very small sample, then a table of random numbers could be used, as illustrated. For all but very small samples, however, using such a table would be unnecessarily cumbersome because a number of programs are available that provide easy-to-use computer-generated random numbers with the same properties as the table.

When an SRS, as illustrated here, can be employed, it should always be used. It is unsurpassed in simplicity of design and calculation of population estimates. Unfortunately, though, obtaining an accurate sampling frame is often not possible. While lists of elements included in vital statistics records, city yearbooks, automobile registrations, telephone directories, etc. often claim to be complete and accurate, they are often out-of-date, incomplete and biased. If flawed lists are used as the sampling frame, then the types of problems that plagued the Literary Digest poll of 1936 are always a possibility.

RANDOM DIGIT DIALING (RDD)

If no unbiased sampling frame can be obtained, random sampling is still possible if the elements of the population can be reached by telephone with random digit dialing (RDD). Before explaining how RDD is conducted, it is necessary briefly to explain how land line telephone numbers in towns or cities are conventionally assigned. The following discussion focuses upon the US, with some mention of differences in other nations. However, the current inter-nation similarities exceed the differences. Historically, several European nations lagged in degrees of telephone coverage, which led researchers to avoid telephone surveys of any type; but most of these differences have now largely disappeared, leading to an upsurge in European telephone surveys.[8]

To begin, local telephone numbers in the US begin with a three-digit prefix that denotes a geographical area. In the UK, the prefix also tends to be a three-digit number pertaining to a geographical area, but it can include as many as five digits, with the additional numbers used to denote a type of phone, such as corporate, freephone (no charge to callers), mobile phone, etc. Following the prefix, telephone companies assign numbers from basic, five-digit working blocks (or four-digit blocks in Australia). A US example would be (860) 486–31XX. For area code 860, this working block is 48631. The telephone company completes a customer's actual phone number by assigning numbers to the XX, usually in chronological order. So, the next assigned number might be 486–3111, then 486–3112, and so on. When any five-digit block is filled, the company opens another block of numbers.

In assigning numbers to individual households, it does not matter whether the number is going to be listed in a telephone directory or unlisted (e.g. an ex-directory number in UK, a private number in Canada). The assigned number is still taken, in order, from the same working block. Therefore, when phone numbers are randomly dialed, unlisted private numbers still have the same probability of being called.

Within an area code (e.g. 860) it is possible to identify the relative number of telephone numbers utilizing the 486 prefix, as well as all other prefixes. Telephone companies will often provide this information, and if they do not the investigator can determine the relative frequency of each prefix by taking a random sample of numbers from the telephone directory. That proportion is then dialed in forming the telephone sample. To take an RDD sample from a larger geographical entity, such as a state or nation, calls are made to area codes and prefixes, again according to each one's percentage of the total population.

Before the ubiquity of cell phones (or mobile phones in the UK), it was possible randomly to select local or national samples by RDD. The growing use of cell phones as people's only telephone, however, has necessitated that samples be drawn from both land line and cell phone numbers. (This problem has arisen in most of the world.) The solution has entailed drawing a second sample of cell phone numbers, from shared service banks of large and small carriers. It is necessary, however, to exclude those sampled individuals or households that also have directory-listed land line numbers.[9] Otherwise, people with both types of phones could be selected from either set while others could only be selected from one or the other. All elements' probabilities of inclusion would then not be identical, making selection non-random.

If a selected phone number corresponds with a single owner – as with most cell phones and/or land lines in a one-person household – then that person is interviewed, following questions that screen respondents to see if they are appropriate for the sample. Respondents are almost always screened to ensure they are over 18 years old, but depending upon the purposes of the study, they might also be screened for education, race, religion, etc. If multiple persons use the same telephone number – as with most land lines in multiple person households – then it may be important to follow randomized procedures in selecting a particular respondent from the household. Otherwise, a bias may be introduced if certain people are more likely than others to answer a phone.[10] (For further discussion of this issue, see "Final step: Selecting a respondent" at the end of the section on multi-stage sampling.)

While changing patterns of telephone ownership necessitated that RDD surveys include both land lines and cell phones, it has not always been clear how to allocate calls between the two frames. The percentage

Sample surveys

of the population relying solely upon cell phones is increasing continuously, and the precise percentage at any given time may not be known. So, even if an investigator wanted to dial land and cell phones in exact accordance with ownership and use patterns, that might not always be possible. In addition, there can be cost differences associated with the two frames that push an investigator to rely more upon telephone numbers associated with the less expensive frame. For the future, however, there are some data to suggest that cell phone only designs may become the best alternative.[11]

When a selected phone number is first dialed, if no one answers, or the desired respondent is not available, it is routine for sample surveys to call back at least one additional time. In order to maximize response rates, some sample surveys will make three efforts, at different times, to reach a respondent. Every sample survey seeks as high a response rate as possible, which argues for multiple call-backs. However, diminishing returns are often experienced as each additional call-back yields proportionately fewer respondents. The final decision about the number of times a phone number will be dialed ultimately depends upon cost considerations.

Refusal rates   In virtually every nation in which telephone surveys are conducted, the rates at which people both answer their telephones, and agree to be interviewed if they do answer, have been falling. For example, in 1997, the proportion of people in the US who agreed to be interviewed after they were contacted was 36 percent. Every careful re-assessment since has shown consistent declines, and by 2012 the proportion of those sampled who yielded an interview was down to 9 percent.[12] The critical question that arises concerns the degree to which people who cannot be reached or who refuse to be interviewed are a distinctive segment of the population. Do such high non-completion rates necessarily bias a sample? The short answer is, no. It is still possible to adjust a sample by selectively weighting certain groups, and the resulting weighted samples still typically appear to produce findings that can be generalized to a population – even with the high refusal rate. Adjusting for nonresponse is explained later in this chapter.

Systematic samples

Systematic sampling involves the mechanical selection of elements when there is no sampling frame, but the size of the population can be estimated and the elements can be arranged in a way that permits them to be numbered. For example, suppose one wished to sample customers who enter a store during a particular time period. No listing of such people would exist, but the owners/managers could estimate how many people typically enter the store each day, so a total N could be estimated. Using the previously introduced formulas, a researcher could establish the sample size (n). The ratio of these two figures produces what is termed a skip interval (k): k = N/n. For example, if N is estimated at 1,000 and n is set at 100, then k = 10 (1,000/100), which means that every tenth customer who enters the store will be selected (for interview, observation, etc.). The first element to be selected is usually set randomly, for example, by selecting a digit from a table of random numbers.

While researchers frequently rely upon systematic samples, with good results, when there is no adequate sampling frame, a problem can arise if the elements are arranged in, or happen to follow, a pattern and this pattern overlaps with k. To illustrate, suppose that in a town there were ten houses per block (due to zoning, developers' preferences, or the like). If k also happened to be 10, that would mean that the sample would be entirely comprised of either corner houses, or non-corner houses, depending upon the starting point. If corner houses are larger, hence more expensive, then occupants of corner houses may be wealthier, and this difference may be relevant. A representative sample should contain corner homes in their proportion of the population, one in ten, but a systematic sample with a fixed skip interval of 10 would either have all corner houses, or no corner houses.

To avoid biases introduced by an ordering of the elements, as above, researchers select random skip intervals that provide the same coverage as a fixed k. So, if N/n = 10, the researcher lets k vary, its value set randomly by a two-digit number between 1 and 19. The mean of a two-digit number between 1 and 19 is 10. So using this random skip interval will yield the same number of elements as a fixed k = 10. Utilizing the random numbers in Table 4.2 and working down the first two columns, the first number selected would be 37 – it is greater than 19 and so it would be ignored. The next number is 08, within the desired range, so the researcher would count eight elements (customers, houses, etc.) before selecting the next element. Note, by relying upon a random skip interval, all elements have an equal probability of being included, thereby meeting the major criterion for a random sample.[13]

Systematic sampling is widely used in urban research when no sampling frame is available because it is often possible to define a population geographically, in a way that permits elements to be counted. An interesting example is summarized in Box 4.2. Note the investigators substituted a random skip interval for a fixed k, avoiding the possibility that an ordering among the elements could bias the sample.

Sample surveys

Box 4.2 Systematic sampling in a Toronto neighborhood

A group of urban researchers in Ontario, Canada, were interested in contrasting the views of short- and long-term residents of a gentrifying neighborhood. Past studies suggested there might be substantial differences in attitudes toward housing and neighborhood associated with people's length of residence. To pursue this possibility, the researchers wanted to sample within a neighborhood that had recently begun to replace deteriorated housing with upscale buildings and to attract more affluent residents. Other studies, which focused upon neighborhoods that had gentrified years earlier, often had too few long-term residents. As part of the gentrification process, almost all of the long-term residents had been replaced by newcomers in these long-gentrified neighborhoods.

This study selected areas within "Little Portugal," a neighborhood just west of Toronto's business district that had only recently begun to gentrify. Because no sampling frames existed for the areas, an SRS was excluded as a possibility. A modified systematic sample was the only alternative open to them that offered random sampling, and that is what they chose.[14]

They began by specifying the specific neighborhoods in Little Portugal that fit their definition of gentrification, and then numbered all of the streets within the selected geographical areas. Step one involved randomly selecting streets from within the chosen neighborhoods.

They estimated that there were about 1,600 housing units in the area, and they wanted a sample of 400, so the skip interval was set at 4. Instead of a fixed k, however, they selected a one-digit random number between 1 and 7. (The mean of a one-digit random number between 1 and 7 is 4.) In this way they avoided the possibility that any pattern followed by the housing would result in a biased sample.

To be specific: An interviewer started at the corner of each selected street, and identified the first dwelling to be included by drawing a random number between 1 and 7. Then the interviewer continued down the street, counting houses in the same manner. At each selected household, questionnaires were left for the "primary household maintainers" to fill out jointly. If no one was at home, a second attempt was made. If the second attempt was not successful either, the researchers substituted respondents from the adjacent dwelling. (Such substituting is not an uncommon practice, though its assumption that next-door neighbors are equivalent to each other is problematic, both theoretically and methodologically.) From the 400 distributed questionnaires, 292 were returned to the investigators, and their analysis answered their research question, showing that there was not a large disparity between the views of new arrivals and long-term residents.

In much Urban Studies research, as we have noted, there is no sampling frame for the population, precluding an SRS, and the geographical area is too large or complex to permit a straightforward systematic sample. In these cases researchers employ multi-stage sampling, which involves two or more separate steps in which selections are made within successively smaller groupings of elements. The first step in a multi-stage sampling design ordinarily entails dividing the population into either strata or clusters.

STRATIFIED SAMPLING

As its name implies, stratified sampling involves dividing a population into relatively homogeneous subsets, or strata. Its use is suggested when there are substantial cleavages within a population in order to ensure that the sample reflects these divisions. They might involve race, gender, place of residence, or any other variable associated with marked differences within the population. When such differences exist, and they are of theoretical importance to a research project, then stratifying the population and sampling within strata is recommended to ensure that the sample will be representative with respect to the stratification-related variable. An SRS is "likely" to produce a sample that represents a population on any variable, but with stratified sampling, for the variable upon which a sample is stratified, "likely" is replaced by certainty.

Stratified sampling is contingent upon the ability to create relatively homogeneous strata, or the advantages of this approach are mitigated. To illustrate, many Dutch studies have generated strata within cities based upon the Netherland's four-digit postal codes. These strata are, in the view of Miranda Vervoort, larger than – and do not correspond well with – neighborhoods that are meaningful to residents. That was an important reason, she speculated, for the failure of many of these studies to obtain theoretically expected findings on people's social ties within their neighborhood. As the first step in conducting a stratified sample, Vervoot was able to more finely delineate urban neighborhoods, creating more than twice the number that had been generated by postal codes. That seemed to be important in enabling her to find neighborhood social ties that were congruent with theoretical expectations.[15]

Whenever strata are being considered, their homogeneity is the first consideration, In addition, the strata must be inclusive enough to encompass every element, and the boundaries of every stratum must be clearly defined so that every element fits into one, and only one, stratum. Thus, the strata must be both exhaustive (including every element) and mutually exclusive (so elements fit in only one stratum).

Sample surveys

After a population is stratified, the next step frequently involves a systematic sample within strata. The immediate question to be answered concerns whether sampling within strata will be proportional, with elements from each stratum selected in proportion to the relative size of the stratum (i.e. the percentage of the population, or sampling frame, it contains). Alternatively, the second step can involve *disproportionate sampling*, the intentional over-inclusion of elements from certain strata. Disproportional sampling is usually followed under either of two conditions:

1) A stratum that is very small in size is of particular theoretical interest. Because it is so small, proportional sampling would yield too few elements to support an analysis so elements within this small stratum are over-sampled.
2) The dispersion around the mean is greater in some strata than others. Recall that measures of dispersion (e.g. Standard Error) are an important determinant of C.I.s, and that measures of dispersion tend to decrease as the sample size increases. By over-sampling from within strata that have greater dispersion, researchers optimize their return on investments of resources with respect to lowering the C.I.

Whenever any group of elements is not included in the sample in the same proportion in which it is found in the population, or sampling frame, the sample must be adjusted by weighting. Disproportional stratified sampling will obviously result in sub-samples that are too large or too small given their percentage of the population, but there are also other common causes of disproportionate sub-samples, such as a higher refusal rate within some grouping of elements (e.g. stratum). Earlier in this chapter we noted high refusal rates that have become characteristic of many surveys, and they necessitate weighting when there are uneven refusal rates across different strata.

Regardless of the source of the disproportionality, sub-groups (or strata) within the sample have to be adjusted by weighting in order for the sample to be regarded as a microscopic reflection of the population. For example, the overall mean of an unweighted disproportionate sample cannot be assumed to correspond with the population mean. In fact, the two means will definitely not be the same if the means of the under- and over-represented subgroups in the sample differ from each other.

Weighting entails assigning values to strata that will compensate for the over- or under- coverage. To illustrate, suppose the population is divided into two strata, A and B, that are of equal size in the population, but A is either intentionally over-sampled or has a lower refusal rate, so that A comprises 60 percent of the sample. To adjust by weighting involves separate calculation of each strata's mean (or other descriptive characteristics). Then the means of A and B would simply be added together and divided by two. This procedure would assign equal weight to A and B, in accordance with their equal size in the population.[16] Adjusting for nonresponse is further discussed in the final section of this chapter.

CLUSTER SAMPLING

Clusters can involve any type of grouping of elements, but they are frequently based upon the location of elements, such as city-suburban, rural-urban, etc. As with strata, each element of the population must be included in a cluster, but in only one cluster. The typical difference between strata and clusters is that while homogeneity is desired within a stratum, heterogeneity is usually preferable in a cluster. In addition, an investigator often has information about the elements included in a cluster, but not about the elements within a stratum; for example, nothing is usually known in advance about a passer-by or household resident who is selected in a stratified systematic sample.

Illustrative of multi-stage cluster sampling is a study by two Australian researchers who wanted to know how easily seniors, living in the outskirts of Melbourne, were able to travel to neighborhood service facilities. They began by dividing the numerous communities in the suburban area into three types (i.e. clusters) based upon their distance from the center of the metropolitan area and their rural-urban qualities. Step one involved selecting one representative municipality from each of the three clusters. The investigators then compiled lists of senior organizations within each selected cluster (i.e. municipality). This produced a list of 61 known organizations. In the next step they randomly selected 30 of the 61 organizations, and then attempted to contact all members of those organizations.[17]

Note, the investigators violated the principle of equal probability of inclusion in the first two steps of their design. Step one disregarded differences in the size of communities and clusters, and step two disregarded differences in the size of organizations. So, all elements did not have the same chance of being included in these first two steps. For example, in clusters that contained larger numbers of municipalities, any given municipality had a smaller chance of being included in the sample than a municipality in a smaller cluster. The investigators acknowledged that their design fell short with respect to randomness, but they felt that it was adequate for conducting a preliminary study of an important policy question.

Final step: Selecting a respondent

Regardless of how a household is selected for inclusion – by phone number, skip interval in a systematic sample, mailed questionnaire, etc. – there should be an established procedure in place to select a specific respondent. Obviously, if the sampling frame consists of individual names, there will not be any question about who to include. And the more the questions to be asked are factual and unambiguous – e.g. how many television sets are currently in the household? – the less it matters who is selected to answer. However, in many studies a potentially multi-person household with unknown composition is selected in the next-to-last step, and the questions to be asked are not cut and dry. Therefore, the research cannot rely upon answers from whoever happens to answer the phone or open the mail because some people may be more likely than others to answer the phone or open the mail, and their responses may not be the same as everyone else's.

Consistent with the principle of mechanical selection associated with probability sampling, the final step in selecting a respondent entails following an established rule. Almost any rule will do; for example, the procedures routinely utilized in this final step include asking for the: respondent with the next or most recent prior birthday; or the youngest male or youngest female in the household over age 18; or the oldest male or female, or so on. Random numbers are often employed in conjunction with any of the above alternatives. For example, using a table of random numbers, the youngest male is identified as the desired respondent if the selected number is odd, or the youngest female if it is an even number. Following any rule seems to matter more than which specific one is followed. In other words, the alternatives that can be followed do not seem to differ greatly from each other in terms of response rates or the representativeness of the household composition they produce.[18]

Panel studies

Panel studies, unlike cross-sectional designs, follow the same sample of elements over a period of time in order to observe change. Most often the sampled people who comprise a panel are surveyed periodically, each such period being termed a wave. The length of the interval between waves depends largely upon the topic of interest. For example, if a panel is comprised of registered voters who are being studied during the month preceding an election, waves may be scheduled only weeks apart. On the other hand, if the objective is to study the effects of childbearing upon a woman's labor force participation, a panel might begin with women immediately after the birth of a child, with waves scheduled multiple years apart.

There are two problems, or issues, that are distinctive to panel studies. The first is the difficulty that can be encountered in obtaining a probability sample. Because the people are being asked to make a continuing commitment, they may be more likely to refuse to participate, and excessive refusals can bias a sample. The second problem that bedevils panel studies, unlike cross-sectional studies, is *attrition*: people included in an initial wave who drop out before later waves are completed. Some die or become incapacitated, others move without a forwarding address, change their minds about continuing, etc. So a panel study may begin with a representative sample, but unequal rates of attrition across subgroups may over time result in a panel that is no longer representative.

To begin, we must note that the same considerations that strongly recommended a probability sample in a cross-sectional study apply equally to a panel study. However, obtaining a probability sample for a panel study is usually more difficult because of higher refusal rates. People are ordinarily more reluctant to make a lengthy time commitment. If any segment of the population is more likely than another to refuse – for example, if employed people are more likely to refuse than unemployed – then the sample will be biased. This places a premium upon recruitment efforts (and, of course, demands weighting to correct for any disproportionalities).

In recent years, a number of panel studies have recruited respondents on-line, usually by contacting people affiliated with on-line organizations of some type. The representativeness of the resulting samples is questionable. This issue is discussed later in the chapter; here we wish only to consider varying approaches that have been employed to increase people's willingness to participate in on-line panel studies. Box 4.3 summarizes the results of two relevant experiments designed to see how different ways of approaching potential participants for on-line Dutch panels affected their refusal rates.

Box 4.3 Recruiting on-line panels

Study one

Two Dutch researchers wanted to see what most influenced people to participate in an on-line panel of people that would be contacted in monthly waves to answer questions about their health, family ties, political opinions, and so on. They began by selecting a probability sample of 5,000 households from a national population register in the Netherlands that served as their sampling frame. A bias would obviously be introduced if people without Internet access could not be included in the panel, so the investigators offered free equipment to selected people who lacked Internet access.[19]

Sample surveys

After selecting the respondents they wanted to include, the researchers designed an experiment in which they systematically varied:

1) Face-to-face versus telephone contact. They had both the addresses and phone numbers of people selected from the registry. Would meeting an interviewer in person lead to a higher rate of volunteering for the panel than a phone call?
2) Incentive offerings to participate of either 0, 10, 20 or 50 euros. (One euro equals about $1.25.) Would larger amounts provide greater incentive?
3) Whether the incentive was offered in advance, or promised to participants at the conclusion of the study. Did people care which?

The dependent variable of this study was, of course, the rate at which people agreed to participate in the panel. The researchers found that:

1) There were few differences attributable to how people were contacted. The investigators decided, therefore, to proceed with telephone interviews rather than in-person interviews as a cost-saving measure.
2) Incentives of any size increased agreement to participate compared to no monetary offering; but the size of the incentive did not appear to make much difference. So, again to hold down costs, they proceeded with the 10 euro payment.
3) The prepaid payment had a much stronger effect upon agreements to participate than a post-participation promise. (A bird in hand..?) Therefore, the investigators assembled the panel by offering a prepaid 10 euro incentive.

Study two

To obtain people's perceptions concerning Dutch national elections, an international group of Political Scientists systematically varied how people were invited to participate in an on-line panel. They followed a complex experimental design in which individuals were randomly assigned to a number of different groups whose cover letters describing the research differed from each other in a number of different respects.

According to their findings, two variables were associated with significant differences. Specifically, people were found to be more willing to participate when:

1) The appeal in the cover letter was altruistic, appealing to respondents' sense of social obligation, rather than egoistic, implying a personal reward for participating.
2) The cover letter was written simply, using words with few syllables and sentences without multiple clauses, rather than in linguistically complex sentences.[20]

The studies described in Box 4.3 were entirely conducted in the Netherlands, and involved on-line panels. However, studies of people's willingness to participate in panel studies have reported similar results in other nations, and with varying invitations to participate in panels that did not rely upon Internet connections.

ATTRITION

It is likely that no panel ever completed its last wave with its initial sample intact. Some people drop out because they were never really committed. They were convinced to begin by the incentives that were offered or by a persuasive interviewer; but after the first wave (or the second), they wanted to exit. Others may become "fatigued" as each wave of the panel seems to present a heavier burden. In addition, people's life situations change: illness, marital change, a new job, and so on, alter their ability or willingness to remain in a panel. Finally, the different topics on which some waves focus can cause some people to drop out if the questions delve into potentially embarrassing subjects: income, sexual relations, or the like. Dropping out can also be temporary. Any of the above circumstances can cause a person who completes at least one wave to miss a subsequent wave, but they may later return to the panel, if that is permitted.[21]

Any substantial degree of attrition reduces the number of respondents, adversely affecting statistical analyses. However, the most serious problem arises when attrition is selective because it biases a sample that was initially representative. Weighting is again recommended, though some patterns of attrition can result in very difficult to correct problems.[22]

Non-probability samples

As previously noted, the accuracy of inferences to populations from non-probability samples are not amenable to precise assessment. This is one of the main ways in which probability and non-probability samples differ from each other. A second major difference concerns how elements are selected: in probability samples it is mechanical while non-probability samples provide a good deal of discretion to the investigator who is selecting elements. (For this reason, non-probability sampling is sometimes referred to as, purposive.) A final difference involves cost. Non-probability samples are virtually always less expensive, which favors them when the research budget is very limited.

Almost any type of casual or informal selection of elements could be described as a non-probability sample. However, there are two principal types of non-probability samples that are utilized in serious research: quota samples and snowball or respondent-driven samples. We will discuss each, in turn.

Sample surveys

Quota samples

Quota samples partially resemble both stratified and cluster samples in that they are typically taken in a particular place: on a street corner, in a large lecture hall, at the entrance to a store, or so on. Logically, this narrows the sampling frame to all those people who happen to cross the street corner when the investigator is selecting subjects, or all the students who are in the large lecture hall, etc., and this places a premium upon the representativeness of the elements that happen to be selected. That representativeness is difficult to estimate in a quota sample, however, because its procedures clearly violate the basic principles of probability sampling: some elements of the population have no chance of being included, and all elements obviously do not have the same chance of inclusion.

Like probability samples, quota samples focus upon the representativeness of a sample. However, they seek purposively to create representative samples rather than rely upon representativeness resulting from following procedures derived from probability theory. To illustrate, suppose a population is assumed to have equal numbers of males and females. If so, then a quota sample will be carefully selected to include equal numbers of males and females. Further, if 40 percent of the population is believed to be comprised of people over age 60, then that proportion will also be sought for the quota sample. Many characteristics of the population that are considered relevant to a study may similarly become criteria for selection.

The first potential deficiency of a quota sample stems from an investigator's ability to select respondents based upon *multiple* characteristics, that is, a number of characteristics considered together. For example, what proportion of the sample should contain males over age 60? That question cannot be answered solely from an examination of each attribute, by itself. It requires focusing upon their joint distribution. The more characteristics that must be simultaneously considered – for example, (1) Hispanic, (2) men, (3) over age 60, (4) who are college graduates – the more difficult it is for an investigator to assemble a representative quota sample. The proportion of a sample that should be comprised of Hispanic men over age 60 with a college degree cannot be ascertained by the separate examination of each of the four attributes; but that is frequently the only information available to the researcher designing a quota sample. So, a quota sample that looks representative if one population characteristic at a time is examined may look biased when multiple characteristics are considered simultaneously.

The non-mechanical selection of potential respondents introduces a second possible source of bias in quota samples. The investigator may calculate that 35 percent of the sample should consist of men over age 60. But which of the possible men over age 60 who happen to appear at the selection site will be selected? Will a researcher's conscious or unconscious biases about race or height or the way men dress lead to the selection of a quota sample that only appears to be representative with respect to men over age 60?

The accuracy of quota samples is apparently quite variable. Despite the potential biases noted above, projections to populations based upon quota samples have sometimes proven to be quite accurate, at a fraction of the cost of probability samples. A great deal of market research continues to rely upon quota sampling, mostly because of its cost advantages. Quota samples are also sometimes utilized by academic researchers, to test hypotheses in pre-tests, that are followed by studies relying upon probability samples. However, there also appear to be many instances in which quota samples have yielded population projections that were shown to be substantially off the mark when compared to probability samples.[23] User beware is the most prudent conclusion.

Snowball / RDS sampling

In Chapter 2 we introduced snowball sampling in relation to ethnographic field studies. At that time we described it as a way of sampling from within a population that was either very small, or very difficult to access, or both. Examples of populations studied by snowball sampling include: illicit drug users, undocumented immigrants, sex workers, etc. (A specific example is described in Box 4.4.) Building a sample in these situations relies upon an investigator making initial contacts with members of the target population, then piggy-backing upon their contacts to build a sample. If the people initially contacted are parts of a clique or distinctive subgroup within the targeted population, then the sample built upon these initial contacts will often not be reflective of the totality. While field study researchers are concerned about avoiding such biases, with snowball sampling there is usually no attempt statistically to assess the representativeness of the snowball-built sample.

Respondent-driven sampling (RDS), like snowball sampling, begins with an investigator's purposive (i.e. non-mechancial) selection of people who are part of a hard-to-reach population. However, RDS usually involves statistical assessments of a sample's representativeness that are not found in most studies relying upon snowball sampling.[24]

The first set of people contacted in an RDS sample are frequently referred to as *seeds*. The seeds are asked about the people they are in contact with and their referrals constitute a second wave that, in turn, nominates a third, and so on. Limitations are usually placed upon the total

Sample surveys

Box 4.4 Sampling young drug users in inner-city Sydney

Joanne Bryant, a professor and director of the University of New South Wales' National Centre in HIV Social Research, was interested in studying young people's understanding of drug use and Hepatitis C. The specific group she wanted to target for the study consisted of young people (16 to 24 years) who lived in inner-city Sydney, Australia, and: were currently illicit drug users, had recently been homeless and had been involved with the juvenile or criminal justice system. Obviously, there could be no adequate sampling frame for this target population, leading her to rely upon RDS.[26]

She began by asking the staff members of an inner-city shelter that specialized in services for homeless youths to recommend people who fit her profile of interests. She especially wanted the names of people the staff thought to be well-connected to others in the target population so she could build a cumulatively larger sample. The staff identified four individuals, the initial seeds, who she subsequently interviewed. She questioned them about how many drug users their age they knew, how often they saw them and whether the young drug users they knew had also been homeless. Based upon the names that were provided by the first four seeds, in the following week Bryant obtained a second wave consisting of 20 more people who fit the profile. Not a bad start; however, subsequent waves grew progressively smaller, and took longer to locate. After nine additional weeks the total RDS sample consisted of only 61 people, though the investigator had hoped for a sample of about 275 people from the target population.

From an analysis of the composition of the networks it appeared that RDS produced a sample that adequately penetrated the target population and produced a representative sample, but one that was much smaller than she had hoped. Why was adding cases so slow and difficult? The main problem, Bryant inferred, was that most of the people who were in the target population were in extremely small networks that had little overlap with the other small networks that existed among these young people. Some of the original seeds were, in fact, isolates who knew of no one to refer. If investigators confront such situations in the future, she recommends that they begin with more than four people in their initial seed group. RDS can still be a useful way to build a sample from such populations, she concluded, but even with a larger number of seeds, investigators should anticipate the possibility of a very lengthy recruitment process.

number of other people that any person already included can nominate so that one person's social circle does not dominate the entire sample.

From the information provided by the people included in each wave, the investigator infers the social networks that appear to be embedded in the target population, their size and the overlap among them. As the sampling continues over time, the known social networks provide a benchmark against which an investigator tries to approximate a probability sample; and the population estimates can be adjusted according to the different probabilities of people in different networks being included in the sample.[25] (This is a special case of weighting, as discussed earlier in this chapter.)

For either RDS or snowball sampling to be effective, people in the targeted population must know each other, or at least be aware of how and where others who share the attribute of interest to the investigator can be reached. If these assumptions do not apply, then RDS and snowball sampling can both be laborious processes, at best, or lead to dead ends. Presented in Box 4.4 is a case study that attempted to build a sample of difficult-to-reach people utilizing RDS. It was mostly unsuccessful, however, because people who fit the profile of interest were apparently not in sufficient contact with each other.

Reaching respondents

The final step in data collection in any sample survey involves obtaining the information of interest from selected respondents. This typically involves asking questions, via interview or questionnaire, but it can also entail making observations. The information can be obtained in person by an interviewer or a researcher who guides respondents through answering a questionnaire. The questions can also be asked and answered by telephone, mail or the Internet.[27]

The way respondents are reached is frequently associated with a particular form by which information is obtained from them. Reaching respondents in person typically involves interviews, for example, while mailed surveys usually entail self-administered questionnaires and both field work and experimentation frequently rely upon direct observation. However, almost any means of obtaining information can (and is) employed with diverse research methods. For that reason, each of the major means of obtaining information from subjects (questionnaires, interviews and observation) are discussed separately, in detail, in the following chapter.

In this section we will describe only the means by which potential respondents are reached. We will also consider the response rates associated with each means, though the figures must be compared with caution because of wide variations in how response rates are calculated. This section concludes with discussions of how response rates are calculated and the ways to reduce the bias that can be introduced when information cannot be obtained from the specific elements selected in a probability sample.

In-person

Having an investigator present to conduct a face-to-face interview or facilitate respondents' completion of questionnaires is usually considered ideal because the in-person investigator is able to observe respondents and make inferences related to their attitudes that can be helpful later in analyzing their responses. In addition, in-person surveys tend to have the highest completion rates, often reporting that 80 to 85 percent of the selected respondents agree to provide the requested information. Perhaps when face-to-face it is more difficult to say no to a person?

However, collecting information from respondents in person is the most expensive way because of the staff time and travel costs it introduces. (Except for special types of medical and psychological research that offer treatment inducements, or on-campus studies in which students are obligated to participate as a class requirement, it is not possible to expect selected respondents to come to the investigator.) If a trained researcher is going to the home of selected respondents, the cost may be five times more than a telephone survey, 25 times more than a mail survey, and hundreds of times more than an Internet survey. The actual costs vary substantially, based upon research design.[28] Nevertheless, given that sending a researcher to the home of respondents will almost always be the most expensive option by far, researchers without large external grants typically rely upon one of the less expensive alternatives described below.

Telephone

The procedures involved in reaching selected respondents by telephone were described earlier in this chapter in the discussion of random digit dialing (RDD). Here we note that while, in principle, telephone surveys are highly efficient, a serious problem has arisen with their use because the ability of telephone surveys to reach selected respondents has been rapidly declining. At one time, response rates for RDD were only a little behind those of in-person interviews. As we have previously noted, however, over the past few decades a number of national surveys in the US and UK that relied upon RDD have reported consistent and substantial declines in response rates.[29] The falloff is due to an increase in both the number of very difficult-to-reach people and in the number of people who are contacted, but refuse to participate.

There is no reason to assume that selected respondents who are not reached or who decline to participate are the same as those who are reached and who agree to participate. Procedures for substituting potential subjects who are available to replace non-reached or unwilling subjects are widely employed, including substituting an immediate neighbor, another person with the same telephone prefix, or the like. However, with respect to the theory behind probability sampling, these substitutions are questionable. On the other hand, without replacement, the extensive nonresponse associated with telephone surveys has the effect of shrinking the sample size which, as previously discussed, raises confidence limits.

Mail

Surveys that rely exclusively upon mail – to reach respondents and for the return of their replies – depend upon self-administered questionnaires, which can make them less expensive than either in-person or telephone surveys. They have two drawbacks, though:

1) Mail surveys have generally tended to have very high refusal rates, necessitating follow-ups which add to their cost. However, even after repeated mailings (e.g. postcards) to remind respondents to return their questionnaires, response rates are typically low.
2) As no researcher is available to provide clarification, the questionnaire must be completely free of ambiguity. This can require extensive pre-testing, which detracts from the potential cheapness of mail surveys. (The preparation of self-administered questionnaires is discussed in the following chapter.)

To mail questionnaires obviously requires a sampling frame of addresses. To serve this purpose, there are government and postal service address files that can be obtained. For example, in the UK there are administrative records (see Box 4.1). In the US, the Postal Service provides a computerized delivery sequence file which contains almost all addresses serviced by the Postal Service, and it has provided a useful sampling frame.[30] It is also possible to develop sampling frames by field enumeration, that is by having investigators walk through the neighborhood in question, noting all addresses or taking a random or systematic sample of addresses. However, if field enumeration is required it reduces the cost advantages of a mailed survey.

On-line

As Internet access has expanded, reliance upon the Internet as a means to reach respondents has also grown because it is very inexpensive.

Sample surveys

An obvious impediment to its use is that it cannot reach people who lack Internet access, except in very limited situations in which an investigator is able to equip selected respondents who do not have Internet connections (see Box 4.3.) In most cases, Web access limits the sampling frame, disproportionately excluding people who are older, poorer and less educated – the subgroup most likely not to have Internet connections.[31]

A second major detraction from on-line surveys is their typically low response rates, often ridiculously low. In a Facebook survey for a Houston bakery and coffee chain, for example, investigators e-mailed 13,270 surveys to people on the store's mailing list (i.e. the sampling frame). After several months, they eventually received 1,067 responses, an 8 percent return rate. Nevertheless, major polling firms have begun to rely more upon on-line surveys, attempting to build large and diverse population pools, then mimicking quota sampling procedures by selecting demographic categories from the pool in proportion to their relative size in sampling frames. The result appears to be representative, but it is still a nonprobability sample, with an unknown margin of error.[32]

Mixed mode

Mixed-mode sampling can refer to the utilization of different modes of sampling with different sub-groups, or strata, within a population; or it can entail uniformly utilizing the same two or more ways of reaching all the selected respondents. Here we will consider examples of each type.

In order to study what variables influenced commuters in downtown Melbourne to use either public transportation or private automobiles, Panndhe and March employed three different modes of reaching people who worked in offices in the city's central business district. Included were: a mailed survey, with addresses provided by office managers (with no response rate provided by the investigators); an e-mail survey, with e-mail addresses provided by colleagues (with a 45 percent response rate); and an "intercept" survey which entailed interviewing people as they left railway stations or public parking facilities (with a 64 percent response rate).[33]

The second type of mixed-mode sample has in recent years frequently combined a Web option with a mailed survey. This combines the two least expensive modes that are also characterized by the highest refusal rates. Investigators have hoped that the combination would increase response rates, but the studies employing both have not had encouraging results. To be specific, a large number of recent studies have added a Web option to mail surveys, enabling the selected respondents to reply by mail or Internet. In principle, having such a choice should increase the response rate. However, an analysis of 16 such studies conducted since the year 2000 showed that including a Web option actually led to a decline in overall response rates, from 58 percent (mail only) to 53 percent (mail or Web); but it was not clear why that happened. Perhaps, the analysts concluded, having to make a choice added to respondents' perceived burden, and they resolved it by discarding the questionnaire?[34]

Nonresponse bias

The completion rate of a survey is the percentage of all completed questionnaires or interviews that are obtained from respondents selected in a probability sample. The formula is deceivingly simple looking: One minus completed surveys (numerator) divided by the total sample (denominator).

$$1 - \left(\frac{\text{completion}}{\text{total sample}} \right)$$

Exactly what that means in any individual survey varies, though, because the major terms in the formula are subject to very different calculations. To understand these differences, it is helpful to begin by noting that there are at least four reasons why any selected respondent does not complete an interview or questionnaire. To be specific, in any survey, some selected respondents:

1) Will not be located due to errors in the sampling frame (e.g. a wrong address).
2) Will not be reached (e.g. never at home during attempts to contact).
3) Refuse to participate, for any reason.
4) Fail to complete a substantial portion of the interview, or questionnaire.

In calculating completion rates, some investigators disregard (1), and subtract such cases from the possible total, reducing the denominator, and thereby increasing the reported completion rate. Other investigators replace elements that cannot be reached – (2) above; and accept even partially completed questionnaires or interviews as completions – (4) above. In sum, they maximally increase the numerator, which also has the effect of increasing the apparent completion rate. So, in evaluating a survey's reported completion rate, it is important to note how that rate was calculated. These variations in computing completion rates can also make it very difficult to compare different modes of reaching respondents (e.g. mail versus telephone) because investigators frequently calculate completion or refusal rates differently.

There is no simple answer to how high a completion rate is minimally accepted. It obviously depends upon how it was calculated. It also depends upon the way respondents were reached because, by convention, lower rates are accepted for mail or on-line surveys. And in any type of survey, the *most important question* is whether non-completions distorted the final sample, i.e. produced a nonresponse bias. With a very high completion rate, the likelihood of nonresponse bias is lessened, but there is not a one-to-one correspondence between completion rate and nonresponse bias.[35] Even a sample with a low completion rate can sometimes be relatively free of bias, while a sample with a high participation rate can still be biased.

The key issue, we have repeatedly noted, is whether the final sample remains representative of the population or the sampling frame from which it was drawn. If there is an association between any of the attributes of respondents and their propensities to respond, they will distort the sample. For example, if the topic is of greater interest to men than women, that may result in men responding in higher proportions; if younger people feel more strongly about an issue (pro or con), that may produce a sample biased with respect to age, and so on.

Bias due to nonresponse patterns can be indicated in a variety of ways. Most simply, it can be suggested by comparing the attributes of respondents to nonrespondents, if any attributes of the elements in a sampling frame can be inferred. If there are no biases, those who responded and those who did not should have the same distributions with respect to age, gender, race, etc. Often, however, the investigator knows virtually nothing about the nonrespondents, and may only have a telephone number, for example. If a survey relies upon a face-to-face interview, then the observations of interviewers concerning respondents who refused to participate can also provide very useful information for analyzing nonrespondent bias.

In situations where no attributes of elements can be inferred, investigators often rely upon data taken from a government census or an extensive survey that is assumed to be very complete, without systematic biases. Such data sources are typically referred to as *gold standards,* and their distribution of attributes becomes the referent. Thus, the attributes of people who complete the survey are expected to be distributed in the same way as in the gold standard, so any discrepancy can indicate nonresponse bias.[36]

Adjusting for nonresponse bias

When nonresponse bias is detected by any of the procedures described above, it is important to adjust sample weights accordingly. This typically entails post-stratification: creating strata, or sub-groups, after the survey is completed. For all strata the question asked is: What would be their percentage of the sample, if each had the same propensity to participate? Table 4.3 shows this adjustment for a hypothetical survey of cell phone ownership that relied upon a gold standard as the referent.

Table 4.3 Adjustment weighting

	% Sample	% Gold standard	% Who own a cell phone
Age 65 and over	22	31	8
Under age 65	78	69	30

According to the figures in Table 4.3, people over 65, who are less likely to own cell phones, comprised 22 percent of the sample. Gold standard figures suggest their actual proportion of the sample probably should have been 31 percent – likely indicating a nonresponse bias.

If cell phone ownership is calculated for the unadjusted sample:

$$(0.22 \times 0.08) + (0.78 \times 0.30) = 0.2516 \text{ or } 25.16 \text{ percent}$$

If cell phone ownership is calculated for the sample with weights adjusted by figures from the gold standard:

$$(0.31 \times 0.08) + (0.69 \times 0.30) = 0.2318 \text{ or } 23.18 \text{ percent}$$

In other words, because people over 65 were less likely to be included in the sample and because people over 65 were also less likely to own cell phones, the unadjusted sample probably projected an incorrectly high rate of overall cell phone ownership for the population. That is why adjusting samples for nonresponse bias is always recommended.

Notes

1 For an excellent anthology that contains an overview of SSM and many of the major early studies, see Martin Blumer, Kevin Bales and Kathryn K. Sklar (Eds), *The Social Survey Movement in Historical Perspective*. Cambridge University Press, 2011.
2 Alan Hunt, "Measuring Morals." *Social History*, 35, 2002.
3 A.L. Browley, "Address to the Economic Science and Statistics Section of the British Association for the Advancement of Science." *Journal of the Royal Statistical Society*, 69, 1906, p. 553. Quoted in John Aldrich, "Professor A.L. Browley's Theory of the Representative Method." School of Social Sciences, University of Southampton, 2008.
4 A.L. Browley and A.R. Burnett-Hurst, *Livelihood and Poverty*. Bell, 1915, p. 174. Quoted in Aldrich, *ibid*.
5 There was bias due to sampling frames, as noted, and in addition, due to selective non-responses. Almost three quarters of the people who received post cards did not return them, and more Democratic supporters were among the non-respondents. For further discussion, see Peverill Squire, "Why the 1936 Literary Digest Poll Failed." *Public Opinion Quarterly*, 52, 1988.

6 Antonia Simon, "Using Administrative Data for Constructing Sampling Frames and Replacing Data Collected Through Surveys." *International Journal of Social Research Methodology*, 17, 2014.

7 See, for example, www.wikihow.com/Calculate-Confidence-Interval.

8 For a discussion of historic and current telephone surveys in Europe, see Anja Mohorko, Edith de Leeuw and Joop Hox, "Coverage Bias in European Telephone Surveys." *Survey Methods: Insights from the Field*, 25, 2013.

9 See, for example, the telephone sampling methods followed by Pew Research Center for the People and the Press: www.people-press.org/methodology/sampling.

10 For a detailed description of the steps involved in RDD in public housing agencies (but which are not unique to this population), see U.S. Department of Housing and Urban Development, *Random Digit Dialing Surveys*. Washington, D.C., March, 2013.

11 Andy Peytchev and Benjamin Neely, "RDD Telephone Surveys." *Public Opinion Quarterly*, 77, 2013.

12 Pew Research Center, *Assessing the Representativeness of Public Opinion Surveys*. May 15, 2012.

13 For further discussion, see Floyd J. Fowler, Jr., *Survey Research Methods*. SAGE, 2013.

14 Emily McGirr, Andrejs Skaburskis, and Eim S. Donegani, "Expectations, Preferences and Satisfaction Levels among New and Long-term Residents in a Gentrifying Toronto Neighbourhood." *Urban Studies*, 51, 2014.

15 Miranda Vervoort, "Ethnic Concentration in the Neighbourhood and Ethnic Minorities' Social Integration." *Urban Studies*, 49, 2012.

16 For further discussion of weighting alternatives in multi-stage samples, see Richard Valliant, Jill A. Dever and Franke Kreuter, *Practical Tools for Designing and Weighting Survey Samples*. Springer, 2013.

17 Benno Engels and Gang-Jun Liu, "Ageing in Place." *Urban Policy and Research*, 31, 2013.

18 These are the findings reported in a methodological experiment involving mailed questionnaires. See Kristen Olson, Mathew Stange and Jolene Smyth, "Assessing Within-Household Selection Methods in Household Mail Surveys." *Public Opinion Quarterly*, 78, 2014.

19 The experiment also included several other variables not included here. See Annette Scherpenzeel and Vera Toepoel, "Recruiting a Probability Sample for an Online Panel." *Public Opinion Quarterly*, 76, 2012.

20 Zoltan Fazekas, Matthew T. Wall and Andre Krouwel, "Is It What You Say or How You Say It?" *International Journal of Public Opinion Research*, 26, 2014.

21 For a review of the causes of attrition, see Peter Lugtig, "Panel Attrition." *Sociological Methods and Research*, 43, 2014.

22 The complex adjustments for attrition are discussed in Part One in, Badi H. Baltagi (Ed), *The Oxford Handbook of Panel Data*. Oxford University Press, 2015.

23 For an assessment of quota sampling, see Erin E. Ruel, William E. Wagner and Brian J. Gillespie, *The Practice of Social Research*. Sage, 2015.

24 For further discussion of the distinctions among snowball and respondent-driven samples see, Leo A. Goodman, "Comment on Respondent-Driven and Snowball Sampling." *Sociological Methodology*, 41, 2011.

25 For further discussion of ways of adjusting RDS samples, see Douglas D. Heckathorn, "Extensions of Respondent-Driven Sampling." *Sociological Methodology*, 37, 2007.

26 Joanne Bryant, "Using Respondent-driven Sampling with 'Hard to Reach' Marginalised Young People." *International Journal of Social Research Methodology*, 17, 2014.

27 For a comparison, as well as examination of each type, see Don A. Dillman, Jolene D. Smith and Leah M. Christian, *Internet, Phone, Mail and Mixed-Mode Surveys*. Wiley, 2014.

28 For further discussion of cost considerations, see Robert M. Groves and Steven Heeringa, "Responsive Design for Household Surveys." *Journal of the Royal Statistical Society Series A, Part 3*, 2006.

29 UK figures reported by Gareth James, "Measures to Understand Non-response in the UK Labour Force Survey." Office for National Statistics, n.d. US figures reported by Paul P. Biemer and Andy Peytchev, "Census Geocoding for Nonresponse Bias Evaluation in Telephone Surveys." *Public Opinion Quarterly*, 76, 2012.

30 See, for example, Bonnie E. Shook-SA, Douglas B. Currivan, Joseph P. McMichael and Vincent G. Iannacchione, "Extending the Coverage of Address-Based Sampling Frames." *Public Opinion Quarterly*, 77, 2013.

31 Pew Research Center, "What the New York Times' Polling Decision Means." July 28, 2014.

32 See Pew Research Center, *op. cit.*

33 Amruta Pandhe and Alan March, "Parking Availability Influences on Travel Mode." *Australian Planner*, 49, 2012.

34 Rebecca L. Medway and Jenna Fulton, "When More Gets You Less." *Public Opinion Quarterly*, 76, 2012.

35 For further discussion, see Robert M. Groves, et al., *Survey Methodology*. Wiley, 2009.

36 For further discussion, see Jennifer Sinibaldi, Mark Trappman and Frauke Kreuter, "Which is the Better Investment for Nonresponse Adjustment: Purchasing Commercial Auxiliary Data or Collecting Interviewer Observations?" *Public Opinion Quarterly*, 78, 2014.

Glossary

Attrition: The number of people who drop out of a panel study between waves.

Bias: Any way in which a sample differs from the population from which it was drawn.

Confidence Interval (C.I.): The area above and below a sample mean (or other descriptive statistic) in which the population mean (or other statistic) likely falls; popularly referred to as the margin of error.

Confidence Level (C.L.): The probability that the population figure lies within the CI.

Cross-sectional Study: Sample elements are observed or questioned at one point in time.

Disproportionate Sampling: Intentional over-inclusion of elements from certain strata.

Element: Each individual person, group or the like that possess the characteristic that defines the population.

Gold Standard: Census documents or surveys believed to accurately describe the distribution of attributes in a population.

Longitudinal Study: Sample elements are questioned or observed over an extended period of time.

Population: All of the elements that share a defining characteristic (e.g. all adults in a nation, all automobiles registered in a city).

Random: Every element has the same likelihood of selection.

Representativeness: The degree to which a sample is a microscopic reflection of a population.

Sampling Frame: A listing of the elements in a population.

Seeds: People included in the initial wave of a panel study.

Social Survey Movement: Surveys conducted in cities across the world at the turn of the twentieth century that attempted to stimulate social reforms.

Standard Deviation: The amount of dispersion around a sample mean.

Standard Error (S.E.): The variability among sample means (usually inferred from the standard deviation of a single sample).

chapter 5

Obtaining data, Part One: Interviews, questionnaires and observation

Outline

- Interviews
  - Unstructured interviews
  - Structured interviews
  - Semi-structured interviews
  - Interviewer effects
  - Interview length
  - Matching characteristics
  - Interview mode
    - Face-to-face
    - Telephone interviews
    - Computer-assisted self-interviews
- Questionnaires
  - Pre-tests
  - Cover sheet

- Question wording problems
  - Leading questions
  - Double-barreled questions
  - Ambiguous questions
- Attitudes or behaviors?
- The social desirability bias and possible solutions
  - Face-saving introductions
  - Randomization techniques
  - Psychological scales
  - ACASI, again
- Response formats
  - Open-ended or closed
- Response categories
  - Grid format
- Mode of delivery
  - Mailed questionnaires
  - Via the Internet

- Observation
  - Direct observation
  - Informed consent?
  - Indirect observation (physical traces)

- Notes
- Glossary

This chapter begins our review of the last step in the data collection process, the means by which an investigator obtains the data of interest from or about a subject/respondent. The principal means discussed in this chapter include interviews, questionnaires and unobtrusive observations. The following chapter concludes this discussion, focusing upon the use of secondary documents and records and mixed methods. With each means of obtaining data we will review the best practices recommendations that can be inferred from recent research.

Interviews

Interviews have been a data collection staple for many years. They originally involved only face-to-face exchanges, and many still do. When interviewer and subject meet face-to-face, it is important for the interviewer's dress and demeanor to fit the situation in order to make an appropriate presentation of self. This could entail carrying a clipboard, sitting behind a desk and being well-groomed or it could entail very casual dress, sitting next to subjects, etc. What is most fitting depends largely upon who is being interviewed, so what would make city hall executives feel comfortable probably would not work well with members of a street gang.

Interviews also vary greatly in terms of the role of interviewers, and the relationship they try to maintain with the subjects providing the information. These differences can be placed along a continuum, varying in the degree to which the interviewer poses specific, previously determined questions and provides the specific alternatives that are to be used by subjects in answering the questions. Interviews vary along the entire range of this dimension, from highly structured to unstructured.

Unstructured interviews

At one extreme along the continuum are *unstructured, or nondirective*, interviews that resemble a relaxed, friendly conversation in which subjects are free to take the discussion in whatever directions they wish. The interviewer does not suggest the terms or conditions they should use to express their views or experiences. In this format, the interviewer provides some initial focus, and then has the primary responsibility of keeping the conversation flowing. This usually requires acknowledging the views expressed by the subject so they know the interviewer is listening to them, and offering enough encouragement for them to continue to talk. The objective is to be supportive without directing the subject. It is often helpful in this regard to "mirror" the respondent's statements by re-phrasing them in the form of a question. To illustrate, if a respondent said that he was not comfortable in the neighborhood, then paused, the interviewer might ask, "So, you are uncomfortable here?"

However, it is important not to rush to fill a silence because quiet pauses, lasting up to about 10 seconds, are common in normal conversation; and when an interviewer responds to silence by displaying unease, it makes the interview feel different to normal conversation. For this reason, when conducting an unstructured interview, if there is a brief silence, investigators may mutely count to ten before overtly attempting to move the interview along. Most of the time a subject will spontaneously resume talking. Correspondingly, to maintain the feel of normal conversation, investigators conducting unstructured interviews are usually advised not to obtrusively record, or take notes, during the interview.

An unstructured interview is recommended when the investigator has a predetermined topic of interest, but is not sure, prior to actually carrying out the research, what variables are most important to consider. To proceed inductively, relying upon input from relevant subjects, unstructured interviews would be best. Alternatively, an investigator may believe that

Box 5.1 Warsaw Poles' view of recent migrants

The assumptions that suggest investigators should rely upon unstructured interviews – anticipating subjects' reluctance or the uncertainty of investigators – were present when a group of British researchers wondered how people living in Warsaw, Poland, had experienced changes in their city's ethnic diversity. They were specifically interested in the effects of changes which occurred after the Soviet Union withdrew in 1989. The central agenda of the investigators was to better understand how Warsaw residents' identification with their city and nation had been impacted by the presence of a variety of "others" – post-1989 migrants – who their subjects considered to be different from themselves; but they did not want to restrict in any way how the Warsaw Poles expressed themselves on the questions of interest.

Not wanting to identify particular ethnic groups for their subjects to consider, and being concerned that their subjects might feel reluctant to express any anti-ethnic sentiments, the investigators selected 30 participants with whom they conducted in-depth, non-directive interviews. Over a period of one year, each subject was interviewed three times in this manner.

During the interviews respondents were encouraged to express themselves freely, and interviewers sought non-invasive means of prompting them to expand upon points of potential interest. To illustrate, one Polish woman living in Warsaw, who had also lived in France, stated that she was concerned that immigration into Poland could result in Warsaw becoming like Paris. She stated that she would "very much not like for Poland to find itself in a situation like it is in France." After she finished the thought, the interviewer responded by asking, "What kinds of risks are you talking about?" The interviewee then explained that she feared an influx of Arabic migrants would form an enclave in Warsaw. She expected that they would want to build a mosque and listen to their Imam more than secular officials, and be unwilling to accept Polish culture.[1]

potential subjects are not likely to be able to readily answer specific questions on the topic of interest. Perhaps they have not thought much about it, or perhaps they may feel a reluctance to come directly to the point. Either assumption can lead an investigator to the same conclusion: utilize unstructured interviews, and that is how a research group proceeded in the study summarized in Box 5.1.

In sum, the most important points to remember about unstructured or non-directive interviews are:

1) They are most recommended when the investigator has a topic of interest, but is unsure of the relevant variables to be examined; or the

investigator believes that respondents may be unable or unwilling to readily provide the relevant information.

2) The non-directive interview should be conducted like a relaxed conversation in which subjects are encouraged to present and clarify their views or experiences with open-ended questions ("What kinds of risks?") that do not suggest the terms or directions the subject should follow in responding.

A word of caution is in order, however, for the young researcher contemplating the use of unstructured interviews. Any analysis ultimately requires the creation of variables common to all cases. When each respondent gets to define what they mean by "other," for example, their views may be difficult to compare. There may be as many views of other as there are respondents. If each one is truly unique, then analysis options are very limited. To find sufficient comparability when unstructured interviews are utilized can be a very difficult and time-consuming task for even the experienced researcher. Finally, conducting unstructured interviews requires specific training that goes well beyond reading a couple of pages in a text. Delving deeply into the opinions and values of a stranger can lead to difficult-to-manage situations.[2]

Structured interviews

At the opposite end of the continuum from unstructured interviews is the structured form. Here the interviewer asks highly focused questions. There is typically an interview schedule with all questions written down. The interviewer cannot deviate from the schedule so if subjects offer opinions unrelated to a specific question, the interviewer will, in a nice way, stop them and bring them back to the specific question. In addition, the *structured interview* usually imposes the form in which the questions are to be answered. It may entail asking subjects whether they like or dislike, approve or disapprove or to indicate their degree of agreement on a Likert scale, as previously introduced. In many respects, being the subject in a structured interview is like filling out a closed form questionnaire, with an interviewer replacing the questionnaire.

Under these structured conditions, the interview is not likely to feel like a normal conversation to the subject – it feels like what it is, a research project – and there is no reason for the investigator not to conspicuously record the subjects' answers. In fact, when conducting structured interviews, investigators often prepare a detailed code sheet on which to record subjects' responses during the interview.

The structured interview is typically chosen when investigators have a clear idea of what the important variables are in the topic they have chosen to study. Working deductively from a theory and/or past research, investigators develop a structured interview to focus upon obtaining only that information deemed to be important prior to data collection. Data analysis is quite straightforward and less time consuming compared to the analysis of data obtained with unstructured interviews. This is one important reason to recommend structured interviews when a research project is under tight time constraints. In addition, because it requires less training to conduct properly, a structured interview is also recommended when investigators are inexperienced.

The advantages of structured interviews can come at a cost, however. Its non-natural feel may lead subjects to hide more and disclose less, and their plug-in answers to previously scripted questions may have little meaning to them. In addition, this format does not permit subjects to raise new issues that are of interest or concern to them, or to express their reactions in ways not anticipated by the investigator. This means that there is no opportunity for serendipitous findings, that is, for discoveries that lead the research in directions that were previously not foreseen by the investigator. So the quality of a study that relies upon structured interviews is very reliant upon the thoroughness of the investigator's preparation prior to data collection.

Semi-structured interviews

In order to obtain some of the relative advantages of each of the preceding polar types of interviews, many investigators opt for a middle road: semi-structured interviews. They encompass a broad array of interview forms, ranging from nearly unstructured to nearly structured, and all points in-between. It is also common for semi-structured interviews to mix open-ended questions (where the subject is free to decide how to answer) with closed-ended questions (which impose response categories).

An effective use of semi-structured interviews, as the primary instrument of data collection, is illustrated by the study of participants in the Gezi Park movement, described in Box 5.2. By way of background, in 2013 the government stated its plans to raze a public park in the center of Istanbul. To try to block the demolition, protesters camped inside the park, and their efforts escalated into a national dissent against government policies.

Interviewer effects

The more unstructured the interview, the greater the opportunity for interviewers to influence how subjects respond to questions, and for variations in how interviewers interpret what subjects are saying.

Box 5.2 Participants in the Gezi Park (Istanbul) movement

On Saturday night, June 15, 2013, the Turkish government decided to forcibly evict the Gezi Park protesters. Two Istanbul Sociologists were in the park at the time, talking to protesters, trying to understand the diverse reasons for their participation. As the police were clearing people out of the park, the two investigators stayed in the area until early Sunday morning, and managed to conduct a total of 14 interviews with the protesters.

The interviews consisted of a mix of open-ended and highly focused questions, with more open-ended questions typically preceding more detailed follow-up questions. The investigators' strategy was to try first to get their subjects talking about why they were in the park with the protesters, and then to hone in on their motivations. For example, many of the subjects responded to the initial question by claiming they wanted to show opposition to government policies. The interviewers then prodded them to elaborate further by posing a number of detailed questions, such as: Who exactly was she battling against? What specific issues led him to camp out in the park?

The investigators only interviewed 14 of the park protesters overnight, but they did observe the entire encampment, and concluded that at least based upon age and sex, their small sample did seem representative of the larger group. Therefore, from the results of their interviews they concluded that there were large numbers of people in Istanbul who felt politically disenfranchised, and they joined the Gezi Park protest movement to show resistance to an authoritarian government.

Even in a highly structured format, however, the way questions are asked – with different inflections or emphases – can influence subjects' answers and, of course, interviewers may be predisposed to hearing certain types of answers, which can lead to differences among interviewers in what they record as subjects' answers. Broadly defined, *interviewer effects* are variations in the answers given by, or attributed to, subjects, that are due (at least in part) to interviewers' socio-demographic characteristics, their presentation of questions or ways in which their own predispositions toward the topics of the interview influence respondents.[3]

Because both reliability and validity are adversely affected, in any large-scale study involving multiple interviewers it is important to examine interview data for the possibility of interviewer effects. There are

two major ways in which assessments of interview data lead to the inference of interviewer effects:

1) If variations in subjects' answers to questions are associated with specific interviewers; for example, some interviewers consistently report
high scores for their subjects while other interviewers consistently
report obtaining low scores on the same issues. This approach to
inferring interviewer effects is illustrated in Box 5.3 below.

2) When the interview involves sensitive questions – for example, asking
about embarrassing or illegal activities – some interviewers have
more high-disclosure subjects while other interviewers' subjects give
more socially desirable answers. In situations of this type, more disclosures imply more honesty and variations in rates of disclosure, by
interviewer, would indicate interviewer effects. (This type of assessment is illustrated later in this chapter, in Box 5.4).

Interview length

It is conventionally assumed that to prevent fatigue from affecting either
the interviewer or interviewee, it is important to keep down the length of
an interview as much as possible. It is also assumed that the willingness
of respondents to participate will be enhanced by briefer interviews.[5]
However, research on this issue suggests that while large differences in
length may have adverse effects, small differences in time to completion
may not matter much. For example, Lynn conducted an experiment in
the UK in which subjects were randomly assigned either to a shorter
interview session (mean completion of 25 minutes) or a longer interview
session (31 minutes). The topics (religion, education, neighborhood
attachment and friendship networks) were the same in both versions.

In this experiment the 6-minute difference in interview length was not
associated with any difference in completion rates or in subjects' willingness to answer additional (post-interview) questions. However, in his
conclusion, Lynn cautioned that if a 6-minute difference was a larger
percentage of the total length – for example, if interviews taking 8 and 14
minutes were compared – perhaps the effects of a longer interview on
participation would have been greater. And, of course, if the time difference between the interview versions exceeded 6 minutes, perhaps that
could have affected the subjects. Finally, he noted, that increased length
might decrease the quality of responses, an issue he did not examine.[6]

Matching characteristics

It is often possible to know in advance the socio-demographic characteristics of the people to be interviewed. Neighborhood profiles may be

Box 5.3 Interviewer effects on US social isolation scores

From the time that social scientists first began to study urban life, many analysts contended that people in cities tended to live in isolation and anonymity. In recent decades, there has been a good deal of interest in the question of whether social isolation has been increasing, given that there is more diversity in communities and more elderly people living alone. The General Social Survey (GSS) is an on-going survey conducted regularly in the US and it contains a module on social isolation in which subjects are asked to provide the names of up to six people with whom they have discussed important matters in the past six months. For subjects who are concerned with maintaining confidentiality, they can provide only the initials of their discussion partners. If they nominate fewer than five such people, interviewers are instructed to probe for additional names, or initials. This is a critical step in identifying the size of a subject's social network. From follow-up questions about subjects' nominees, the interviewers obtain information about the size and nature of each subject's social network.

In a re-analysis of GSS surveys conducted in several different years, investigators found that some interviewers turned in forms on which a larger than expected percentage of the subjects they interviewed appeared, on average, to experience high levels of social isolation (i.e. to have small and fragmented networks). Many of their subjects reported that they had not discussed matters of importance with anyone, or if they had, it was only with one or two persons, at most. Other interviewers, by contrast, were reporting that their subjects had larger networks, that is, subjects who, on average, had more discussion partners. How could this difference among interviewers occur?

The investigators posed several possibilities. Some interviewers may do a better job of motivating subjects to recall all the people with whom they have had important discussions. Or, some interviewers may be less inclined to probe for additional names because each name requires a number of follow-up questions. Perhaps the interviewers get tired, or are in a hurry to finish? In any case, if an interviewer appears unenthusiastic or inattentive, it will certainly be a cue to the subject to disengage.[4]

available; there may be published documents, such as census reports for the zip or postal code; or it may be possible for investigators to cruise the neighborhood(s) involved prior to beginning the study. If the socio-demographic characteristics of potential subjects are known in advance, then the researcher must decide how important it is for interviewers to have matching characteristics: Blacks to interview Blacks, women to interview women, and so on. The assumption is that if there is a significant status similarity between subjects and interviewers then subjects will feel freer to disclose their feelings and past experiences because they will believe the interviewer has shared these experiences and can, therefore, better understand them. It is also assumed that "insiders" will be less likely than "outsiders" to miss subtle cues, and that they will be more able to probe, without making subjects uncomfortable.

Several decades of research have generally indicated that matching of interviewers and subjects has benefits: that subjects provide more complete information and fail to answer fewer questions when the interviewer shares their characteristics. However, the differences that are apparently due to matching of subjects and interviewers have often been reported as small in magnitude.[7] In addition, it has often been difficult to estimate with precision how much effect to attribute to the characteristic being matched (or not matched), and how much may be due to other qualities the interviewer and subjects may or may not share. For example, if the pair share a relevant interest or attitude, that may create a connection between them that is more significant than similarities or differences in gender or race.[8]

There is also some evidence that female interviewers may be more effective at eliciting sensitive or embarrassing information from both male and female subjects. As previously noted, one important type of interviewer effect involves variations in subjects' disclosures of sensitive information. How variations in the interviewer's gender can be related to rates of such disclosures is inferred from an interesting experiment described in Box 5.4.

Interview mode

Historically, the face-to-face interview was the dominant mode, and many researchers continue to favor it in collecting interview data. Technological innovations have led to increased alternatives, though, first to the use of telephones and more recently to computer-assisted, self-administered interviews. We will note the relative strengths and weaknesses of each of these alternative modes.

Face-to-face

There are numerous advantages to relying upon an in-person interviewer: that person may be able to persuade reluctant subjects to be interviewed, may be able to help clarify the intent of ambiguous questions, may be able to connect with subjects and thereby elicit more

Box 5.4 Gender of interviewer effects

In this experiment, 17-year-old male and female subjects were interviewed by a pre-recorded voice of either a male or female in their early
twenties. These were computer-assisted self-interviews, so there were
no face-to-face contacts. The only information subjects had about the
interviewer had to be inferred from their voice. In a pre-test, the investigators had a sample listen to the voices and there were no significant
differences in the race/ethnicity, educational attainment or regional
accent they attributed to the male and female voices. As a result, the
investigators could infer that any differences between the interview
results of male and female subjects were probably due to the gender of
the voice asking the questions.[9]

The interview schedule contained a lengthy list of questions involving negative behaviors, and subjects were asked how often they had
engaged in each of them. Examples included: damaging property,
selling marijuana, getting into physical fights, etc. The assumption was
that people would not ordinarily "fake bad": claim to have engaged in
negative behaviors if, in fact, they had not, so the number of such
actions a subject was willing to admit to was taken as an indicator of
the subject's truthfulness in answering the interview questions. Therefore, if subjects on average had higher rates of admission when they
were interviewed by persons of the same sex, it would imply that such
matching was effective.

The results showed that the gender of the interviewer had no significant effect upon female subjects, but it did produce substantially
higher rates of disclosure for male subjects. In order to explain their
findings, the investigators examined a large number of other gender-
effect studies that had included diverse subject samples. They found
that, overall, female subjects had less to disclose than males – that is,
they were less likely to have engaged in the negative behaviors – but
they had relatively high disclosure rates, regardless of the interviewers'
gender. In other words, females committed fewer negative acts, but
more readily admitted them to either males or females, so there was
less opportunity for the gender of the interviewer to have an effect.
Males had higher rates and were more selective about confessing to
them, typically opening up more to female interviewers. In conclusion, if
getting males to admit to sensitive behaviors is the objective, investigators
would be wise to rely upon the voice of a female interviewer.

candid replies, and may be able to provide observations that provide
context for interpreting subjects' answers. For example, it may be helpful
to have an interviewer's notes concerning how subjects were dressed,
the condition of their homes, or the like. In many studies, in fact,

interviewers are instructed to record observations of this type in the interview schedule or on a companion document.

However, face-to-face interviews are expensive, in terms of time and money, and more than mechanically recorded interviews, they involve the risk of interviewer mistakes, or even falsifications: instances in which interviewers cut short a session, as described in Box 5.3, or even invent answers that they assign to a subject. There are statistical procedures for analyzing patterns in the responses attributed to subjects that appear able to detect many, if not all, falsifications, and when detected those subjects can be re-interviewed by someone else.[10] Of course this further increases the cost of face-to-face interviews.

If the interview involves questions that subjects are likely to consider sensitive or embarrassing, then the most important criterion in evaluating different interview modes concerns their relative efficacy in inducing subjects to candidly provide the requested information. A review of the research involving different modes follows.

Telephone interviews

The telephone has for many decades been a prevalent mode for conducting interviews. It permits data to be obtained from each subject faster and cheaper than in-person interviews. The disadvantage is that when strangers are connected solely via a telephone line, the interview can feel impersonal and/or anonymous, and frank disclosures by a subject can be discouraged as a result. On the other hand, not having directly to face another person may make it easier for people to give honest answers. If they had to directly face an interviewer, perhaps they would be too uncomfortable to admit to certain things. It may be that the relative advantages and disadvantages of telephone (compared to face-to-face) interviews may balance out because some studies have concluded that telephone interviews were superior; some studies have reported that face-to-face interviews were better; and some studies have found no significant difference.[11]

Computer-assisted self-interviews

In recent years, computer-assisted self-interviewing (*ACASI*) has grown greatly in popularity. It entails having respondents listen to pre-recorded questions on earphones and then enter their answers on a laptop. One important reason for its increased usage, apart from the availability of the requisite technology, is that it appears to promote more disclosure than either face-to-face or telephone interviews. Why and how computer-assisted self-interviewing works so well is examined in the experiment described in Box 5.5.

Box 5.5 New Yorkers' self-disclosures when computers ask the questions

A number of studies have reported surprisingly high rates of reporting sensitive information when respondents self-administer a computer-assisted interview (ACASI). Included have been diverse studies that examined cocaine and marijuana use, failing in school, etc. The issue that interested a group of interdisciplinary investigators was: What is it about ACASI that leads to greater reporting of socially undesirable behaviors? To examine the possibilities, Laura Lind and colleagues had an interviewer record questions for ACASI presentation, and they took videos of that person that they projected onto an animated face, creating a "virtual interviewer." This same person also conducted the face-to-face interviews.[12]

The subject pool consisted of 235 adults (mean = 31 years old) in New York City. They were all asked the same series of questions about alcohol use, sexual behavior, and so on, but they were randomly assigned to one of three experimental conditions that differed from each other in how the questions were presented. The same person always asked the questions, but sometimes the questions came "live" from the interviewer, sometimes they were recorded as described above, and some of the recordings came with an animated version of the interviewer's face asking the questions. Three experimental conditions are of special interest to us here:

- Group One: Face-to-face interview.
- Group Two: Animated face, recorded interview.
- Group Three: ACASI.

The investigators found some variations in which of the three conditions produced the most disclosures based upon the specific type of question asked. Overall, however, ACASI (Group Three) was associated with the highest disclosure rates. Notably, ACASI scored higher than Group Two, even though it also involved computerized self-administration. From this experimental design, the investigators were able to conclude that it is apparently the absence of any interviewers' facial representation (actual or animated) that makes ACASI most effective.

In sum, we have reviewed a large number of studies whose results consistently suggested that the most effective mode for eliciting confessions of embarrassing, or negative, behaviors is computer-assisted interviewing, especially if the questions are asked by a female (voice).

Questionnaires

A questionnaire, as we are defining it, is a self-administered and self-contained form, meaning that it is designed to enable a subject to complete it without any assistance. It includes both questions and instructions pertaining to how those questions are to be answered. The questions can be answered by lengthy essays, but response alternatives are typically provided and the respondent is asked only to choose one (e.g. circle the alternative that best fits). Interaction between subject and researchers is minimized; in fact, if the questionnaire is mailed, there will be none.

Because the prototypical questionnaire involves little or no interaction between subject and researcher, there is no feedback from subjects and little or no opportunity for subjects to raise questions about the questionnaire. There is a risk, therefore, that subjects can misinterpret the intent of any question and that their misunderstandings will go undetected. To minimize this risk, it is critically important to conduct a pre-test before presenting a (final) questionnaire to one's subjects.

Pre-tests

To carry out a pre-test, investigators usually try to select as subjects people who resemble those to be included in the actual study, but are not eligible to be included because they live outside of the district, are too old, or the like. The closer the pre-test subjects are to the actual test subjects the better, but procedures should be in place to ensure that the same person is never included in both because the pre-test experience will "contaminate" the subject's responses.

While, or immediately after, people in the pre-test fill out the questionnaire, it is important to discuss the specific questions with them to make sure they understood the investigator's intents. It is similarly important to discuss the response alternatives provided to ensure they provide subjects with an adequate means of responding to the questions. From this feedback, an investigator can prepare new drafts of the questionnaire until the problems are resolved. If during the actual study subjects misinterpret questions or find the response alternatives are not meaningful, it will spoil the data, but the investigator will have no way to know that until it is too late. When the data are analyzed and the results do not make sense, there is nothing an investigator can do at that point. So, the moral is clear: pre-test. Always pre-test even if it only involves a small sample.

Cover sheet

Most questionnaires are accompanied by a cover sheet that begins by informing subjects of the objective of the study. The first thing potential subjects will want to know is what they will be asked about, and who is doing the asking. Specifically, a good cover sheet should:

1) State the objective(s) of the research. What does the investigator want to know about? In this introduction, it is important to avoid emotionally laden terms or anything which even subtly suggests the investigator may have a bias. For example, to state that it is a study of people who fail to obey downtown traffic signals implies a negative view of that behavior because of the word, "fail." If an investigator's position is implied, potential subjects who disagree with that position may be more inclined to refuse to participate, biasing the sample. Or, as we will describe later in this chapter, it may suggest how the investigator hopes subjects will answer, and they will often try to please the investigator.
2) Identify the investigator's affiliation (a research institute, university, or the like) so that potential subjects will know the questionnaire is not linked to the sale or marketing of some product. If the questionnaire is to be mailed, the investigator's affiliation should appear on the outside of the envelope.
3) Describe how people will be expected to answer the questions, e.g. circle the alternative that best fits; and provide an honest estimate of the amount of time it should take most subjects to complete the questionnaire.
4) Look professional. If it is sloppy in appearance, grammatically incorrect or difficult to understand, potential subjects will be more inclined to discard the questionnaire, and refusal rates will be increased.
5) If the questionnaire involves sensitive information, it is important to assure subjects that their response will be treated confidentially, and describe the procedures that will ensure confidentiality. (See the discussion of this issue in Chapter 1.)
6) Finally, the cover sheet should convey the investigator's thanks in advance; and if a summary of results will later be available to subjects (a nice touch), the cover sheet should tell people how to request it.

Question wording problems

The proper wording of questions is both an art – developed from long practice – and a science in which problems to avoid have been identified. Here we will describe the most important rules for constructing questions.[13]

Leading questions

A *leading question* is phrased in a way that suggests how a respondent ought to answer it. One way to circumvent this problem is to avoid using words or terms with implicit value judgments ("Did you fail to . . .") and to avoid wording questions in a way that respondents may feel puts them into a dubious category ("Are you the sort of person who . . .").

Another type of leading question that can be more difficult to detect involves asking respondents if they would be in favor of some desirable outcome, without noting the possible costs of that outcome. To illustrate, SurveyMonkey posted an on-line questionnaire asking people their perceptions of air pollution in their cities. Many of the questions did well in noting the possible costs of desirable solutions; for example: "Power stations and factories should switch to cleaner processes even if consumer bills and prices have to go up." People replied on a five-point Likert scale: Strongly Agree; Agree; Unsure; Disagree; Strongly Disagree. However, other questions did not note costs, for example: "Recycling programs should be put in place and promoted across the whole city." Why would a respondent not agree with the question phrased in this manner? It sounds good and is free of cost.

A related problem associated with question wording is *acquiescence*: the tendency for people to select Agree more than Disagree responses. The way questions are worded can increase or decrease this tendency. For example, more people will select Agree in response to the question, "immigration is good for the city's economy," than will choose Disagree to the question, "immigration is bad for the city's economy." It is not clear why this acquiescence bias occurs. Perhaps it is easier to agree and people get lazy? Perhaps they want to please the investigator and think that agreeing is the way to do that? In any case, it is important to reverse the direction of some of the questions (as in the above immigration example) in order to keep respondents from simply agreeing over and over.[14]

Double-barreled questions

Double-barreled questions present two questions combined into one, making it very difficult for many people to answer. For example: "Would you prefer dividing the city into two administratively separate zones in order to better plan transportation improvements?" How could that question be answered by someone who wanted to create separate zones, but wanted to do so in order to improve the delivery of social services rather than transportation planning?

Double-barreled questions frustrate respondents and can lead them to give thoughtless answers, just to get the questionnaire over with, or they may even refuse to complete the questionnaire. The solution to the problem is usually to divide the double-barreled question into two separate questions. For example:

> Would dividing the city into zones, in your opinion, improve
> transportation planning?
> If yes: Would you be in favor of creating separate zones?

The same questions could then be repeated for the delivery of social services, or any other interest of the investigators.

Ambiguous questions

Ambiguity is probably the most prevalent flaw in questionnaire items, and perhaps the most difficult to detect. It is especially likely to arise when a question is amenable to different interpretations, and none of the alternative responses clarify which meaning was intended. In ordinary conversation, people can rely upon inflections, tones and facial expressions to clarify the other's intentions. In a self-administered questionnaire, however, the printed words stand alone. Unless the investigator is very careful about question wording, subjects may give different interpretations to the same question, making it impossible to compare their responses.

To minimize ambiguity, it is helpful to keep questions as specific as possible. This often entails dividing them into separate questions, as in the case of double-barreled questions. The single best way to detect and minimize ambiguity, however, is again to pre-test. Having subjects explain how they interpreted each question is the surest way to identify ambiguities.

Attitudes or behaviors?

The self-contained questionnaire is ideally suited to measuring people's attitudes, which are conventionally defined as pre-dispositions to act. Some investigators assume that measures of people's attitudes and their actual behaviors are largely interchangeable; that the correlation between them is so high that if one wants to be able to predict how people will behave in a situation, it is adequate to probe relevant attitudes in a questionnaire. Other social scientists, however, regard the presumed strong connection between attitudes and behavior as the *attitudinal fallacy*; and they refer to the related assumption that self-reported behavior in a questionnaire is a good proxy for observations of actual behavior as an accounting fallacy.[15]

Critics of the reliance upon attitudinal indicators do not contend that there is no relationship between attitudes and behavior. In fact, numerous studies report that there is at least a modest relationship between attitudes, as measured in questionnaires, and people's behavior, as actually observed. However, it is typically only a modest relationship; not so large as to enable investigators to assume that it is not problematic to utilize attitude measures as proxies for observed behavior. Even if people honestly and accurately report their attitudes, there are often intervening events and situational factors that may lead people to behave in ways that seem inconsistent with their previously expressed attitudes. For example, when Americans' church attendance is asked in questionnaires, the self-reported rates typically exceed those obtained from other behaviorally based measures. Further analysis suggests that the inflated self-reports are a function of some people's strong religious identities.[16] These subjects re-interpret the question as asking how religious they are, and in response they check a higher frequency of attendance alternative than is warranted by their behavior. Based upon their attitudes, they would regularly attend church; but competing claims upon their time on Sunday mornings often lead them instead to sleep in, meet friends for breakfast, etc. In sum, if an investigator is primarily interested in explaining or predicting people's behavior, and is relying upon attitudinal questions in a questionnaire, a word of caution is in order.

There is some evidence that self-reports of behavior correlate more strongly with behavior, as objectively measured, than do attitudes. However, when the topic involves sensitive issues – such as abortion, bankruptcy, church attendance, etc. – analyses of public records showing actual rates indicates a marked tendency for people, in self-report questionnaires, to under-state "undesirable" behavior while over-stating "desirable" behaviors. Again, the conclusion is to be cautious about assuming that self-reports accurately recount people's actual behavior, regardless of whether the questions focus upon self-reports of attitudes or behavior. The alternative, discussed later in this chapter, is to rely upon direct observation, where it is feasible.

The social desirability bias and possible solutions

One important reason for the less than perfect relationships between either attitudes or self-reported behavior, on the one hand, and people's actually observed behavior, on the other, is the *social desirability bias*: the tendency for respondents to avoid answering questions in a way that may make them look bad to others and/or to overly ascribe favorable traits to themselves. If the questions that were posed to people asked them about behaviors that may potentially be embarrassing for them to admit to or pose a risk to subjects because the actions in question are illegal, it is important to assess the possibility that the social desirability bias was operating in the way they answered the questions. A social desirability bias is generally inferred from low rates of admission to sensitive questions. The reasoning here is parallel to that previously described in relation to interviews, namely, that people will not ordinarily fake bad in filling out a questionnaire. So, in comparing two or more ways of asking sensitive questions, the one that produces higher numbers of admissions is considered to be better.[17]

Several approaches have been developed to reduce, if not eliminate, this potential bias. The simplest is probably to assure respondents that they will be anonymous, and that is reassuring if respondents believe it. However, they may feel that the investigator knows their name and address and used it to mail or deliver the questionnaire. As a result, they may wonder, how am I really anonymous? That takes some explaining in the cover sheet if the investigator is counting on respondents believing that their responses will be anonymous.

Face-saving introductions

Another relatively simple way to address social desirability is to include a face-saving introduction to potentially embarrassing questions. For example, in asking a group of Swedish adults if they had engaged in any political activity (voted, signed a petition, contacted an elected official, etc.) during the past year, the face-saving introduction to the question acknowledged that many people feel that they have little time for involvement in political issues. Then the questionnaire proceeded to ask whether they had engaged in any of the political activities that were listed. When the face-saving mode of asking was compared to a neutral, matter-of-fact way of introducing the question, it was found to markedly decrease the amount of political activity in which respondents claimed to have engaged. This result suggested that it reduced social desirability effects.[18]

Randomization techniques

In order to reduce social desirability effects, a number of techniques have been devised specifically to shield respondents from any legal consequences of their admissions. *Randomization techniques* instruct respondents to select certain answers, whether or not they are true, based upon random events that they alone know about. For example, respondents may be instructed to shake a die, and if it comes up one, to lie in answering some question, but to tell the truth otherwise. Or they may be asked to answer a question truthfully unless their mother's birthday falls in certain months of the year. The logic behind all of these randomized response techniques is that respondents may feel that it protects them from any sanctions because no one could know for sure whether they told the truth in answering a specific question because they shook a die or flipped a coin or the like in private.

However, because the investigator knows the probability of occurrence of the random events these techniques introduce, the investigator

Obtaining data, Part One

can later eliminate the random error by statistically adjusting the obtained findings. The results can be generalized from the sample to a population, but not applied to any individual in the sample.[19] Given that the objective of most social science research is to describe a population, the absence of individual applicability is not usually a problem.

Randomization techniques have sometimes been found to reduce the social desirability bias in questionnaire responses, but when they have it has typically been to only a very small degree. Its limited efficacy is probably because asking respondents to employ these techniques before they answer specific questions calls attention to the questions and may make respondents more fearful of offering honest answers than they would have been otherwise. Another potential disadvantage is that randomization techniques require lengthy and sometimes complicated instructions in the questionnaire's cover page and that could lead some recipients of the questionnaire to decline to participate.[20]

It might be better to utilize randomization techniques in an interview rather than a questionnaire so that an interviewer could instruct a subject as to when to flip a coin, roll a die or the like – outside of the interviewer's vision. The interviewer could then clarify how the technique protects the subject from potentially incriminating admissions. However, the apparent reduction in social desirability effects in interviews utilizing randomization techniques has also been relatively small.

Psychological scales

There are a number of psychological scales that have been developed to indicate whether anyone taking a paper and pencil test, including a conventional questionnaire, is lying or faking good. To illustrate, the MMPI-2 (Minnesota Multiphasic Personality Inventory, version 2) has a "lie scale" consisting of questions that ask respondents whether they have stolen things, snuck into a movie without paying, and so on. If respondents are trying to fake good, their denial of having committed any of these actions will exceed the averages that have been developed from testing large, national samples. A similar approach is involved in Paulthus Deception Scales. They contain a number of questions that ask respondents for self-descriptions. Again, by comparing the answers of people in any sample to national norms, it is possible to infer whether or not any respondent's answers likely contain inflated self-views.

When any of these scales are used in questionnaire studies, investigators typically select a subset of the questions in the scale, and embed them throughout the questionnaire. These questions only add a couple of minutes to the time required to complete the questionnaire. The scale items are analyzed separately, and the results of this analysis inform an investigator of how strongly a social desirability bias was operating. It is also commonplace to exclude from the primary data analysis the questionnaires of respondents with scale scores that exceed some criterion. Subjects' scores can also be useful as a way of comparing the effectiveness of different interviewers.

ACASI, again

Finally, self-administered computer-assisted (i.e. ACASI) questionnaires, taken in private with no bystander present, have been reported to be most effective in increasing respondents' willingness to offer socially undesirable answers. This research finding mirrors the results previously described for interview studies in which computer-assisted interviews elicited more socially undesirable answers than face-to-face interviews. If computer-assisted questionnaires are too expensive for a study to utilize, or too sophisticated for most of the target subjects, even a low-tech MP3 player with ear phones is sufficient in conjunction with self-administered and self-contained answer sheets. In this case, a prerecorded voice explains how and where subjects should mark their responses on an answer sheet.[21] And as has been consistently reported in other studies, the self-administered form apparently best reduces the social desirability bias because it is associated with the greatest number of socially undesirable admissions.

Response formats

Formulating the questions to be asked in a questionnaire is half of the investigator's task. The other half involves deciding how respondents are to answer the questions. Although the two tasks can be separated for purposes of discussion, in fact they must be developed together because certain types of questions call for specific ways of responding.

Open-ended or closed?

The first issue for an investigator to resolve concerning a response format is whether it will be an *open-ended format*: respondents will be permitted to formulate and freely express their answers; or a *closed format*: subjects will be constrained by a set of alternatives provided by the investigator. There are also many intermediate options that offer a mix of open and closed formats. This discussion will only examine the two extremes.

The advantage of an open-ended format is that respondents are able to answer questions in a way that seems most appropriate to them. Perhaps they would like to respond to a question along an approve-disapprove dimension, but a closed format might only provide them with an agree-disagree alternative. Their responses may not be meaningful as a result. Or their complete answer to a question may be full of contingencies that the answer sheet did not provide. For example, suppose people were asked how they would feel about adding a subway stop in their neighborhood. In a closed format, they might be asked to express a degree of liking (L) or disliking (D) for such a stop; but, what if a respondent would like such a stop only if: the station were below ground level, the trains connected to the city's bus terminal, and riders would not have to pay more than a set amount? How would this person select an L or D option?

An open format enables an investigator to better understand how respondents feel about an issue. They get to express their feelings or attitudes without format constraints. However, this advantage can also be a disadvantage. Respondents may offer many different and non-comparable replies to the same question. Any type of extensive analysis requires that like responses be combined so that categorical variables can be compared. This can entail a very difficult and time-consuming coding process after the questionnaires have been collected.[22]

Recommendation: Investigators with limited experience conducting research or who face time constraints should stay with a closed format, but rely upon a pre-test to make sure that the response alternatives presented provide meaningful alternatives.

Response categories

If an investigator chooses a closed format, the first question to be addressed is, how many response categories should be presented? The popular Likert scale, as previously introduced, provides five categories: a strong alternative at each end, and a neutral-uncertain point in the middle. Does this require making distinctions that are too difficult for most people? Or, would more alternatives be better by permitting subjects to offer more differentiated responses and to express more intense opinions?

Assessments of this issue yield somewhat inconsistent results because the conclusion can vary according to who is in the subject pool, what issues are being examined, the dimensions along which the response categories are arranged, and so on. However, for the most part, there appear to be gains when the response categories are increased from two (A or D, L or D, etc.) to five (i.e. Likert); but people's ability to distinguish among more than five categories seems to decline, and the reliability of their answers is correspondingly reduced.[23]

Grid format

When a series of questions, in a closed format, share the same core wording and response alternatives, investigators often place them together in order to save space or to help the subject complete the questionnaire quicker. For example, there could be a series of questions asking subjects how much they trust their: city government, local police, city newspapers, etc. A large number of questions of this type could be presented in a *grid format*. Table 5.1 illustrates a portion of a typical grid.

While it offers economies, a common problem with this design is that subjects may respond to what the questions share in common, i.e. trust, and not carefully distinguish among the specific entities. In other words, people answer each question according to their overall degree of trust. Their replies might indicate no trust in any of the entities or full trust in all of them, but they are not reliable answers. In addition, questions posed in a grid format may be particularly susceptible to acquiescence. Some experts have concluded that the grid format should be used very sparingly, or not at all.[24]

Mode of delivery

A self-administered questionnaire can wind up in the hands of potential respondents in a variety of different ways. If the geographical boundaries of the desired sample are known, for example, the simplest way to reach potential respondents is to make the questionnaire available at sites in the neighborhood(s). This could entail leaving copies of the questionnaire at local coffee shops and book stores, having them inserted into a neighborhood newspaper, and the like.

The problem with this approach is that it will not ordinarily be possible to generalize to any population from the sample of returned questionnaires. Not only can an investigator expect to have few of the questionnaires returned, but the investigator may have no way of correcting for biases in the sample, which will almost certainly exist. Further, the investigator has no way of verifying who actually filled out the returned

Table 5.1 A grid illustrated

Q: How much would you say you trust:	Circle one alternative				
	No Trust	*Little Trust*	*Unsure*	*Some Trust*	*Full Trust*
1) City government	1	2	3	4	5
2) Local police	1	2	3	4	5
3) City Newspaper	1	2	3	4	5

questionnaires and under what conditions they were completed. This approach is rife with opportunities for "mischief;" for example, a group of friends may find a stack of questionnaires late on Saturday night, and decide to have fun filling them out. In sum, because of a variety of problems, this is not really a viable option under most conditions.

Mailed questionnaires

Historically, many studies that employed questionnaires sent them to pre-selected people or addresses, by mail or post. It can be cost effective, but the main drawback is the typically low response rate. It is not uncommon for the return on the first mailing of a questionnaire to be in the single digits![25] As discussed in Chapter 3, response rates are not always the most important criterion by which to judge the adequacy of a survey. One would also want to assess and try to adjust for biases in the sample. However, at some point, returns can be too low to permit adequate assessment of biases.

Because response rates to a first mailing are typically very low, it is best practice to rely upon multiple follow-up mailings. Each subsequent mailing can increase the response rate, but typically by a diminishing amount. It is uncommon, therefore, to rely upon more than two follow-ups to an initial mailing. Recognize, though, that each mailing adds to the cost, detracting from a major advantage of mailed questionnaires.

Via the Internet

If potential subjects have an affiliation or an interest in common – based upon a shared occupation, religion, hobby, or the like – they may be particularly inclined to visit certain websites. This introduces a possibility that has been increasingly relied upon in recent years, namely, posting the questionnaire on an Internet site. The quality shared among visitors to the site has sometimes been found to increase return rates, and if access to the site is limited that can probably reduce the potential for mischief. It also resolves the problem of how to return completed questionnaires. Serious sampling issues can remain, though; see the discussion in Chapter 4.

A number of studies have examined Web questionnaires and compared them to other modes of delivery with less than perfectly uniform results, though overall they do suggest better returns with the Internet mode.[26] A major concern yet to be fully resolved concerns the relative quality of responses to digital questionnaires. One of the major issues – subjects' differentiation in their responses – is examined in the study described in Box 5.6. The study has limitations, notably the use of a grid format, but its results are consistent with those reported in other studies.

Box 5.6 Responding by Web versus mail

The regional government of Andalusia, Spain, was interested in understanding the circumstances of adults who were eligible to vote in Andalusia, but were residing in other countries. The regional government funded a study in which over 15,000 former residents were selected from government records, contacted by post, then given two ways to answer a mailed questionnaire: by mail, postage paid, or the Web.[27] For comparability, the questions that appeared on each screen in the Web version exactly mirrored the pages of the paper questionnaire that was mailed. The questionnaire contained a mix of open and closed questions, the latter involving rating scales that offered between two and ten response categories.

Given a choice, more subjects utilized the Internet to respond, but there were enough of each mode to permit a comparison of the postal and Web returned questionnaires. The evaluation focused upon differentiation, the number of different response categories used by subjects in their answers. More differentiation suggests that a subject was thinking more about the meaning of questions, and trying to give the best response. Very weak differentiation would be indicated if, for example, a subject simply went down one column in answering every, or most, questions.

The analysis indicated that those who responded by post were somewhat more likely to select the "easy" choices, those at the extremes and middle (that would be 1, 3 and 5 on a Likert scale.) The number of affirmative (i.e. agree) answers was also a bit higher among the postal returns, indicating acquiescence, as previously described. Overall, differentiation was higher in the Web returns, but only to a small degree. Also favoring the Web returns was the fact that it included a higher rate of completely answered questionnaires.

In sum, questionnaires posted on the Web generally have higher return rates than conventional mailed questionnaires, though both often suffer from sampling deficiencies. The quality of responses in questionnaires conducted via the Internet also seem better than those sent by post, though the differences appear to be small in magnitude.

Observation

There is a broad range of research that can be termed, at least in part, observational. An investigator's observations are often part of an experiment conducted in either a laboratory or natural setting. In this type of study, the investigator manipulates an independent variable and then relies upon direct observation of subjects in order to obtain measures of the dependent variable. Observations of this type were discussed in conjunction with experimentation in Chapter 3.

Observation is also intimately involved in ethnographic, or field studies, in which the observer is also, to some degree, a participant in the activities of the people being watched. There is typically no intentional manipulation of any aspect of the social setting because the objective in ethnographic research is to avoid reactivity. An investigator's observations while serving also as a participant were discussed in association with ethnography in Chapter 2.

Excluding experimentation and ethnography leaves two types of observation not connected to a primary research method. The first is direct observation of people's behavior, in which (unlike ethnography) the investigator is not a participant and (unlike experimentation) no variable is manipulated. The second type involves indirect observation, and it typically entails focusing upon physical traces that are by-products of people's behavior. We will discuss each, in turn.

Direct observation

Direct (non-participant) observation is usually conducted unobtrusively, that is, without the awareness of the people who are being viewed. A group of people being studied in a natural setting will not ordinarily tolerate the presence of an outsider who is conspicuously observing them, but is not affiliated with the group in any way. In effect, there is no social role for a direct non-participant observer in a natural setting. The people being watched will chase the outsider away, if they can; move, if they cannot; or at the least, alter their behavior so that much will not be visible to the outsider.

One of the major reasons that an investigator would want to rely upon direct, but unobtrusive, observation is a distrust of the ability of other methods to obtain the desired information. An investigator might believe that people will be motivated to color their self-reports (due, for example, to a social desirability effect), or that people will not be able accurately to recall their behavior. Either concern would lead an investigator away from a conventional questionnaire or interview. These concerns led a research team to conduct a study relying upon direct, non-obtrusive observation, as described in Box 5.7.

In reflecting upon the research on the Australian shoppers, it is helpful to ask: Would the people who were observed relying upon their car, rather than walking, candidly admit to their "laziness" in a questionnaire or interview? Even if motivated to be truthful, would they be able accurately to recall how much they typically walked between stores?

Box 5.7 Shoppers in Australian cities

Three Australian researchers were interested in how supermarkets influenced the flow of pedestrians in shopping centers of small cities in New South Wales. By way of background, they noted that pedestrian flows were the "lifeblood" of town centers. Therefore, it was important to understand how supermarket locations could affect that flow. Many cities have considered relaxing the controls on the location of super-markets. How might doing so affect overall patterns of pedestrian movement?

A survey of residents in the area was an obvious method to employ. However, the investigators did not want to depend upon what they termed "the vagaries of memory." They chose to rely upon covert observation to ensure that the recorded behavior of people would be "as accurate, natural and un-self-conscious as possible."[28]

The investigators selected two cities and prepared land-use and built-form maps for both shopping centers. Every two hours, between 8 am and 6 pm, one of the investigators walked through a pre-defined route that cut once through all the public spaces and noted how many pedestrians were passed on the route. Every time a pedestrian was passed, the investigators placed a dot on the map: the *trips-and-dots* method. (By walking the route every two hours, it was unlikely any investigator would pass the same pedestrian again, and arouse suspicion.) In addition, in each city, they selected a pedestrian who entered the study area at a different point, and covertly tracked that pedestrian at a distance. The routes of all pedestrians were recorded and the investigators noted their gender and approximate age.

Among their more notable findings, the investigators reported that most people did not walk more than one to two city blocks (250 meters). When they drove to a supermarket, and that supermarket was not within the walking range (one to two blocks) of other stores, they did not visit those other stores. The investigators concluded that city planners should be sensitive to these findings in taking steps to improve the activity on city center streets.

Another reason for relying upon direct, unobtrusive observation in a study is in order to construct a social-spatial map of a particular geographical area that is of theoretical or practical interest. The objective of the research is to describe the social ecology of the specific area: its physical structures, and the types of activities that predominate in it. It could be a central business district, an ethnic enclave or a red-light (i.e. prostitution) district. For example, to describe the social ecology of red-light districts in Belgian cities, an investigator spent days and nights

over a period of years diagramming and describing: physical arrangements (e.g. vacant buildings, abandoned cars, etc.), the conduct of people
on the street (loitering, arguing, etc.) and the nature of interactions
between them (buying and selling, arguing, etc.). He supplemented his
diagrams and descriptions with photographs.[29] Others conducting similar
studies rely greatly upon preparing maps of the area.[30]

Informed consent?

Unobtrusive observations can obviously violate human subject protocols
requiring the informed consent of subjects (see Chapter 1). However,
seeking informed consent from subjects is incompatible with the objective of conducting non-reactive observations. One defense of proponents is that, in many instances, unobtrusive observations do not provide
information about any identifiable individual. In other studies, individual
identification is possible, though. For example, the investigators could
have recognized the Australian pedestrians they were surreptitiously
following. Some of the men who were seen paying prostitutes in the
Belgian red-light districts could also have been recognized by the investigator. Identifying individuals was probably irrelevant to all of these investigators; but is it safe to assume that it would always be irrelevant?

A second defense of by-passing human subject protocols is that these
direct observational studies put subjects at minimal risk, while the information obtained from the research can be very beneficial. From the
findings of the study of the Australian shoppers, for example, city planners might want to carefully consider where they permit supermarkets
to locate in relation to other retail complexes. The findings of the study
of red-light districts has public policy implications for the regulation of
red-light, and other types of vice, districts. Nevertheless, seeking the
prior approval of human subject committees is always recommended
(and the investigators in most of these studies do manage to obtain such
approvals).

Indirect observation (physical traces)

The most distinctive feature of this form is that it relies upon the observation of physical traces, or other by-products, of people's behavior
rather than upon observations of that behavior itself. An early and influential advocate for studies of this type was a book entitled *Unobtrusive
Measures*. As one of many illustrations of the advantages of such indirect
observations, the authors described observing the erosion of tiles in front
of museum exhibits as a way of inferring the relative popularity of different exhibits. The more people spent a long time in front of an exhibit,
shuffling their feet, the more the tiles would show wear. They viewed tile

erosion as a more valid way of measuring popularity than one that would be obtained by asking visitors to recollect the exhibits at which they spent the most time.[31] One could probably obtain the same information by directly, but surreptitiously, observing museum visitors, but it would be much more time consuming, and more prone to sampling and other types of errors.

One specific line of inquiry that was stimulated by the emphasis upon unobtrusive measures relies upon examinations of people's garbage. In the early book, the authors described a study in which an investigator counted empty containers of alcoholic beverages in people's garbage. When the number of discarded bottles was tabulated for different communities, it disclosed that there was no difference between dry

Box 5.8 Studying garbage in New York City

Taking the unobtrusive study of people's garbage to a logical next step, Anthropologist Robin Nagle spent some years as a regular sanitation worker in New York, including some time spent driving a garbage truck. With this background, plus her academic training, she convinced the New York Department of Sanitation to appoint her as "Anthropologist in residence." She then proceeded to study sanitation workers as well as the products they were collecting in people's trash. Her studies of the workers would best fit in our previous discussion of ethnography (Chapter 2), but her studies of the garbage, itself, is very congruent with the indirect observation-unobtrusive measures tradition.

Nagle's primary research agenda has been to document the relationship between garbage and cities: what demands trash places upon urban areas, and how the content of that trash provides a window into city life. For example, she found almost every conceivable item among the trash: furniture, electronics, clothing, etc. It is a "throw-away" culture, she concluded, and that is perhaps necessary in a city comprised of small apartments where residents are constrained to toss things out as the only alternative in order to make more space.[32]

A physical record of people's daily lives is also reflected in their trash. Nagle notes that divorces are associated with photos of former spouses being torn and discarded; drinking problems are reflected by an increase in the number of empty wine or whiskey bottles; the birth of a child corresponds with the appearance of disposable diapers in the garbage. And by tabulating the rates with which people are discarding various types of objects, it is possible to construct a mirror into a city's patterns of life.

communities – which prohibit the sale of alcohol – and non-dry communities. People living in dry communities can purchase alcohol elsewhere and consume it at home, but choosing to live in a dry community presumably reflects something about the image of themselves residents choose to convey. Following this assumption, is it reasonable to expect that people living in dry communities would be as willing to self-report their alcohol consumption? In other words, would relying upon questionnaires or interviews have led to the same findings?

The contents of garbage can, of course, yield by-products of many types of activity, not just alcohol consumption. An interesting recent example is provided by an Anthropologist's study of the trash collected in New York City. It is summarized in Box 5.8.

Unobtrusive observations, as illustrated by the research described in the previous boxes, can be very effective means of obtaining data about people's behavior that is not filtered by their memory or candor. By itself, however, the information generated by unobtrusive observations can be subject to different interpretations. Do many empty whiskey bottles in their garbage indicate that people who live there are consuming more alcohol, or is it evidence that they invite lots of people to parties in their homes? To clarify such ambiguities, Webb and Campbell recommended that unobtrusive measures, of all sorts, be utilized in conjunction with other methods, in order to provide multiple confirmation. Many studies of this type are today referred to as mixed-method and we turn to this topic in the following chapter.

Notes

1 Lucy Mayblin, Aneta Piekut, and Gill Valentine, "'Other' Posts in 'Other' Places." *Sociology*, 49, 2015.

2 See, for example, the discussion in, Juliet Corbin and Janet M. Morse, "The Unstructured Interactive Interview." *Qualitative Inquiry*, 9, 2003. See also, Herbet J. Rubin and Irene S. Rubin, *Qualitative Interviewing.* Sage, 2011.

3 Franke Kreuter, "Interviewer Effects," in Paul J. Lavrakas (Ed), *Encyclopedia of Survey Research Methods.* Sage, 2008.

4 Anthony Paik and Kenneth Sanchagrin, "Social Isolation in America." *American Sociological Review*, 1, 2013.

5 For further discussion of this issue, see Floyd J. Fowler, *Survey Research Methods.* Sage, 2013.

6 Peter Lynn, "Longer Interviews May Not Affect Subsequent Survey Participation Propensity." *Public Opinion Quarterly*, 78, 2014.

7 Robert M. Groves, et al., *Survey Methods.* Wiley, 2009.

8 See the discussion in Reuben A.B. May, "When the Methodological Shoe is on the Other Foot." *Qualitative Sociology*, 37, 2014.

9 The 17-year-olds in this study were under state supervision, hence represent a special population. However, the results are consistent with those obtained with other samples. Jennifer Dykema, et al., "ACASI Gender-of-Interviewer Voice Effects on Reports to Questions about Sensitive Behaviors among Young Adults." *Public Opinion Quarterly*, 76, 2012.

10 For further discussion of falsification, see Natalja Menold and Christoph J. Kemper, "How Do Real and Falsified Data Differ?" *International Journal of Public Opinion Research*, 26, 2014.

11 For a summary of this research, see Susanne Vogl, "Telephone Versus Face-to-Face Interviews." *Sociological Methodology*, 43, 2013.

12 Laura H. Lind, et al., "Why Do Survey Respondents Disclose More When Computers Ask the Questions?" *Public Opinion Quarterly*, 77, 2013.

13 See David F. Harris, *The Complete Guide to Writing Questionnaires*. I&M Press, 2014. See also relevant chapters in, Stanley Presser, et al., *Methods for Testing and Evaluating Survey Questionnaires*. Wiley-Interscience, 2004.

14 For further discussion, see Allyson Holbrook, "Acquiescence Response Bias," in Lavrakas, *op.cit.*

15 For further discussion, see Colin Jerolmack and Shamus Khan, "Talk is Cheap," and "Toward an Understanding of the Relationship Between Accounts and Action." *Sociological Methods and Research*, 27, 2014.

16 See Phillip S. Brenner, "Exceptional Behavior or Exceptional Identity?" *Public Opinion Quarterly*, 75, 2011.

17 Social desirability is analyzed in, Roger Tourangeau and Ting Yan, "Sensitive Questions in Surveys." *Psychological Bulletin*, 133, 2007, and Frauke Kreuter, Stanley Presser and Roger Tourangeau, "Social Desirability Bias in CATI, IVR and Web Surveys." *Public Opinion Quarterly*, 72, 2008.

18 Mikael Persson and Maria Solevid, "Measuring Political Participation." *International Journal of Public Opinion Research*, 26, 2014.

19 For further discussion, see Ben Jann, Julia Jerke and Ivar Krumpal, "Asking Sensitive Questions Using the Crosswise Model." *Public Opinion Quarterly*, 76, 2012.

20 See Elizabeth Coutts and Ben Jann, "Sensitive Questions in Online Surveys." *Sociological Methods and Research*, 40, 2011.

21 Simon Chauchard, "Using MP3 Players in Surveys." *Public Opinion Quarterly*, 77, 2013.

22 For further discussion of open and closed formats, see Willem E. Saris and Imtraud N. Gallhofer, *Design, Evaluation and Analysis of Questionnaires for Survey Research*. Wiley, 2014.

23 For a review of studies, see Melanie A. Revilla, Willem E. Saris and Jon A. Krosnick, "Choosing the Number of Categories in Agree-Disagree Scales." *Sociological Methods and Research*, 43, 2014.

24 For further discussion, see Don A. Dilman, Jolene D. Smyth and Leah M. Christian, *Internet, Phone, Mail, and Mixed-Mode Surveys*. Wiley, 2014.

25 *Ibid.*

26 See, for example, Martyn Denscombe, "Item Non-response Modes." *International Journal of Social Research Methodology*, 12, 2009.

27 Vidal Diaz de Rada and Juan A. Dominguez, "The Quality of Responses to Grid Questions as used in Web Questionnaires." *International Journal of Social Research Methodology*, 18, 2015.

28 Stephen Wood, Tim Sneesby and Robert G. Baker, "Maintaining Town Centre Vitality in Competitive Environments." *Australian Planner*, 49, 2012, p. 175.

29 Ronald Weitzer, "The Social Ecology of Red-Light Districts." *Urban Affairs Review*, 50, 2014.

30 See Ellen K. Cromley, "Mapping Spatial Data" (Chapter 4), in Jean J. Schensul and Margaret D. LeCompte (Eds), *Specialized Ethnographic Methods*. AltaMira Press, 2012.

31 Eugene J. Webb and Donald T. Campbell authored a highly influential book, entitled *Unobtrusive Measures*, in 1966. With some additional authors, they revised and expanded the book, same title, in 1999 (Sage).

32 Robin Nagle, *Picking Up*. Farrar, Strauss and Giroux, 2013.

Glossary

ACASI: Computer-assisted self-interviewing.

Acquiescence: Tendency for people to select more agree than disagree responses.

Attitudinal Fallacy: Assumption that self-reports of behavior correspond perfectly with actual behavior.

Closed Format: Subjects answer questions by selecting from alternatives provided by the investigator.

Double-barreled Questions: Combine two separable questions into one.

Grid Format: Places questions that share wording and response alternatives together.

Interviewer Effects: Variations in subjects' answers that are due to the interviewer asking questions.

Leading Questions: Phrased in a way that implies how the questions should be answered.

Open-Ended Format: Respondents are free to answer a question in their own terms.

Randomization Techniques: Based upon chance events, subjects are instructed to lie in answering certain questions.

Social Desirability Bias: Tendency for respondents to answer questions in a way that makes them look good.

Structured Interviews: Ask highly focused questions and pre-arrange ways of answering.

Unstructured, or Nondirective, Interviews: Encourage subjects to express themselves in a relaxed manner resembling normal conversation.

chapter 6

Obtaining data, Part Two: Multi-/mixed-methods and secondary sources

Outline

- Multi-methods
- Mixed-methods
  - Mixed-method types
  - Mixed-method limitations

- Secondary sources
  - Matching data to a research question
  - Agencies of city government
  - Large-scale, regularly conducted national surveys
  - Large-scale, regularly conducted cross-national global surveys

- Special analyses
  - Ecological inference
  - Meta-analysis

- Notes
- Glossary
- Appendix One: AAPOR transparency requirements

As the term is widely used today, *mixed methods* involves a combination of quantitative and qualitative data gathering and/or analysis within the same study. Although there are exceptions, there is a marked correlation between how data are collected and how they are analyzed. A conventional questionnaire with fixed response alternatives, for example, will ordinarily be analyzed quantitatively while the data generated by a participant-observation field study will typically be analyzed qualitatively. *Multi-methods*, by contrast, involves *any* two (or more) methods of data collection and/or analysis. Both could be quantitative or qualitative. For example, if data were collected from an experiment and a survey that both examined the same question, and all data were analyzed quantitatively, the research would qualify as multi-method, but not mixed method. As a result, mixed-method studies can be regarded as a special type of multi-methods research, though in recent decades it has attracted the most attention across the social sciences, including Urban Studies.

Multi-methods

There is a long tradition in Urban Studies, and the social sciences more generally, of utilizing two or more methods of data collection and analysis in the same research project. For example, in the 1920s, Nels Anderson – part of the Chicago School of Urban Sociology – spent several years studying homeless men (who were then called hobos) living in Chicago. To understand their backgrounds and orientations toward life, and to distinguish among various types of homeless men, he carefully recorded several hundred case studies. In addition, he spent a period of years living with, and living like, the homeless men he was studying.[1] His use of participant observation and a case study method would classify Anderson's early research on hobos as multi-method (both qualitative), but not mixed-method. Studies of the latter type did not regularly appear in urban research for many decades.

Several developments in the social sciences increased interest in multi-methods later in the twentieth century. Especially notable were contributions by Social Psychologist, Donald Campbell. He was involved as the co-author of two very influential publications. The first, with a psychological focus, urged investigators to measure personality traits, utilizing multiple types of data, such as peer ratings, paper and pencil

Obtaining data, Part Two

tests and self-reports.[2] Only quantitative approaches to analyzing psychological variables were advocated, but this multi-method paper later led a wide range of investigators to consider how confidence in their findings might be increased if those findings were confirmed by different methods, even if all were of the same genre.

Campbell's second notable publication entailed his (and Webb's) argument for the use of unobtrusive measures to study a broad range of psychological and social behavior.[3] In advocating for the use of these indirect, non-reactive indicators of people's behavior, the analysts claimed that they were best employed in conjunction with more conventional modes of collecting data, such as interviews or questionnaires. They invoked the term triangulation to describe the multiple perspectives that are obtained when several methods are employed because they thought it was analogous to navigators' use of multiple points to fix the locations of their ships. This second paper continued to emphasize quantitative approaches, and so they primarily encouraged multi-method rather than mixed-method research; but from their examples, some of which included qualitative data, they also opened the door to a mixing of quantitative and qualitative methods.

Today, quantitative analysts often combine methods, such as surveys and experiments. Similarly, qualitative analysts often combine methods, such as participant observation and open-ended interviews. However, as long as the methods employed are entirely within either the quantitative or qualitative categories, the studies are classified as multi- rather than mixed-method. Box 6.1 describes a study that illustrates how the line between the two categories can be crossed as a research project unfolds.

When Mehta's investigation began by relying upon case studies of streets, photography, participant observation and in-depth interviews it would have been classified as multi-method: employing more than one method, all of which were (in this case) qualitative. When a quantitative index was developed and used to examine the correlation between city streets and sociability, the research project became a good example of a mixed-method study.

Mixed-methods

During the last third of the twentieth century, some of the groundwork for combining quantitative and qualitative methods was laid by the decline of several theoretical paradigms that had advocated for either exclusively quantitative or exclusively qualitative analyses. As they lost much of their dominance to greater theoretical pluralism, it also opened up possibilities of greater methodological pluralism. In place of qualitative methodologists deriding "bean counters" and quantitative methodologists boasting

Box 6.1 Studying sociability on Boston's city streets

Vikas Mehta, an Architecture professor with an interest in how people use built-up city spaces, conducted an extensive analysis on three streets in the metropolitan Boston area. Using techniques and protocols he "borrowed" from urban researchers in the social sciences, he spent nearly six months studying people on the sampled streets. His objective was to understand everyday social behavior in a city's public spaces.

Mehta began by conducting case studies of the selected streets from whatever information sources he could find, and he took photographs and studied them, all to familiarize himself with the areas to be studied. He then employed two types of observation. The first was direct observation. He located himself at a discreet vantage point from which he could view people without being seen. At other times he was a participant-observer, interacting with people on the street, going into local stores, noting who was on the street and what they were doing. Later he engaged people in open-ended interviews, asking them how they felt about the street, how familiar they were with it, and so on.

He was especially interested in active social behaviors, such as talking to others, eating, walking pets, etc. And he wanted to know why they occurred more on some streets than on others. For this Mehta concluded he needed a quantitative measure of sociability so he constructed an index of how much activity people were engaged in and how much people were engaged with others on the street. He calculated Cronbach's alpha (see Box 7.2 in Chapter 7) in order to show that his index was reliable, and finally he correlated the sociability index with features of the streets in order to see what made streets conducive to more or less sociability. Among the variables he found to be most relevant were: feelings of safety, opportunities for enjoyment, comfort and convenience.[4]

of the superiority of their more precise conclusions, social scientists from both backgrounds became increasingly interested in trying to combine the two approaches in order to attain the advantages of each.

Around the turn of the twenty-first century, interest in mixed methods dramatically increased. There were a number of important precursors, but software developments were particularly notable. Data analysis software that was being developed made it dramatically less cumbersome to quantitatively analyze qualitative data that had previously been extremely cumbersome to analyze quantitatively.[5] For example, the QDA Miner offers computer-assisted software for the analysis of textual data, such as recorded interviews, news transcripts, open-ended responses to survey questions, and even still images. It codes the data, offers rapid means to search the data and presents a variety of frequency analyses. It also links to statistical software packages that facilitate a variety of quantitative analyses.[6] The effect of such software developments was to make it dramatically easier for investigators relying upon qualitative data to add a quantitative dimension to their research.

As a result of paradigm changes and analytical developments, quantitative and qualitative researchers reached across what had formerly been a very difficult-to-cross divide. By 2007, there was so much interest in mixed methods that a specialty journal (*Journal of Mixed Methods Research*) was founded, devoted to publishing studies that showed the best practices of, and most effective uses of, mixed methods. In 2014, the Mixed Methods International Research Association was formed and connected to the journal.[7] The Association brought together mixed-method researchers from across the world to its first annual meeting, held in Boston, and the next meeting took place in 2016 in Durham, UK.

As researchers from around the world focused upon mixed methods, it led to another difference between mixed- and multi-method studies. In the latter, the methods that are combined have not typically been scrutinized apart from their individual components. For example, if a study utilized a survey and an experiment, the study would usually be evaluated according to the adequacy of the survey and the experiment, each separately assessed. The way they were combined was not a separate issue. By contrast, as mixed-method research has grown in popularity across all the social sciences, very much including Urban Studies, it has been receiving specialized examination as a distinct method.[8]

Mixed-method types

While it is reasonably clear what distinguishes a multi- from a mixed-method study, the latter includes a wide range of studies that differ from each other in several important respects. And there is some disagreement concerning what is the most important feature that defines a study as mixed method. The first distinction concerns exactly what qualitative and quantitative features are combined. Mario Small presents three possibilities:

1) Types of data that are collected (e.g. response frequencies, field notes, etc.)
2) The way the data are collected (experimentation, participant observation, etc.)
3) How the data are analyzed (coding of case studies, regression analysis, etc.)

As we have previously noted, there is a correlation among these three aspects of a study, but it is a less than perfect correlation, so that data typically considered qualitative is sometimes analyzed quantitatively, data collected in a manner associated with quantitative data is sometimes analyzed qualitatively, and so on. As a result, it is sometimes difficult to classify a study based upon only one of the above criteria.

To reduce the possibilities somewhat, Small has argued that the mixing of quantitative and qualitative approaches and techniques with respect only to (1) or (2) above should qualify a study for mixed-method status.[9] Their combination in (3) above should designate a separate category: mixed-data analysis study. However, there is as yet little consensus concerning exactly what it is about data that a mixed-method study must entail.

Mixed-method studies can also be differentiated from each other by the order in which qualitative and quantitative methods are employed. In some cases, one data set builds on the results of another. These are often referred to as *sequential designs*.[10] To illustrate, after data have been statistically analyzed, an investigator may collect qualitative data in order to better understand how to interpret the quantitative analysis. This could, for example, entail following up on a survey questionnaire (quantitative) by selecting a sub-sample of respondents for open-ended interviewing (qualitative). It is also very common for qualitative data collection to serve as a pilot study that is followed by a quantitative design that builds upon the insights of the preliminary study. The pilot study might, for example, help an investigator to infer the issues that are most important to examine in a questionnaire. This type of mixed-method study is illustrated in Box 6.2.

Finally, it is also possible to classify mixed-method studies along a continuum according to their emphases.[12] At one pole of the continuum are studies that are primarily quantitative and tack on some qualitative data or method. These studies typically quantify the variables being studied and test hypotheses mathematically or statistically. The qualitative add-on is designed to offer depth and richness to quantitatively based conclusions. At the opposite pole on the continuum are studies that are primarily qualitative in design. The quantitative data or method is employed as a supplement that is expected to provide more precision in conjunction with qualitative explanations.

Finally, there are designs in which the qualitative and quantitative dimensions proceed along parallel lines, from the start to finish of a study. Neither is primary. Often referred to as a *convergent design*, it entails collecting both types of data at the same time, and then analyzing them together. This can entail merging of the two data sets, or separate but parallel analyses in which insights derived from one type of data are used to explore or analyze the other.

Differences in emphases and sequence often go together. When both quantitative and qualitative methods are involved from the beginning to

Box 6.2 Developing a resident satisfaction index in German cities

A group of investigators wanted to develop an index that would measure the satisfaction of residents with the city in which they were living, and also enable them to compare cities in this regard. They believed that satisfaction was an important variable because the more satisfied residents are with their city, the more they are likely to be politically active citizens and the more they will act as "ambassadors" for their city in attracting tourists.

Their first step was to figure out what to ask people with respect to satisfaction with their city. What variables might make the most difference? They met with 20 experts from diverse urban specialties in one of the cities, Hamburg. The investigators conducted lengthy interviews with these experts, asking them what they thought would be the most important considerations in such a study. This qualitative step provided them with a range of possible variables pertaining to a city's cultural activities, public space, housing costs, and so on.

From discussions with the experts, the investigators developed a 38-item questionnaire asking people how satisfied they were with these attributes in the city in which they lived. It included a five-point Likert scale on which respondents indicated their degrees of satisfaction. A total of 611 people completed the questionnaire.

The investigators' ultimate goal was to develop a brief index for comparative urban research so they had to reduce the 38 questions to a more manageable total. They utilized exploratory *factor analysis*, a statistical technique that is designed to reduce a large number of variables/items into a small number of clusters, called factors. Each factor can then be used as an index and it is labeled by inferring the common content of the variables it includes. (This technique is further discussed on pages 214–17, in the following chapter.) From this analysis they obtained a factor that they labeled "urbanity and diversity" and found that it had the greatest impact on residents' satisfaction. People wanted to live, they concluded, in a city with lots of cultural events and good shopping that is also open to, and tolerant of, differences among people.[11]

end of a study, each is likely to be similarly emphasized. Box 6.3 illustrates a mixed-method study in which both types of data were collected and analyzed in a convergent design and neither qualitative nor quantitative data or analyses were emphasized more than the other.

Unlike several earlier studies that reported that contemporary malls pushed smaller, non-mall shops out of business, these investigators found the opposite. Perhaps because of their methodological pluralism – involving

Box 6.3 The Accra shopping mall in Ghana

Two investigators in Ghana were interested in understanding the role of enclosed retail malls in local economies in general, and in Africa in particular. As a case study, they selected a large indoor shopping mall in Accra, Ghana's principal city, that contained a wide range of international retail stores. Their central question was: How does such a mall impact the traditional, informal local economy which in cities like Accra continues to employ most of the labor force?[13]

They utilized a wide range of data gathering methods. Most of the data that were subsequently analyzed quantitatively were generated by:

1) Questionnaires given to 2,000 shoppers in the mall. These data enabled them to tabulate the shoppers' socio-demographic characteristics and their reasons for coming to the mall (shopping, restaurants, meeting people, etc.).
2) For a sample of ten shops in the mall the investigators obtained three years of sales tax revenue records (2012–2014) and then assessed the trend of these contributions to state revenues.

Qualitative data were simultaneously collected by:

1) Observations of 24 "informal" merchants who set up stalls outside the mall, selling food, clothing, mobile phones, etc. They remained open for business later than the mall and offered better credit arrangements than mall stores.
2) Conducting open-ended interviews with managers and operators of stores in the mall.

In all of the interviews, subjects were encouraged to relate their experiences and attitudes in an open-ended way. The data obtained from interviews and observations were later analyzed qualitatively in order to infer themes and to capture the "complexity of meanings."

Finally, the investigators turned to the central question of how the Accra mall impacted local populations. (It was an important question, because other malls like it were being developed in many African cities.) They concluded that as a result of rising incomes, more high-income Africans were shopping in the mall. However, with the growth of the mall, there was also expansion of the smaller, informal stalls and stores that surrounded the mall, and their longer hours and better credit terms were serving a lower-income population.

quantitative data for the mall stores and qualitative data for the informal stalls – they were able to ascertain that the mall's formal stores and the informal stalls located outside the mall each served largely different clienteles; but there were a number of inter-connections between the two types of retail trade, and they appeared to be of benefit to each other. For example, the mall's popularity led to expansion of local bus routes to convenience mall shoppers, but these buses were also utilized by people coming to shop primarily at the stalls outside. The authors attributed their insights to their multiple perspectives.

Mixed-method limitations

We have described a number of research projects which illuminate the potential contributions of mixed-method research. We have also described professional activities (i.e. journals and associations) that are committed both to nurturing and promoting mixed-method research. The future development of this method faces some potentially difficult-to-surmount limitations, however, and they should be noted before this topic is concluded.

The first issue of concern is epistemological and it involves some fundamental differences in what "knowing" implies in qualitative and quantitative traditions. As we have previously noted in several contexts, most quantitative approaches emphasize prediction, and value research designs that facilitate causal inferences. By contrast, many qualitative methods are designed to promote a full understanding of the situations in which people are acting, and the way these people define those situations. And they often reject quantitative views of causation as artificial and simplistic. While there may be some middle ground between these approaches, it is probably Pollyannish to believe that they can be completely reconciled.

One interesting manifestation of the difficult-to-transcend gulf between quantitative and qualitative approaches is provided by the concept of triangulation. In quantitative traditions, it entails multiple confirmation of findings; that is, arriving at the same point with multiple measures. Implied is the possibility of a "single reality" that is defined by arriving at the same point with multiple measures. On the other hand, in most qualitative traditions, triangulation implies comprehensiveness or completeness of an explanation, or understanding. The objective is to synthesize divergent views in order to overcome the weaknesses, biases or incompleteness of any one approach.[14]

As both quantitative and qualitative methodology grows ever more complex and specialized, any individual investigator becomes less and less likely to possess all the requisite skills. Collaborators who bring different skill sets to a research project would seem the logical solution. However, collaboration among investigators whose fundamental orientations are not compatible can pose quite a challenge.

Secondary sources

A great deal of urban research is conducted utilizing *secondary data*: data that were previously collected, by someone other than the investigator, and usually collected for some purpose that differs from that of the current investigator. The objective when the data were collected may have been to study a different question, or it may not have been related to research at all. The alternative, of course, is *primary data*: collected by the investigator for the current research project. What is primary data for one investigation can become secondary data in later studies.

The major reason for relying on a secondary data source is cost. The precise cost depends upon how primary data would have to be collected, but to assemble a large data set is very expensive. Even if the research does not require extensive travel or much labor, each case that is included in a data set can cost hundreds of dollars. For many investigators, the expense quickly becomes prohibitive. In addition, if the research is designed to cover a lengthy time period, there may be no choice but to utilize previously collected data.

Consider also that it makes little sense to spend the time and money necessary to build a primary data set if previously gathered data can be found with which to address the research question. Even if the already existing data must be purchased, it is almost certain to cost less than it would cost investigators to collect them. Further, many data sets involving government records, census reports, and the like can be obtained for little or no cost. And it is possible that a data set already exists that, practically speaking, is better than any the investigator could reasonably expect to create.

Matching data to a research question

The drawback in utilizing secondary data sources is that they were not usually assembled to address the question an investigator is now asking. Remember, they were previously collected for a different purpose, and that purpose may not have even been research-related. Even if data were previously assembled to address the same research question, the population that was studied might have been different, or it may have encompassed a different geographical area, or the variables may have been measured differently, or the time period in which it was collected may not correspond with the current investigator's research design. The investigator then faces a difficult decision: Is the secondary data set so good in some respects that it is worth changing some aspect of the current research in order to utilize it? How consequential is the different population, the different time period, or the like?

If an investigator lacks sufficient funds for primary data collection or if, except for some minor details, a secondary data set seems very suitable, then investigators often make concessions. To illustrate, after some deliberation they may conclude that they were primarily interested in how some variable changes, so the different time period in which the secondary data were collected may not be that consequential to the objectives of the current research project. They may then adjust the research design to accommodate the secondary data.

The one realm in which little compromise is possible concerns measurement of the major variables. Does the secondary data set provide adequate measures? If the variables that would ideally measure the major concepts are not in the secondary data set, are there good *proxy measures*? That is, measures of variables that could be substituted for the missing variable because of a high correlation between them; for example, educational levels are often used as proxies for income. The investigator must specifically assess whether it is possible to derive valid measures of the major variables of interest from the available data set, and this may require detailed examination as some of the following case studies illustrate.

An investigator also has the responsibility of assessing all of the methodological steps that were involved in originally creating the data set. This includes such issues as how the data were originally collected, for example, the adequacy of the sampling process; the care or carelessness with which data were tabulated and stored; the way responses were coded, etc. Sometimes secondary data sets lack full descriptions of how the above issues were handled. If so, the investigator must make every effort to obtain the information from the primary data gatherers. Any shortcomings in data that are used in secondary analysis become the fault of the secondary as well as the primary analyst. If you use a data set, you "own" its problems.[15]

It would also be very desirable to know the funding source. Who paid for the data collection, if it was not a government agency? This information can be very useful in inferring whether there may be systematic biases in the data. For example, if the funding source is tied to a specific social objective or a public policy position, the investigators that were selected to conduct the research may have been selected because they expressed positions that were consistent with those of the funding organization. Such positions do not necessarily mean there was any bias in the collection or analysis of the data, but an investigator would like to independently verify the absence of bias, to the degree possible. Unfortunately, many data sets available for secondary analysis do not provide this information. For survey data, in particular, there is a growing demand for making a great deal of descriptive information routinely available. AAPOR, the American Association for Public Opinion Research, has been at the forefront of this effort with a transparency initiative whose major objectives are described in an appendix to this chapter.

There are an enormous number of highly diverse data sets that are potentially available for secondary Urban Studies. Space necessitates that the following pages contain only a very small sample. The studies are presented according to data source in order to provide readers with an idea of the kind of treasure troves that could be available if they look.

Agencies of city government

Included here are documents produced by city planning and zoning agencies, city councils, police and fire departments, etc. The people who put together these data and wrote reports were not usually thinking about using the data for serious research. The problem that can arise, therefore, is that the included data are not in a form that can readily be used for research purposes. The advantage of these data records, if they are – or can be made to be – research friendly, is that they were originally assembled for a city (or cities), hence it is not necessary to try to extrapolate figures for an urban area from a document that was originally prepared to describe a larger geographical area, such as a state or region.

Our first illustration, described in Box 6.4, involves the use of two secondary sources, both of which were obtained from the Police Departments in Chicago and Boston. The study also illustrates the kinds of problems investigators typically must confront before they are able to use the documents with any confidence. They are not usually good to go, right off the shelf.

From the study described in Box 6.4, note that in order to use the police data set, the investigators had to settle for gunshots as their measure of violence. Perhaps a broader measure including assaults, rapes, arson, and so on would have been preferable; but secondary data sets seldom provide ideal measures. Note also that the investigators did due diligence prior to using the police statistics, that is, they searched the literature for evidence that the measures they planned to employ would likely be reliable and valid.

A very different use of a different type of data obtained from agencies of a city government is described in Box 6.5. Here the information, from

Box 6.4 Gang violence in Chicago and Boston

In order to analyze gang violence, a vexing social problem in most large US cities, a group of investigators asked police in Chicago and Boston for copies of their relevant statistical records. They wanted data from two cities so that they could first analyze one of the cities (Chicago) and then try to replicate their findings in the second city (Boston).[16]

As is typically the case, the specific data available for each of the cities were not identical. To measure their dependent variable, from Chicago the police records included only homicides, almost all of which (95 percent) were committed by firearms. For Boston, the most comparable variable included fatal and nonfatal gunshot wounds. From other studies that showed homicides and nonfatal shootings to be very much alike – differing from each other mostly due to extrinsic variables, such as response time of medical assistance – the investigators concluded that they could treat the gunshot data from Boston and Chicago as providing comparable dependent variables in their analysis.

The investigators also confronted the possibility of measurement error in the police records. If a mayoral election was imminent, for example, a police department might be pressured to hold down homicide statistics in order to assist an incumbent. However, the investigators found a recent study of police reports of gang homicides in large US cities. This study reported that the police measures exhibited both internal reliability and external validity; and that validity was highest in cities with specialized gang units, a feature shared by both the Chicago and Boston departments. This enabled the investigators to conclude that they could use the police statistics, as planned.

Their second data source involved maps of the turf boundaries of gangs. Officers in both departments that were most familiar with the gangs in their cities prepared maps that showed areas that particular gangs occupied or, in some instances, areas which were shared by more than one gang. One of the major hypotheses the investigators wanted to test was whether the geographical proximity of gangs (independent variable) was associated with rates of gang violence (dependent variable). The maps seemed perfect for this purpose. They found that rates of homicide were higher in Chicago when gangs shared turf, and then they replicated this finding by showing that rates of fatal and nonfatal gunshots were higher in Boston when the turf of gangs was adjacent to each other. (Prior conflict between gangs was also an important independent variable.)

agencies in Sydney, Australia, was not taken at "face value" like the police statistics. This information, some of which could only be obtained via a freedom of information request, was analyzed in order to reveal what the investigators considered to be "hidden" value systems.

Box 6.5 Refusing proposals for Islamic schools in suburban Sydney

In many parts of the world, an increase in Muslim migrants has created local tensions. Although the principles of cultural diversity are often publicly pronounced, official decision-making often seems inconsistent with those principles. An interesting case in point is provided by proposals to build Islamic schools in suburban Sydney. By way of background, all religious (as well as non-religious) schools are eligible for state funding in Australia as long as they meet: (1) state curriculum guidelines, which are well-defined, and (2) local council requirements, though what the latter assessment should entail has not been well described in planning or policy instructions.

After two proposals for the construction of Islamic schools were rejected on technical grounds by two different local councils, two investigators decided to try to uncover the how and why behind the rejections. The data they obtained for secondary analysis included: planning documents from both councils, assessment reports, council meeting minutes and letters submitted in support or opposition by local residents. One of the councils initially refused to hand over some of the material, but it was later obtained by a freedom of information submission.

The investigators assumed there was more going on in these documents than met the eye, so they conducted *discourse analysis*: a technique for probing beneath any type of textual or visual material to infer underlying meanings and the role of power differences in communication.[17] This type of analysis can be qualitative, quantitative or mixed method. From their explorations, they inferred latent and hidden values that appeared to strongly influence what were presented as rational-technical decisions. For example, there seemed to be apprehension that building an Islamic school would attract more Muslims to a neighborhood, and the increase would lead to inter-ethnic conflict and an increase in crime.[18]

Large-scale, regularly conducted national surveys

In a number of nations, large-scale surveys are conducted at regular intervals, sometimes yearly, other times in alternating years, or there may be even longer intervals. They provide potentially very valuable data for people doing research on cities and city life. While cities (with few exceptions) are not their focus, their samples include sufficient numbers of respondents from urban areas to permit a secondary analysis of an urban sample. Most of these surveys have a particular focus: crime, health, income, etc. However, they typically include a wide range of questions about people's lives and experiences that permit investigators to analyze issues other than the ones initially focused upon. In addition, many of the studies periodically include special modules which can be of particular relevance to urban research.

These surveys differ from each other according to whether the same people are included each time the survey is repeated. *Cross-sectional surveys* collect data from specific respondents one time only. If the survey is repeated, a different sample is included with each repetition. However, if probability sampling is followed, then the discrete cross-sectional surveys can be compared in a trend analysis. The alternative to cross-sectional surveys are *longitudinal surveys* which follow the same group of people over a period of years. There are two major types of longitudinal surveys: *cohort studies* which follow a group of people who share some significant attribute (e.g. age at first marriage), and *panel studies* which begin with a wider range of subjects, often selected to be representative of a large population. Each wave of a panel study is usually self-contained, meaning that it can be used, by itself, as a data source without reference to other waves. In addition, if a panel study covers a sufficiently long time period, it is possible to identify and follow cohorts, as illustrated in Box 6.6.

All of the various large-scale, regularly conducted studies are most often directed by a research institute connected to a university. Most of the funding is usually provided by a government, and is sometimes supplemented by funding from a private agency or foundation. The data are widely available, and at little cost. In some cases, however, a would-be user must be affiliated with a university, private firm or government agency that is a dues-paying member of some organization in order to access the data.

To find surveys of this type that may provide useful data for secondary analysis in one's specialty area, the first step is probably to consult one of the large repositories of such studies. In the US, the Inter-University Consortium for Political and Social Research (ICPSR) has the most extensive collection of large-scale surveys and census reports. In the UK, the largest collection of digital research data in the social sciences is held in the UK Data Archive at the University of Essex. To find relevant surveys, it could also be very helpful to look at articles in professional journals in one's specialty area and note the sources of the data used in their analysis. This information will almost always be provided in a data and methods section of a published journal article.

Following are brief summaries of a few of the more notable large-scale, regularly conducted surveys, presented in alphabetical order. A great deal of additional information about each is readily available via the Web. After these summaries, research will be outlined illustrating how several of these surveys have provided useful data for analyses of urban issues.

- Beginning in 1991 with 5,500 households (over 10,000 individuals) in England, the survey later added thousands of households from Scotland, Wales and Northern Ireland. It contains an extremely broad range of topics, including: adolescent activities, family migrations, income, retirement, etc. It is available from the UK Data Archive at the University of Essex.
- CSEW – The Crime Survey for England and Wales. This is a cross-sectional survey that began in 2001. Conducted annually for the government by a private research organization, it provides data on unreported crime to supplement police reports. It also provides information on characteristics of offenders, their relation to victims, and people's attitudes toward crime, police and the courts.
- DMHDS – The Dunedin Multidisciplinary Heath and Development Study. This cohort study in New Zealand began with a sample of about 1,000 infants born in 1972–73 in Otago, an urban area of about 200,000 people. The cohort that remained in Otago and their offspring have been surveyed every 2–3 years since, with an extremely high retention rate of 96 percent. It provides detailed information on lifestyles, parenting, changes among teenagers, etc. It is conducted out of the University of Otago.
- GSS – The General Social Survey. Another continuing cross-sectional survey, it began in 1972 and has been housed at NORC/The University of Chicago. As its name implies, it asks a wide range of questions of a representative US sample. Each survey also includes a special module dealing with religion, politics, race, and so on. It has been very widely used in social research.
- NELLS – The Netherlands Life Course Study. Starting in 2008 with approximately 5,000 respondents in the first wave, this panel study also includes an over-sample of ethnic minorities. The social issues NELLS has consistently focused upon include: social cohesion, inequality, norms and values. Administered by Radboud University, all disseminated materials from the study are in English (see also Box 6.7).
- PSID – The Panel Study of Income Dynamics. Beginning in 1968 with about 5,000 families, PSID is the longest-running household panel study in the world. Now covering multiple generations, PSID includes representative US samples both of families and of children born into those families. It provides extensive longitudinal data on: employment, wealth, marriage and childbearing, etc. It is available from the University of Michigan (see also Box 6.6).

The first illustration to be presented of a secondary analysis relying upon data from one of the above large-scale, regularly conducted national surveys involves a study of racial separation and integration in metropolitan areas of the US Its primary source of data was the PSID (see above).

Box 6.6 Racial diversity in the metropolitan US

Most studies of racial (Black-White) and ethnic diversity in US metropolitan area neighborhoods have been based upon cross-sectional studies, and they show increased overall diversity over time. However, these studies may not adequately capture changes that occur over people's life-courses. Previous research has shown that people are most likely to move to different neighborhoods at certain times, especially when they leave their birth families to form their own families and settle into the neighborhood in which they will raise their own children. It is only by comparing such cohorts that it is possible to gauge how the experience of neighborhood diversity may have changed between generations.

To pursue this line of inquiry, Wagmiller linked data for individuals from PSID (see above) living within a metropolitan area with data for the neighborhoods in which they were living. A PSID file makes it possible to link individuals to the census tract in which they live, and these tracts are frequently used as a proxy measure for neighborhood, that is, the socio-demographic characteristics of the census tract are taken as those of the neighborhood. These census tracts, which typically contain about 4,000 people, are the smallest units for which much census data is available. They may or may not correspond closely with any particular neighborhood, as sociologically conceived; but they often provide the best available measures in secondary analyses.

Wagmiller examined different cohorts over nine-year intervals, beginning with their move out of the home of their birth families. (They were, on average, 22 years old at the start of the observation period.) Comparing different cohorts across time, he found that for White and Black cohorts the neighborhoods they moved into became much more diverse ethnically, but not much more diverse racially. More recent cohorts of both Blacks and Whites are less likely, than their earlier counterparts, to move into neighborhoods that are almost entirely comprised of people of the same race as themselves; but that is largely because both are more likely to move into neighborhoods that are ethnically mixed, primarily involving persons of Hispanic and Asian backgrounds.[19]

Box 6.7 Neighborhood effects on ethnic minorities in Dutch cities

Studies in the Netherlands and elsewhere have shown that ethnic minorities living in resource-poor neighborhoods tend to be less satisfied with how their lives are going than natives. In addition, their economic positions tend to be lower than natives and they are inclined to feel that they have less social support than natives. Given that economic position and perceived social support are both related to life satisfaction, does living in a disadvantaged neighborhood also have an effect upon how satisfied minorities are with the way their lives are going?

To examine their central question, two Dutch investigators took a probability sample from NELL (see above), stratified to over-represent people living in larger cities because that is where more minorities were located. They took their sample only from the 2009 wave because it intentionally over-sampled people from Turkey and Morocco, the origins of the largest minority groups in the Netherlands. In other words, they treated the 2009 wave as though it was a cross-sectional survey.[20]

Their dependent variable, life satisfaction, was measured with four items from a previously developed scale. With their data, they found that the four items had strong loadings on the same factor and that it was reliable, with a Cronbach's alpha of 0.86. (Both factor analysis and Cronbach's alpha are discussed in Chapter 7.) They were able to measure economic position with measures of income and occupational standing, and social support with measures of the migrants' perceived social contacts and feelings of loneliness. Finally, they were interested in neighborhood deprivation, but had to settle for the percentage on welfare as a proxy measure. It probably would have been preferable to focus more directly upon a neighborhood's resources, but no better measures were available in the data set.

The investigators' analysis indicated that, as expected, minorities' life satisfaction was directly related to their economic positions and to their perceived social support. These same relationships also held for natives, but because natives scored higher on both variables, their satisfaction with the way their lives were going was also higher. The degree of deprivation of the neighborhood in which Turkish or Moroccan migrants lived did not have any additional effect upon their life satisfaction. That is, net of economic position and perceived social support, neighborhood deprivation did not matter with respect to life satisfaction. If the investigators had a measure of neighborhood deprivation that was better than the percentage on welfare, perhaps the results would have been different. But, a major problem with secondary data analysis is that one cannot always find ideal operationalizations of the major variables in the data set.

A similar topic – neighborhoods comprised of ethnic minorities – is examined in the next illustrative study. However, this research project involved Dutch cities and focused not upon diversity or integration, but upon whether certain features of minorities' neighborhoods had an impact upon their life satisfaction.

Large-scale, regularly conducted cross-national global surveys

There are a number of large-scale surveys that are conducted at regular intervals across large sections of the world. These are cross-sectional studies that can be utilized to compare nations at the same point in time or to describe trends within and across nations. They also contain sufficiently large urban populations that can be identified and used to create urban sub-samples with which to examine diverse issues pertaining to city life. Described below are a few of the most notable of these surveys. (All have home pages that are easily reached via the Web and provide a good deal of additional description.)

- AmericasBarometer carries out surveys in 28 nations, including all of North, South and Central America, plus several Caribbean nations. It examines these nations yearly or bi-yearly. It is a project of the Latin American Public Opinion Project (LAPOP) at Vanderbilt University. Since 2004 it has generated data, and publications, on a wide range of economic, political and social attitudes and experiences.
- OECD Database – The Organization for Economic Co-operation and Development is an affiliation of 34 economically developed nations that gathers and compiles yearly data on member nations and many of their metropolitan areas. It primarily provides standardized statistical data on such issues as: tourism, labor force, gender, poverty, etc. rather than attitudinal surveys. It also provides extensive statistics for 70 of the largest metropolitan areas in the US.
- The World Values Survey (WVS) is conducted yearly by the WVS Association, a global network of social scientists that was founded in 1981 and is headquartered in Sweden. Utilizing a common questionnaire, every survey is conducted in nearly 100 nations, focusing upon people's beliefs and values, and how they are changing. It also enables investigators to create rural and urban sub-samples.

In order to illustrate the types of questions that data from these surveys can be used to address, two such studies are summarized in the following research boxes.

Box 6.8 Dissatisfaction with city life in Latin America

Many previous studies examined whether rural residence produced happiness while living in a city led to malaise. In some cases, there appeared to be no difference in happiness while other studies reported that rural residents experienced happiness at a level exceeding their urban counterparts. These studies included international samples, but Latin American nations were largely left out. Seeking to see how these nations fit, Valente and Berry selected a sample of Latin American nations included in WVS and AmericasBarometer.[21]

First, they used data for the eight Latin nations included in WVS. They also utilized WVS statistics on: population size of people's place of residence (to measure rural or urban), people's self-reported happiness, and a number of other individual characteristics, such as income, religion, friendships, etc. These individual characteristics can affect happiness, and they can be correlated with rural-urban living, so they were controlled – that is, their effects were statistically removed – in the analysis. The investigators found no rural-urban differences in happiness within this sample, net of the individual characteristics.

Next, they repeated the analysis because nothing beats replication, especially when samples are not very large. The second analysis contained the somewhat larger sample of nations (12) that were included in AmericasBarometer. One difference between the two analyses: the WVS divided population size (the independent variable) into six levels while AmericasBarometer employed only three. Both data sets' measures of happiness and of the individual characteristics were very similar, though. The results of the second analysis mirrored those of the first, namely, once the individual-level variables were controlled, there were no rural-urban differences in people's happiness.

We turn next to a very different kind of study than those previously considered here because it is based almost entirely upon data pertaining to neighborhoods rather than individuals; that is, it does not contain the kind of attitudinal or behavioral self-reports associated with surveys. Rather, it is based entirely upon correlations between behavioral by-products and socioecological variables, and from these correlations it makes inferences about people's attitudes and motivations.

Special analyses

When utilizing secondary data sources, in particular, there are a couple of issues that frequently arise that require special analysis. We will briefly discuss two of them. The first is a unit of analysis issue and it is most

Box 6.9 Neighborhood fast food and economic impatience

Over the past several decades there has been a proliferation of fast food restaurants throughout most of the economically developed world. At the same time, the rate of household savings has declined. A group of investigators wondered if there was a causal connection. Among people who live in neighborhoods where there are more fast food restaurants does personal savings as a percentage of income decline? A connection was theoretically suggested to the investigators: fast food may be associated with impatience and the continuous repetition of fast food experiences may lead people to be less willing to defer many kinds of gratification, hence they spend more and save less.

In the first of a series of studies, they began with a sample of the 30 nations in the OECD database (see above) and for each year between 1978 and 2008 that the data were available, noted the population size and the household savings rate. They obtained figures from McDonald's on the number of franchises in each country, and then calculated the number of McDonald's per capita. They recognized that a broader range of fast food restaurants would have provided a better measure of exposure to fast food restaurants, but for the OECD sample that was the best they could get. Nevertheless, they found, as hypothesized, that as the number of McDonald's per capita increased, the household savings rate decreased.

In a subsequent study, the investigators examined only US neighborhoods, and were able to obtain a fuller measure of all fast food restaurants and calculated their neighborhood concentration, using zip codes as the proxy for neighborhoods. Consistent with the findings of the first study, they found the same relationship between exposure to fast food restaurants in a neighborhood and household savings. They concluded on an interesting note. In non-experimental studies, such as this one, reverse causality is a difficult to reject possibility. It seems unlikely, but could being financially impatient (and therefore less likely to save) lead people to move into neighborhoods with higher concentrations of fast food restaurants?[22] Still other possibilities are raised in the following discussion of ecological inference.

likely to arise when an investigator has aggregated data, but would like to make inferences about individuals. It can sometimes arise in primary research, but it is especially common in secondary analyses. The second issue to be considered for special analysis occurs when an investigator would like to combine data from two or more non-identical surveys in which there are some variations in question wording, question order, response alternatives, or the like.

Ecological inference

It is often the case that an investigator is interested in studying the behavior of individuals – for example, buying fast food, moving from city to suburb, voting, or the like – and is following a theory of individual behavior; but the data available for secondary analysis exist only for aggregates. In other words, the secondary source set has data pertaining to fast food purchases, geographical moves or voting, but they have been tabulated and presented by zip codes, census tracts, cities, etc. To assume that any relationship that is observed between two aggregated variables will also stand in the same relationship to each other among individuals is sometimes, but not always, true; and when it is not, the erroneous inference is described as the *ecological fallacy*.

To illustrate, consider the previously described relationship between the concentration of fast food restaurants in a neighborhood and the rate of household savings in that neighborhood. Both are aggregated variables, describing supra-individual units. If one assumes that the aggregated relationship is obtained because individuals who more frequently eat in fast food restaurants become generally impatient and are then less likely to save, one may be committing the ecological fallacy. How could the aggregate relationship not also be true for individuals? Consider some possibilities. Perhaps the local residents who most frequent the fast food restaurants are actually more likely to save because they spend less eating out than their neighbors who eat in full service restaurants. But suppose these frugal diners are a small percentage of the neighborhood and they have more neighbors spending more at restaurants and therefore saving less. In this case, even though the relationship between fast food and savings was negative at the aggregate (i.e. neighborhood) level, it would be positive for individuals.

Note also that even if the same relationship among variables could be found at both individual and aggregate levels, it is especially problematic to make inferences from the aggregate level to explain the link between variables at the individual level. For example, perhaps it is the sheer availability of fast food restaurants that leads people in the neighborhood to frequent them and thereby save less. The independent variable would then be availability rather than people's impatience cultivated by frequenting fast food restaurants.

Does the foregoing discussion lead to the conclusion that aggregate data can never be used to make individual-level inferences? There is some debate among methodologists concerning whether given the typical aggregate data set, an analyst can drill down to make inferences about individuals. Whether it will be possible in any case depends largely upon how much information was lost in the aggregation process, and the insight into the variables that one brings to the analysis. The issue is complex, and our objective here is primarily to caution the reader about falling into fallacious reasoning. For the interested reader, we note that Gary King has developed a method and supplementary software that have produced some promising results with regard to ecological inference.[23]

Meta-analysis

A problem unique to secondary analysis arises when an investigator finds surveys, or other types of data sets, that examine the research question of interest, but have serious flaws. Most commonly their samples are too small, though the drawbacks can entail a lot of missing data or any other methodological shortcoming. A solution in such instances may be to combine the studies in a *meta-analysis*: a study of studies that produces a weighted average of the included studies.

There are many potential advantages to a meta-analysis. By increasing the overall size of a sample, the robustness of any statistical analysis is ordinarily increased, and by combining samples it may be possible to generalize the results of a meta-analysis to a more diverse population. In addition, if there are different findings among the studies, an analysis of the differences can increase insight into the workings of the variables under investigation. Note, however, that if the individual studies included in a meta-analysis have serious flaws, combining them will not necessarily eliminate all of the problems.[24]

The key step in a meta-analysis is identifying a statistical measure shared by the studies to be included. It is referred to as the *effect size*, and can be thought of as a quantitative reflection of the strength of a relationship. For example, if the studies utilized a correlation coefficient such as Pearson's r, the effect size can be denoted by r^2. It is known as a coefficient of determination and it denotes the proportion of variance shared by the variables. However, effect size can be shown by utilizing dozens of different statistics, and what is best utilized depends upon the statistics that were employed in the separate studies.

Given the nature of meta-analysis, it has been most widely utilized in conjunction with quantitative data that permit statistical analysis. There have been some re-analyses of qualitative data sets, but such endeavors are probably intrinsically limited because qualitative studies rarely have anything like a full data set. When qualitative studies are published, and hence become better known, their methods discussions are almost never as complete as those of most quantitative studies.

Regardless of methodological approach, however, one serious problem in generalizing from any meta-analysis is that investigators are usually limited to published studies. How would they know about unpublished

studies? However, it has been well-documented that studies reporting insignificant or negative results are less likely to be accepted for publication.[25] This creates a bias in which the significance of effects are overstated because the studies that failed to find them are not published, hence less available for meta-analysis. In the days before most correspondence was electronic, after a journal declined a research paper, it was mailed back to the investigator who submitted it, and probably wound up thrown into a cabinet. Thus, the bias that it created has often been referred to as the "file drawer" problem.

Notes

1 Nels Anderson, *On Hobos and Homelessness*. University of Chicago, 1998.
2 Donald T. Campbell and D.W. Fiske, "Convergent and Discriminant Validation by the Multitrait-multimethod Matrix." *Psychological Bulletin*, 56, 1959.
3 Eugene J. Webb and Donald T. Campbell, *Unobtrusive Measures*, 1966. Rand McNally, 1966, and Webb, Campbell, et al., *Unobtrusive Measures*. Sage, 1999.
4 I have taken a few liberties in discussing the order in which Mehta moved from method to method; but my changes were small, and did not alter the basic thrust of the study. Vikas Mehta, *The Street*. Routledge, 2014.
5 For an overview of these developments, see Johnny Saldana, *The Coding Manual for Qualitative Researchers*. Sage, 2015.
6 QDA Miner in a "lite" version is available on-line, at no charge, from provalisresearch.com.
7 For a review of these developments, see Donna M. Mertens, "A Momentous Development in Mixed Methods Research." *Journal of Mixed Methods Research*, 8, 2014.
8 For further discussion, see Michael D. Fetters, "Haven't We Always Been Doing Mixed Methods Research?" *Journal of Mixed Methods Research*, 10, 2016.
9 Mario L. Small, "How to Conduct a Mixed Methods Study." *Annual Review of Sociology*, 37, 2011.
10 The sequencing of sub-studies can all be part of one investigation, or they may be part of a series of studies. See John W. Creswell, *Research Design*, Sage, 2013.
11 Sebastian Zenker, Sibylle Petersen and Andreas Aholt, "The Citizen Satisfaction Index (CSI)." *Cities*, 31, 2013.
12 See R. Burke Johnson and Larry B. Christensen, *Educational Research*. Sage, 2014.
13 Martin Oteng-Ababio and Isaac K. Arthur, "(Dis)continuities in Scale, Scope and Complexities of the Space Economy." *Urban Forum*, 26, 2015.
14 This discussion of triangulation is indebted to Mandy M. Archibald, "Investigator Triangulation." *Journal of Mixed Methods Research*, 10, 2015.
15 For further discussion of secondary data analysis, see Chapter 6 in, Dahlia K. Remler and Gregg G. Van Ryzin, *Research Methods in Practice*. Sage, 2014.

16 Andrew V. Papachristos, David M. Hureau, and Anthony A. Braga, "The Corner and the Crew." *American Sociological Review*, 78, 2013.

17 For further discussion, see James P. Gee, *An Introduction to Discourse Analysis*. Routledge, 2014.

18 Laura Bugg and Nicole Gurran, "Urban Planning Process and Discourses in the Refusal of Islamic Schools in Sydney, Australia." *Australian Planner*, 48, 2011.

19 Robert L. Wagmiller, Jr., "Blacks' and Whites' Experiences of Neighborhood Racial and Ethnic Diversity." *Urban Affairs Review*, 49, 2013.

20 Thomas De Vroome and Marc Hooghe, "Life Satisfaction among Ethnic Minorities in the Netherlands." *Journal of Happiness Studies*, 15, 2014.

21 Rubia R. Valente and Brian J.L. Berry, "Dissatisfaction with City Life?" *Cities*, 50, 2016.

22 Sanford E. DeVoie, Julian House and Chen-Bo Zhong, "Fast Food and Financial Impatience." *Journal of Personality and Social Psychology*, 105, 2013.

23 Most of the included papers are statistically very sophisticated, but the best reference is, Gary King, Ori Rosen and Martin A. Tanner, *Ecological Inference*. Cambridge University Press, 2004.

24 For further discussion, see Harris M. Cooper, *Research Synthesis and Meta-Analysis*. Sage, 2016.

25 See, for example, David Lehrer, et.al., "Negative Results in Social Science." *European Political Science*, 6, 2007.

Glossary

Cohort Studies: Studies that follow a group of people who initially share a significant attribute.

Convergent Design: Qualitative and quantitative data are both collected and analyzed at the same time.

Cross-sectional Surveys: Collect data at one point in time.

Ecological Fallacy: The assumption that relationships among aggregates are the same as among individuals.

Effect Size: The strength of a relationship as inferred by meta-analysis.

Longitudinal Surveys: Follow the same sample of people over time; the main types are cohort and panel studies.

Meta-Analysis: A study that combines data from previously conducted studies.

Mixed-method: Studies that combine quantitative and qualitative data collection and/or analysis.

Multi-method: Studies that combine two or more methods, both of which are either quantitative or qualitative.

Panel Studies: Follow the same sample of people in successive waves.

Primary Data: Collected by an investigator specifically to study a particular issue.

Proxy Measures: Substitute for variables of theoretical interest not measured in a study.

Secondary Data: Data previously collected for a purpose other than the one they are now being employed to serve.

Sequential Designs: A mixed method study which begins either qualitatively or quantitatively, then adds the other approach.

Appendix One: AAPOR transparency requirements[*]

The following information is always expected:

1 Report who sponsored the research and who conducted it. If different from the sponsor, the original sources of funding will also be disclosed.
2 Provide the exact wording and presentation of questions and response options whose results are reported. This includes preceding interviewer or respondent instructions and any preceding questions that might reasonably be expected to influence responses to the reported results.
3 Provide the definition of the population under study and its geographic location.
4 Show dates of data collection.
5 Describe the sampling frame(s) and its coverage of the target population, including mention of any segment of the target population that is not covered by the design. If possible estimate the size of any segment(s) not covered and explain why it cannot be covered. Indicate if no frame or list was utilized.
6 Provide the name of the sample supplier, if the sampling frame and/or the sample itself was provided by a third party.
7 Describe the methods used to recruit the panel or participants, if the sample was drawn from a pre-recruited panel or pool of respondents.
8 Describe the sample design, giving a clear indication of the method by which the respondents were selected, recruited, intercepted or otherwise contacted or encountered, along with any eligibility requirements and/or oversampling. If quotas were used, report the variables defining the quotas. If a within-household selection procedure was used, describe it. Include sufficient detail to determine whether the respondents were selected using probability or non-probability methods.

Obtaining data, Part Two

9 Note all method(s) and mode(s) used to administer the survey (e.g. ACASI, mail survey, Web survey) and the language(s) offered.

10 Sample sizes and a discussion of the precision of the findings. For probability samples, the estimates of sampling error will be reported. To avoid confusion, do not use the term "margin of error" or "margin of sampling error" in conjunction with non-probability samples.

11 If weighted estimates are reported, describe how the weights were calculated.

12 If the results reported are based on multiple samples or multiple modes, the preceding items will be disclosed for each.

13 Contact for obtaining more information about the study.

---

* This listing of requirements is edited and abridged. For the complete listing, go to: www.aapor.org/Standards-Ethics/AAPOR-Code-of-Ethics.aspx.

Measurement, reliability and validity

Concepts and indicators

Let us begin by briefly recalling the definitions of some previously introduced terms: *Concepts* are abstractions that combine like elements into a category. They often include an exemplar, or prototype, that is regarded as a special representation of the concept, and helps to clarify it. To illustrate, consider neighborhood as a concept. It usually denotes a local community that is in some way connected to a larger area, such as a city; but like most concepts it includes somewhat different places that are sufficiently alike to be subsumed under the same rubric. A number of real, and sometimes imagined, communities are often presented as exemplifying a neighborhood. Despite some differences among them, they are typically described as encompassing people living in an area that is meaningful to them – e.g. it has a name – and shared lifestyles.

Because of their abstract nature, we cannot encounter concepts with any of our primary senses. They cannot be seen, touched, etc. Our information about them relies upon *indicators*: manifestations of concepts that can be observed or measured. To illustrate, attendance at local block parties might be an indicator of the degree to which a place was a neighborhood. How often locals used a distinct name to refer to the place might also be an indicator of the degree to which it was a neighborhood. From indicators of this type we could acquire information about a neighborhood, but we would only know about it through these indicators.

When concepts can be linked to indicators they are typically described as *constructs* in order to differentiate them from those concepts which do not have an empirical referent. Mermaid, for example, fits the definition of a concept, but not a construct because it would not be possible to devise indicators from which to know about mermaids. It is a concept without empirical referents.

Finally, when there are multiple indicators of a construct, and they are combined into a single measure, the result is an *index*. The more complex a concept/construct being measured, the more an index is recommended rather than a single indicator. (The complexity of concepts is discussed in the following section.) The preceding terms are summarized in Box 7.1.

Operationalism

The position we are presenting here concerning the separation of constructs and indicators is widely shared by contemporary social scientists, but not by everyone. The alternative is a strict operationalist position which equates constructs and indicators. This position is historically associated with the physicist Percy Bridgman who, beginning in the 1920s, wrote a number of influential books.

Box 7.1 Concept, construct, indicator and index

- Concept: An abstract idea about a class of objects or events.
  |
- Construct: A concept that appears to have an empirical (i.e. "real world") referent.
  |
- Indicator: Way of measuring, or operationalizing, a construct.
  |
- Index: A measure that combines two or more indicators.

Devising indicators

There are two different ways in which researchers devise indicators: deductively or inductively. Deductive development, working from the more abstract to the more concrete, usually entails following a theory. To illustrate, a group of Sociologists were interested in measuring what they termed the concentrated disadvantage of neighborhoods. From prior research, they knew that this would involve at least three dimensions: employment, education and marital-family patterns. When specific conditions of all three dimensions coincided in a neighborhood, they reasoned, concentrated disadvantage resulted. To measure this concept, they developed an index that calculated unemployment rates, high school graduates, single-mother families, etc. for each neighborhood in their study.[1]

Alternatively, researchers sometimes observe something, think it is interesting, and speculate about what it may be a manifestation of; and this leads inductively to the creation of potential indicators of a construct. To illustrate, a group of Geographers interested in the urban development of Mediterranean cities noted that there seemed to be clusters of private residential swimming pools in various parts of Athens, Greece. They wondered what these pools might indicate. They proceeded to utilize high resolution Google Earth imagery to produce a census of all residential pools in the Athens metropolitan region. They next examined the socio-economic characteristics of each sub-area of Athens in relation to the number of swimming pools it contained. They found a high concentration of pools in the wealthiest areas, and very few anywhere else. They concluded that swimming pools could be considered a "proxy" – that is, an indicator – of socio-economic status, and that the degree of concentration of these pools could be regarded as indicating the amount of social class segregation.[2]

Bridgman essentially reduced meaning to measurement. To illustrate, he wrote that the length of any object is determined by a set of operations involving rulers, and other means, and it is these operations that define length, both conceptually and in terms of measurement. Thus, Bridgman

Measurement, reliability and validity

concluded that concepts or constructs were synonymous with the set of operations by which they were measured.[3]

In the years since Bridgman's writings were published, a few prominent social scientists endorsed his position, but the predominant view today is that there is always a residue of meaning left out of the operationalization of any construct.[4] So, the concept of global cities entails more than the number of regional finance offices in a city; social class segregation cannot be equated with the presence or absence of residential swimming pools in a neighborhood. Implications of the separation of concepts and indicators are further noted in a following section on validity.

Single or multiple indicators

There are some constructs that can probably be adequately measured with a single indicator. Demographic characteristics may be the best example: age, gender, race, etc. There also appear to be some attitudes that can be viewed as discrete constructs and measured satisfactorily with a single indicator, such as a question in a questionnaire. However, assessing the reliability and validity of single indicators can pose special problems, making the creation of an index (with multiple indicators) generally preferable.

The desirability of multiple indicators is particularly pronounced when an investigator is trying to measure a complex concept. They are the most abstract concepts because they are created by combining concepts. As a result, they contain multiple components, or dimensions, usually requiring multiple matching indicators. To illustrate, global cities are a complex concept, conjoining the less abstract concepts of global and cities, and merging the financial and cultural dimensions on which an international hierarchy of cities rests. To measure the place of cities in this global order requires at least two sets of indicators corresponding to cities' roles in maintaining the international flows of (1) finance and (2) culture. Thus, one set of indicators pertain to the presence of transnational banks and the very sizeable financial services firms that retain regional offices in large cities throughout the world. Another set of indicators corresponds to the movement of theatrical productions, musical tours, and the like across venues in linked cities throughout the world.[5] It is difficult to imagine one indicator that would adequately measure a concept as complex as global cities.

Creating an index

An index, as we have noted, consists of two or more indicators that are combined. For example, to measure a city's global standing, financial and cultural activities could be combined. To measure the affordability of a neighborhood, one might combine (1) the cost of rental apartments and (2) the cost of homes. Creation of an index ordinarily requires that numerical values be assigned to each indicator, and the index is the sum of their separate values. There are complex statistical techniques for determining the weight assigned to indicators, but for now we stay with the simple case in which they are weighted equally. In the case of neighborhood affordability, an investigator could rank apartment rentals and home costs of every neighborhood, then place each set of costs into three categories: high, medium and low. One easy way to create three categories from a ranking is to divide the total number of cases by 3, and place equal thirds in each category. A value of 3 is usually assigned to the high category (when there are three choices), 2 is assigned to the medium category and 1 to the lowest. So, if a specific neighborhood was seen to be high (i.e. 3) on the cost of rental apartments and medium (i.e. 2) on the cost of homes, that neighborhood's affordability index score would be 5.

Information is sometimes obtained via an index (or indicator) from individuals, but objective of the study is to assign scores to neighborhoods, cities, or other larger geographical entities. In such instances the average of all respondents from an area is usually taken as the score for the geographical area, and then it is possible to compare neighborhoods, cities, or the like. For example, an average of how frequently residents of a neighborhood walk to local restaurants or to friends' homes could provide the walkability score assigned to their neighborhoods.

While building up from individuals to an aggregate is usually not problematic, drilling down from an aggregate to individuals can be very precarious. This problem arises when data are available only for an aggregate, such as a neighborhood or a census tract, but the investigator would like to make an inference about the behavior of individuals. For example, the data may provide information about the number of ethnic minorities in a community and the crime rates in those communities. From the correlation between the two, an investigator might want to make assertions about whether individuals from minority groups are more or less likely to commit crimes. However, one cannot safely assume that whatever relationship is observed among variables at the aggregate level will also pertain to individuals. See the discussion of the ecological fallacy in Chapter 6.

In sum, we "know" constructs (global cities, neighborhood socio-economic status) only through an observable indicator (international firms, private swimming pools) or index. All research must, therefore, rely upon indicators to present descriptions of constructs, or to test hypotheses concerning the relationship between constructs. There are

Measurement, reliability and validity

two major criteria against which any indicator or index is assessed: reliability and validity. We begin with reliability, and will turn next to a discussion of validity.

Reliability

Reliability, as previously introduced, generally refers to the consistency across time of an indicator or of a way of operationalizing a construct. The reliability of an indicator would be perfect if there were no changes over time in its results – except for those that were due to actual changes in the phenomenon being studied. In other words, as long as a construct stayed the same, a reliable indicator of it would continue to yield the same result.

To be more technically precise, think about a "true" score of any concept. It cannot empirically exist, but we can imagine it. Based upon the properties of the concept, over time it might change very rapidly (e.g. moods) or hardly at all (intelligence). What we can observe are changes in the values of an indicator that can also change rapidly or slowly. Because of various types of measurement error, the (observed) score on the indicator will probably never be identical to the true score. A measure is reliable, mathematically, to the extent that variation in its values mirror those of variation in the true score. So, an indicator could be highly reliable despite frequent fluctuations in its values if the concept it was measuring was also believed to be highly changeable.

Test-retest

In principle, reliability would be most suitably examined by repeating the same measure at two (or more) different times, a procedure that is typically referred to as *test-retest* reliability. One statistic that is commonly employed to examine the degree of congruency between the two repeated measures is Spearman's Rank-Order Correlation Coefficient (rho). It is included in the commonly used statistical software programs such as SAS and SPSS. A description of rho is presented in Box 7.2.

The first question that arises in employing test-retest to examine reliability concerns what is an appropriate interval between the two tests. The answer depends first upon how the construct being measured is viewed. The more it is viewed as prone to change, the shorter the interval should be because the reliability of an indicator ought not to be reduced by actual changes in the phenomenon being studied.

To illustrate, consider neighborhood walkability: how much the people in a neighborhood walk, rather than ride, to get to stores, restaurants, friends' homes, or so on. Past studies have shown that the amount of walking usually correlates with a neighborhood's: population density,

Box 7.2 Correlation between two ordinal variables (rho)

Many variables studied in urban research are measured at the ordinal level, meaning that the measure provides a ranking from high to low, but the numbers assigned to the ranks lack many of the familiar mathematical qualities of numbers. The commonly utilized Likert scale, for example, presents five response alternatives that are frequently assigned numerical values: Strongly Agree = 5, Agree = 4, and so on. Because the numbers assigned to the alternatives are arbitrary, there is no reason to assume that the magnitude of difference between Agree (4) and Don't Know (3) is equal in magnitude to the difference between Don't Know (3) and Disagree (2). All we can say is that Agree represents a greater degree of agreement than Don't Know which, in turn, represents a greater degree of agreement than Disagree, and so on. In other words, the responses can be ranked relative to each other – like the order in which people finish a race – so the numerical values assigned to them are, therefore, ordinal. (If the runners' exact times were measured, the absolute differences among them would be known, and the measurement would correspondingly be described as interval level.)

In trying to establish the test-retest reliability of an ordinal variable, Spearman's Rank-Order Correlation (rho) is appropriate, and widely used. Like the more familiar Pearson Correlation, its values can be positive or negative, and range from –1 to +1. In assessing test-retest reliability, a strong positive relationship would be expected. What is strong? There is no established cut-off, but there are two minimal criteria to consider. First, rho can be squared to determine the proportion of variation in the rankings of one test that can be explained by the rankings in the other. To explain at least 50 percent of the variation, one would therefore require a rho over 0.70.

The second minimal requirement is that the correlation should be statistically significant, that is, exceed a pre-determined level of chance. By convention, that probability level is usually set at 0.05. There is a sampling distribution of rho for any sample size, and the 0.05 level would mean that the obtained relationship would occur by chance no more than five in 100 times.[6]

traffic volume, street connectivity and other variables, all of which are known not to typically change very much over a short period of time.[7] Therefore, one could permit substantial time to elapse between utilizing an indicator to take a measure of neighborhood walking and a later retest with the same indicator and still expect the two to be highly correlated.

Measurement, reliability and validity

On the other hand, the number of homes being renovated as part of gentrification projects can vary a great deal over a short period of time. To assess the reliability of an indicator of renovation-gentrification by test and retest, a more condensed time interval would therefore be advisable so that actual changes would not lower the correlation between indicators at the two time periods. If an investigator waited a long period before a re-test and found the correlation between measures was very low, it would be difficult to decide whether the measure was unreliable or if true change had occurred.

In addition, it is important for enough time to elapse to permit forgetting to occur, if the indicators developed for an investigation are obtrusive (for example, derived from a questionnaire or interview). If people can recall how they answered questions the first time, then a desire to appear consistent may lead them to select the same response at a later time, even if their attitudes or habits have changed in the interim. That tendency to avoid the appearance of contradicting oneself will artificially inflate the apparent reliability of an indicator. How long it takes for people to forget how they answered a question depends, in part, upon the salience of the issue. The more a question pertains to something in the forefront of people's thinking, the longer they are likely to remember the question and how they answered it. Working in the opposite direction, the longer the overall length of a questionnaire or interview, the quicker people may forget how they answered any one set of questions. Thus, when obtrusive measures are involved, an investigator needs to balance forgetting against the occurrence of actual change in deciding upon an interval between test and retest.

If the indicators that were developed for an investigation relied upon inconspicuous methods, such as surreptitious observations, published documents or GIS analysis, then people's rate of forgetting would be irrelevant to a determination of the interval between test and retest. The only concern would be that the time interval selected should not be so long that actual change (in the construct) occurs.

While it clearly captures the essence of reliability, and is therefore desirable, test-retest is often impractical. For example, if an investigator is employing a questionnaire, it will be necessary to obtain responses from the same people, but after an appropriate time interval it may not be possible to reach most of the originally included people. In addition, inferences drawn from indicators in a field study are typically not subject to a reliability-across-time assessment. It is not even clear what that would mean in an ethnographic investigation, given that behavior, in that type of analysis, is usually viewed as tied to a situational context rather than being a discrete entity that can be repeatedly measured outside of that context.

When test-retest is precluded by circumstances or considered to be inappropriate, there are a number of alternatives that can be employed to assess reliability, depending upon whether indicators are quantitative or qualitative.

Internal reliability

Internal reliability assessments are the most frequently used alternatives to test-retest when a quantitative indicator is being utilized, and the indicator has multiple components (i.e. it is an index). The logic underlying internal reliability is that if at time one the components of an index do not consistently correspond, or correlate, with each other, then they are also unlikely to be consistent with each other across time. Such consistency implies that an index is stable, not given to random fluctuations. The *absence* of such stability would make it problematic to infer consistency among indicators across time. Hence, technically speaking, demonstrating the internal consistency of a measure is a necessary, but not sufficient, requirement for inferring its reliability across time.

One of the most commonly used statistics to assess the internal consistency of scale is Cronbach's alpha. It is offered in the most widely used statistical software packages, and it is briefly described in Box 7.3.

To illustrate the use of Cronbach's alpha to assess internal reliability, let us return to the walkability of neighborhoods. If a neighborhood is generally conducive to walking, then we might argue that residents should specifically be inclined to walk to stores, friends' homes, restaurants, etc. Conversely, if the neighborhood is not conducive to walking, then residents should not walk to stores, friends' homes, etc. Consistency among the specific parts of the index would imply that when people are more likely to walk to stores they are also more likely to walk to friends' homes, and so on. The creation of an index of walkability and the way its internal reliability was assessed is discussed in Box 7.4.

In addition to Cronbach's alpha, there are several other statistical analyses that could be utilized to assess internal reliability when investigators have a potentially large number of indicators that they would like to combine in an index. One of the most widely used of these statistics is factor analysis. It is a very efficient technique for sorting items – responses to questions on a questionnaire, observations of people's behavior, etc. – into clusters, categories or dimensions that are called factors. For each factor, it also provides a multiple item index, with weights assigned to each item. It is a very appropriate technique when studying a complex concept that is thought to entail a number of sub-concepts. However, it can be of dubious value if the investigator does not work deductively, from a theory about the concept.

Box 7.3 Cronbach's alpha

Cronbach's alpha is generally considered a test of the (internal) reliability of an index by assessing the correlation among items presumed to measure the same construct. (These items could be observations, questions on a questionnaire, or the like.) Because it expresses a ratio between variances, its values range from 0 to 1, with higher values suggesting greater reliability. As with rho, to which it is related, an alpha value over 0.70 is typically a minimal expectation for reliability. This reliability estimate also provides an approximation of the measurement error of an index. The greater the error, the less consistency across time is to be expected.

In other words, a high alpha score indicates internal consistency, which implies that the items are all measures of the same construct. If so, then the index is capable of being consistent over time, that is, reliable. A high alpha (over 0.70, at least) is therefore necessary, but not sufficient, to assume that an index is reliable.

Alpha is also a very useful statistic in deciding which of the potential items actually to include in an index. It provides part-whole correlations, that is, correlations of each item with the total index. By deleting those items with the lowest correlation, alpha is increased. This process can be continued until alpha reaches an acceptable level. Some analysts contend that alpha should not exceed a value of about 0.90 because higher values suggest that some items in the index may be redundant.[8]

Most types of factor analysis begin with a correlation matrix, expressing the correlations among all the items (or variables) that have been included. If there are moderate to strong correlations among them, the issue to be examined is whether these correlations arose because the correlated items are manifestations of the same dimension of the concept. To illustrate, suppose an investigator wanted to devise a measure with which to classify urban neighborhoods. From an appropriate data source, the investigator might be able to obtain data on a very lengthy list of potential characteristics, dealing with: housing conditions, average incomes, availability of restaurants and shopping, quality of municipal services, minority concentrations, and so on.

One question that would immediately arise is: Do all these items measure the same thing or are urban neighborhoods comprised of multiple dimensions? If the latter, they may be related to each other, but nonetheless separable. In other words, are urban neighborhoods a unitary variable, or are they comprised of multiple components? Preparing a correlation matrix, showing how all items are correlated with all other

Box 7.4 The reliability of a neighborhood walkability index

Two urban planners in Granada, Spain were interested in developing a walking index that focused upon what people thought would be the most important considerations in their decisions to walk rather than ride to places in their neighborhoods.[9] The investigators' review of the literature disclosed that past studies had relied upon a number of different indicators of walkability, making it difficult to compare their findings. For this project they wanted to create an index that would subsume the multiple components of walkability utilized in prior research. Toward this end they prepared a questionnaire which contained four (potentially) distinct dimensions of people's inclinations to walk:

- Accessibility: distance to destination, slopes, etc.
- Safety: lighting, traffic speed, etc.
- Comfort: trees, cleanliness, etc.
- Attractiveness: public spaces, shops and restaurants, etc.

In total they created a list of 28 separate indicators associated with the four categories noted above. Then they asked a sample of 125 respondents in Grenada to fill out questionnaires rating how important they considered each of the 28 items. To answer, respondents selected one of five Likert scale alternatives, each scored as 1 to 5. By summing the numerical values assigned to each of their 28 answers, respondents were given a total index score. For example, in the unlikely event any respondent selected "Very Important" as the answer to all 28 questions, that person's total score on the scale would be 140 (28 × 5).

The investigators analyzed people's responses to the 28 walking questions using Cronbach's alpha. They obtained a value of 0.91, nearly ideal, because it showed a very high degree of internal consistency among the respondents' answers, but probably not so high as to imply redundancy in the index. This high degree of internal consistency implied that the questions were all addressing the same construct, so that people's total scores were probably not the result of random replies. The index could, therefore, provide consistent results across time.

items, would be a good place to begin to answer this question, and that is where most types of factor analysis begin. It attempts to answer the question of whether the correlations among items arose because the items are manifestations of the same underlying dimension, or subdimension. The degree to which an item is an indicator of an underlying dimension is expressed by a factor loading that has the same range of values as correlation coefficients (i.e. 0 to +/−1).

Despite some overarching similarities, in terms of the statistical operations that are involved, and the underlying theoretical approach, factor analyses can be divided into two major types. Each is described in Box 7.5

Both Cronbach's alpha and factor analysis require that an investigator begin with a substantial number of individual indicators. Both entail data reduction. When an investigator has a more limited number of indicators, one of the most widely used ways to assess internal reliability is the split half method. It entails dividing the indicators into two groups, and

---

Box 7.5 Types of factor analysis

There are two primary types of factor analysis. The first is named *exploratory factor analysis (efa)*. Here the investigator begins without any explicit hypothesis about the relationships between items and factors or among factors. As its name implies, it is exploratory, and relies upon the obtained factor loadings to identify the factor structure of the data. The investigator works inductively. While efa is widely used, it must be used very cautiously. The factor loadings that one obtains are a function of the items that were included in the analysis. It is, in effect, a kind of summary. So, if theoretically important variables were left out of the original data list, the summary will be very incomplete. The absence of important subdimensions could distort the theoretical picture.

In sum, efa can be very useful in reducing a lengthy list of potential indicators into a factor index in which each indicator is weighted appropriately. However, factor analysis provides results and the investigator always provides the interpretation of those results, that is, the factor analysis yields the factor structure and loadings, but does not identify the factors in a substantive way. Therefore, it can be very problematic to rely upon an exploratory factor analysis without a theoretical model because it can lead to bizarre conclusions.

The second type of analysis is called *confirmatory factor analysis (cfa)*. It is utilized in a more deductive manner to test hypotheses derived from previously established theory. Each factor is expected to be related to a specific set of items, and this expectation is the basis for the selection of items. The cfa is thus a test of a hypothesized theoretical model. It also enables an investigator to rely upon more complex statistics than an efa in order to more thoroughly evaluate the model. Over time, as research and theory building about an issue continue, investigators are often able to replace efa by cfa.[10]

---

then examining the relationship between the two groups (or halves). For example, suppose one had four questions pertaining to neighborhood walking, and they involved how frequently people walked to: (1) stores, (2) restaurants, (3) a place where they worked, and (4) friends' homes. A researcher might place questions 1 and 3 in one group, and 2 and 4 in the other. In effect, there would be two "sub" indexes, each consisting of two indicators. The strength of the relationship (e.g. correlation) between the two sub-indexes would provide a measure of split half reliability; and if it were sufficiently high, all four indicators would be combined into a single index with some reason to believe that it could be stable across time.

Inter-rater reliability

The statistical techniques thus far discussed in relation to assessments of reliability presuppose quantitative data. With qualitative data, the stability or consistency of an indicator is often assessed by examining the degree of agreement between two (or more) observers who have been trained to use a specific coding scheme. In the absence of such training, the biases that observers bring to a situation can affect what they perceive. For example, in one study Japanese and American researchers observed the same group at the same time, but the Japanese researchers (whose culture places more emphasis upon collective undertakings) reported that they detected more communal activities among the observed subjects than did their American counterparts.[11] These inconsistencies in how they coded or evaluated what they saw implies that the indicators being used were probably too prone to subjective bias to provide uniform results across time.

Assessing *inter-rater reliability* obviously requires a research design in which there are two trained observers present in the same situation. In Chapter 2, for example, we described a study in which two ethnographers worked as judges in debates between students in inner-city high schools. The "training" in this instance involved discussions between the two judges concerning the kinds of behaviors of other judges they would focus upon, and how they would classify these behaviors. In other studies, observers are trained in how to use a coding scheme that involves indicators of their subjects' behavior.

Inter-rater reliability can be thought of as expressing the degree of agreement between coders. The higher the percentage of times they code the same observation in the same way, the greater the reliability. However, the percentage of agreement, by itself, is an overly simplified way of calculating reliability because some agreement between coders will occur by chance. It is a function of how many categories, or values, are being coded. If, for example, the two raters were classifying observations

Measurement, reliability and validity

into four alternatives that occurred with roughly the same frequencies, then the two coders would agree – solely by chance – about 25 percent of the time. Therefore, inter-rater reliability is most accurately calculated by estimating how much above chance the two raters agreed.[12]

One widely used statistic for showing the degree of above chance agreement between raters is Krippendorff's alpha. (It is available in most of the statistical software packages.) It is applicable in a wide range of studies, whenever agreement between raters is to be assessed. For example, it is used to compare agreements in rating observations, but also in the coding of open-ended interview data or the content analysis of textual data. Krippendorff's alpha, like other alphas, has a range of 0 to 1, in which 1 indicates perfect agreement, 0 indicates no agreement. Again, the higher a positive value of alpha, the greater the implied degree of internal reliability of an indicator or index. However, it is also possible to obtain a negative value for this alpha, which indicates systematic disagreement between raters in excess of what would be expected by chance.[13] Obtaining a negative value would mean that the raters were poorly trained in using the coding protocol.

Validity

Validity is defined in a number of ways, but most fundamentally it refers to the congruence between a construct and an indicator. The greater the degree of congruence, the more the indicator can be said to measure the construct it purports to measure, and therefore, the higher the degree of validity. Remember, we "know" constructs only through their indicators. Therefore, it sometimes takes a good deal of creativity to analyze the congruence between a construct and its indicator(s). By contrast, note that from an extreme operationalist position, the notion of validity makes little sense. It is relevant only when the concept is held to have broader meaning than the indicator(s). If the operationalization defines the concept – if intelligence is held to be whatever an IQ test measures – then any indicator is necessarily valid.

Validity assessments fall into two categories. In the first are mostly subjective appraisals that are usually categorized under the term *face validity*. In the second category are more rigorous examinations that typically establish formal criteria. The latter are usually categorized under the term *concurrent validity*, and sometimes called *criterion validity*. We will discuss each grouping, in turn.

Face validity

Face validity entails a subjective assessment of the indicator, or index, in relation to a theoretical understanding of the construct. On the face of it, so to speak, does the indicator look right? With respect to the walkability of a neighborhood, for example, do the specific questions or observations to be employed as indicators appear to be getting at the theoretical meaning(s) of the construct?

It is obviously very important for an investigator to assess the face validity of an indicator or index at the very beginning of a research project. If it does not feel right or seem right, then it probably should be abandoned, and the investigator would need to go back to the drawing board. However, note that this is a subjective evaluation, hence prone to bias. And because it is the investigators that are gauging the face validity of the measure, it is likely to pass their muster; after all, they are the ones who created it. Face validity should therefore be considered a weak assessment of an indicator's validity.

One variant of face validity that introduces a little more rigor into the assessment is termed *content validity*. It entails a theoretical examination of all of the components of a construct in relation to an index. The process usually begins with a careful evaluation of a construct in order to create a checklist of its parts, or dimensions. Then any proposed index is examined against the checklist to see if it contains all the facets of the construct. If an index seemed very complete, that would imply content validity.

Face or content validity can also entail the use of expert judgment. Step one entails the selection of experts and, depending upon the nature of the construct, the expert pool could include scholars who have written about it, practitioners, people who have experienced it, or so on. If one wished to create a quantitative summary of the validity of an index in this way, it would be possible to calculate the degree to which experts agreed that an index measured all of the components of a construct.

Construct validity

Construct validity (sometimes referred to as criterion validity) begins with a careful scrutiny of the theory from which the construct was derived. The objective is to infer how the indicator or index in question ought to be related, following the theory, to other indicators of the same or a related construct. Two somewhat different types of assessment are involved, each of which is described below.

Concurrent validity

Concurrent validity typically involves examining the relationship between the indicator of interest and another indicator of the same construct whose validity has previously been demonstrated, or is assumed. The new indicator is usually proposed because it is easier to use, requires less time, captures some previously untapped dimension of the construct, or in some other way is potentially better than the one previously regarded as a valid measure. Despite some difference between the two indicators, there still ought to be a significant relationship between them; and the observed relationship between the two indicators constitutes the test of concurrent validity.

A related form of assessing validity entails utilizing two different indicators of a construct and assessing whether each is related to other variables in the manner expected by a theory. Doing the analysis twice is almost like a replication, and it suggests that both indicators are valid measures. To illustrate, Brian McCabe was interested in measuring how much people trusted their neighbors. He used data from a survey that contained two potential measures of trust. The first was a direct question that asked, generally speaking, how much the respondent trusted people in the neighborhood. It offered four alternatives, varying from a lot to not at all. The second potential measure of trust was indirect and specific, asking respondents how likely they thought a neighbor would be to return their wallet, if it was lost with $200 in it. This question also provided four alternatives, from very likely to not likely at all.[14]

The hypothesis to be tested concerned whether being a home owner, rather than renter, was associated with more trust in neighbors. From past research and established theories, the investigator expected that home ownership would strengthen people's neighborhood bonds and that would build trust. The survey from which McCabe obtained data for the study contained a number of other variables potentially related to trust, such as how long the respondent had lived in the neighborhood, the overall rate of neighborhood turnover, and so on. These other variables were held constant when the home ownership hypothesis was tested. To be specific, the analysis was run twice, separately using each of the two measures of trust. The results showed a strong relationship between trust and home ownership, net of the other variables, when either the direct or indirect indicator of trust was employed. In fact, the results were virtually identical in both analyses. Thus, the validity of both indicators was shown by the replicated findings.

Predictive validity

Predictive validity, as its name implies, entails extrapolating from the theory from which the construct was derived in order to make an informed guess about how it might relate to another construct. The prediction sometimes involves a future condition; people who score highly on the indicator in question should score higher (or lower) on some future condition. To illustrate, if an indicator of neighborhood attachment has predictive validity, then people who score higher should be less likely to move out of the neighborhood. A meaningful test would probably require tracking people over a period of years. If the time interval was too short, it would not permit enough people to move for a difference between high and low attachment residents to be observed.

While predicting a future state is an excellent way to assess predictive validity, it is often impractical. It may be difficult, for example, to keep track of which people move out of a neighborhood. This difficulty leads to a second type of assessment of predictive validity that entails deducing from the theory what other variable(s) the indicator in question should logically be related to, with all variables being measured at the same point in time.

The differences between predictive validity and concurrent validity are sometimes very small, and can come down to matters of emphasis. The similarities between them are illustrated by the research summarized in Box 7.6.

Investigator triangulation and legitimation

In mixed-methods research (described in the previous chapters) validity can also entail *investigator triangulation*: the congruence in findings that are obtained when an investigator uses different methods of gathering and/or analyzing data. As historically used in navigation and cartography, triangulation usually involves relying upon at least two reference points in order to ascertain a third. To be consistent, then, investigator triangulation would have to entail the use of at least two different research methods, one or more quantitative and one or more qualitative.

Every mode of data collection and analysis has weaknesses and biases. When a finding transcends different methods, it suggests that the finding is not an artifact of the method employed. To some experts, this confirmation of findings can be roughly equated with validity. The two or more methods employed are regarded as providing evidence analogous to when two or more indicators are assessed within a single quantitative method.[16]

To other experts, however, combining qualitative and quantitative data creates additional complexities that are not encountered when only quantitative data are involved. Because their combination alters the conventional meaning of validity, they recommend utilizing an entirely different term, and often propose legitimation as the alternative. One major difference between validity and legitimation is that the former is assessed at one point in a research project, namely when indicators are being developed. *Legitimation*, by contrast, involves a continuous process of examining the consistency between the qualitative and quantitative components of a study at each stage of the research process.[17]

Box 7.6 The validity of an indicator of urban sprawl

Thomas Laidley noted that sprawl has been extensively studied because of its association with urban problems, including: automobile-reliant travel, more carbon emissions and hazardous pollution. On the other hand, sprawl is also associated with more affordable housing because both rental and ownership costs tend to be higher in more densely populated areas. However, much of the research on sprawl has lacked precision, in Laidley's view, because of its reliance upon overly simplistic indicators of sprawl, such as the proximity of jobs to residential areas or how close development occurred in relation to the city's central business district. Cities can vary from each other in these respects due to many variables besides sprawl, leading to inconsistent, as well as imprecise, results. And finally, he felt that past studies had often examined sprawl in urban subareas, such as census tracks, that were so large that pockets of both high density development and sprawl could be lost within them.[15]

For his study, Laidley divided metropolitan areas in the US into blocks, the smallest geographical units available. He developed precise measures of population density from which he set thresholds as cut-off points, and then classified metropolitan areas by the sum of the density of their blocks. To assess the validity of this operationalization of sprawl, he proceeded to examine its correlation with: (1) previously developed measures of sprawl (which would suggest concurrent validity as we have defined it); and then examined whether, from his index, he could extrapolate to metropolitan area scores on (2) conventional pollution, carbon dioxide emissions and housing affordability (which would imply predictive validity, as previously defined).

Laidley found large and significant correlations between his new measure of sprawl and a half dozen indicators that other investigators had previously used. All of the correlations were statistically significant, and many were substantial in size. This finding suggests concurrent validity. Most importantly, he also found that the new measure had a stronger relationship than the previously used indicators with the criteria variables that sprawl was theoretically expected to predict: pollution, carbon dioxide and housing affordability. Further, it is not just that the correlations between the new sprawl indicator and these presumed consequences were relatively higher, but in an absolute sense they were very robust, suggesting high predictive validity for the new measure.

Notes

1 Christopher J. Lyons, Maria B. Velez, and Wayne A. Santoro, "Neighborhood Immigration, Violence, and City-Level Immigrant Political Opportunities." *American Sociological Review*, 78, 2013.

2 Luca Salvati and Margerita Carlucci, "Latent Sprawl, Divided Mediterranean Landscapes." *Urban Geography*, 36, 2015.

3 Percy W. Bridgman, *Reflections of a Physicist*. Philosophical Library, 1955.

4 One of the most influential advocates for not equating concepts and indicators was Paul F. Lazarsfeld. See, *On Social Research and its Language*. University of Chicago, 1993.

5 Many of these studies are summarized in Mark Abrahamson, *Global Cities*. Oxford University Press, 2004.

6 For a detailed discussion of the rank-order correlation, see Ferris Ritchey, *The Statistical Imagination*. McGraw-Hill, 2007.

7 For further discussion of measures of walkability, see Li Yin, "Assessing Walkability in the City of Buffalo." *Journal of Urban Planning and Development*, 139, 2013.

8 For further discussion, see Mohsen Tavokol and Reg Dennick, "Making Sense of Cronbach's Alpha." *International Journal of Medical Education*, 2, 2011.

9 Ruben Talavera-Garcia and Julio A. Soria-Lara, "Q-PLOS, Developing an Alternative Walking Index." *Cities*, 45, 2015.

10 For further discussion of both types of factor analysis, see G. David Garson, *Factor Analysis*. Statistical Associates Publisher, 2013.

11 For further discussion of inter-rater reliability, see D'Lane Compton, Tony P. Love and Jane Sell, "Developing and Assessing Intercoder Reliability in Studies of Group Interaction." *Sociological Methodology*, 42, 2012.

12 See the discussion in *ibid*.

13 For further discussion, see Andrew F. Hayes and Klaus Krippendorff, "Answering the Call for a Standard Reliability Measure for Coding Data." *Communication Methods and Measures*, 1, 2007.

14 Brian J. McCabe, "Homeownership and Social Trust in Neighbors." *City and Community*, 11, 2012.

15 Thomas Laidley, "Measuring Sprawl." *Urban Affairs Review*, 1, 2015.

16 For further discussion, see Mandy M. Archibald, "Investigator Triangulation." *Journal of Mixed Methods Research*, 10, 2015.

17 For further discussion of the legitimation process and its relation to validity, see Anthony J. Onwuegbuzie, R. Burke Johnson and Kathleen M. T. Collins, "Assessing Legitimation in Mixed Research." *Quality and Quantity*, 45, 2011.

Glossary

Concepts: Abstractions that combine similar elements; they may or may not have an empirical referent.

Confirmatory Factor Analysis: Utilizes factor analysis deductively to test a theoretical model.

Construct Validity: An assessment of whether the relationship among indicators is consistent with the theory from which they were derived.

Constructs: Concepts which have an empirical referent, measurable with indicators.

Content Validity: Examines whether all the components of a construct are included in an indicator or index.

Exploratory Factor Analysis: Working without a theory, an investigator relies upon obtained results to identify a factor structure.

Face Validity: A subjective appraisal of whether an indicator looks right in relation to a construct.

Factor Analysis: A statistical technique that sorts subject responses into like clusters, termed factors (see appendix).

Index: A measure of a construct that combines indicators.

Indicators: Observable manifestations of a construct.

Internal Reliability: Relies upon consistency among indicators to infer their possible consistency across time.

Inter-rater Reliability: The consistency with which trained researchers agree in coding observations or written materials; consistency implies the possibility of reliability across time.

Investigator Triangulation: Assesses the congruence in findings when an investigator relies upon mixed methods.

Legitimation: An alternative to validity in mixed-methods research, it examines the congruence between the qualitative and quantitative components.

Reliability: The consistency across time of an indicator, net of changes in the construct.

Test-Retest: A reliability assessment that entails repeating the same measure.

Validity: The degree to which an indicator actually measures the construct to which it is linked.

chapter 8

The research report

Outline

- Section headings
  - Abstract
  - Executive summary
  - Introduction
    - Citation form
  - Methods
  - Results
  - Discussion
    - Recommendations
  - References

- Writing style
  - Formality

- Notes

Section headings

It is customary for research reports published in professional journals or submitted to universities in order to fulfill academic requirements to be divided into the following six parts, or sections: Abstract, Introduction,

Methods, Results, Discussion, and References. A perusal of articles in scientific publications indicates some variability in the number and names of headings, though. For example, the Methods section is sometimes called Methods and Data, and the Results and Discussion sections are sometimes combined and referred to as Findings. Research reports that are not intended for a scientific audience – for example, research paid for by a client, or carried out by an agency – differ somewhat in their form and content. The major differences between them will be explained.

In deciding how many sections to employ and what to call them, the most important consideration is how best to report what one has done and found and what it means. Clarity in presenting a particular study is paramount, and sections of a report should be formulated accordingly. However, the content of the major sections we will describe here provide a reasonably comprehensive checklist of the information that must typically be conveyed in a report. And they conform with the format expected by readers of these publications. Thus, these standard sections provide a useful point of reference even when the dictates of a particular study suggest some modification.

Abstract

An abstract is a brief statement of the most important findings and most relevant methodological features of a study. It is presented first, usually at the top of the first page. In essence, it is a summary that is presented before, rather than after, the main body of a paper. It is typical for an abstract to contain about 100–150 words – about one dozen typed lines. If it is possible to summarize the study in fewer words, so much the better; but the problem faced by most beginners is exactly the opposite, namely, a tendency to be too wordy. Remember, an abstract is a summary and, like any summary, it is useless if its length approximates that of the report which it is supposed to be condensing.

One major function of an abstract is to provide a reader with just enough information to decide whether to read the entire paper. For people who are doing a survey of the literature prior to designing their own study, it is extremely helpful to have a brief abstract so that obviously irrelevant papers can be quickly discarded. If the abstract is not accurate as well as brief, it is obviously a disservice rather than an aide to those who read it.

For those who are preparing their first abstract, a model is presented in Box 8.1. It provides a guide, and beginners can fill in the blanks according to their specific study.

Box 8.1 Model abstract

This paper reports a study of . . . _____.
The major finding is that there is no apparent relationship between. . .
_____ and . . . _____.
The data for this analysis were obtained from . . ._____.
The results are interpreted as indicating . . . _____.

The model presented in Box 8.1 above will more or less fit many different studies, and it provides a succinct form for presenting the most important information up front.

Executive summary

Most client- or agency-centered research includes an executive summary in place of an abstract. It would be unusual to include both. They are alike in that each provides a brief summary of a research project in front of the actual report. However, an executive summary is typically a good deal longer than an abstract, one to two pages probably being its typical length.

In the executive summary, it is important to devote a few lines to the main points in each section of the report, and to present that information in the order it is presented in the report. Remember, the executive summary should focus only upon the main points. It should be concise, but it should also be certain to describe: the issue that was explored, what problems led to undertaking the study, the findings and their limitations, and what decisions are being recommended as a result of the findings. In addition, within an executive summary, it is often helpful to summarize key findings in a table, chart, or the like.[1]

Introduction

The introduction to a scientific paper usually provides some historical description of how the research question has been treated. If there is a seminal figure associated with the line of research, that person or the tradition should be noted, and followed by a discussion of the studies that can be considered the precursors to this one. What did they find? What was problematic about their findings that led you to conduct this study?

The nature of the particular study being reported will often provide a pragmatic basis for deciding how much theoretical background to include in an introduction. If the principal concepts of a study have been formulated only recently, they will usually afford limited opportunities for historical discussion. On the other hand, when the concepts of a study have been the subjects of longstanding analyses, some discussion of the continuity, or discontinuity, seems unavoidable. Sometimes writers must decide the issue according to their own inclinations. How extensive a theoretical history should be, in these circumstances, is a matter of personal taste.

In any event, an introduction should emphasize the bearing of recent studies on the formulation of the research hypothesis. It should explain how past findings have led to an interest in the specific question(s) being posed. If any methodological procedures have been shown to have an important effect upon substantive findings, then these methodological considerations should also be discussed. It is often difficult to decide how much of the discussion belongs in the introduction and how much in the methods section. Generally, the more technical the content, the more it belongs in the methods section. The more it pertains to theoretical inter-pretations, the more it belongs in the Introduction.

In a non-scientific paper, the background of the issue being investi-gated is also reviewed, but more emphasis is placed upon the particular problem that led to the study being conducted. For example, was there an increase in street crime that led the police to commission a study to try to understand why the increase occurred? Did tax revenues suddenly decline, prompting a city to undertake an analysis of what led to the decline? This research purpose should be noted both in the abstract and introduction.

Citation form

The introductory section of a scientific paper, as noted, invariably con-tains a literature review. In a scientific paper, there are formal rules for citations and reference sections. Papers submitted to meet university degree requirements must typically follow these same rules, though there can be some university-specific regulations, and students are wise to consult them prior to preparing a paper. The same advice applies to students writing a research paper as a course requirement.[2]

Throughout the social science literature, the citation style of the American Psychological Association is most commonly followed through-out the world.[3] That also specifically includes many journals devoted to Urban Studies. The second most common style found in Urban Studies (and most Sociology) journals is that of the American Sociological Asso-ciation.[4] The citation formats of the two styles are extremely similar, though.

In the main body of a research report, references are partially pre-sented, by noting the last name of the author, date of publication, and page number if the reference is to a specific quotation. To illustrate, if the author's name is mentioned in the text, the date of publication is enclosed in parentheses after the author's name: "According to Smith (2007), most city agencies are highly bureaucratic." If the author's name is not mentioned in the text, both name and date are placed in parentheses: "Most city agencies are highly bureaucratic (Smith, 2007)." If a specific passage is being quoted, then the page on which it appears goes after the date, separated by a colon: "Most city agencies are highly bureaucratic (Smith, 2007: 180)." If the author had more than one publication during the year, they are identified as a and b (and c, etc. if necessary). Thus: (Smith, 2007a) for the first citation to Smith's work published in 2007.

If a citation has two authors, both are included (Smith and Jones, 2014). In APA style, if there are three to five authors, all authors are named in the first citation; for any further citations, only the first author is named, but the existence of others is noted (Smith, et al., 2014). Otherwise, the same rules for citation form in the text that apply to a single author also apply when there are multiple authors.

If a number of different authors are referred to simultaneously in the text, all of them are enclosed within a single pair of parentheses, and separated from each other by semicolons: "Most city agencies are highly bureaucratic (Jones, 1975; Smith, 1978)." When different publications of the same author are referred to, and the years of publication are the same, the citations are distinguished from each other by chronological use of an alphabetic letter inserted after the date. For example, if Jones published two papers in 1975, and both of them are cited, the first would be (Jones, 1975a); and the second (Jones, 1975b).

When there are more than two authors of a cited work, only the first author's last name is presented, followed by et al. For example, if White, Phillips, and Davis are the authors, the citation is (White et al., 1979). When there are only two authors, both are cited; thus, (Grove and Black, 1966). Finally, no matter how many times the same work is cited, it is given the same citation in the text each time. *Ibid.*, *op. cit.*, and the like are not used.

This citation form has the disadvantage of cluttering the body of a paper, and they can be distracting, interrupting the reader's flow. However, it also has a lot to recommend it. For the writer, it means that footnotes/endnotes do not have to be re-numbered when revisions add new citations. For readers familiar with the area in which the paper is written, this brief citation in the text is often sufficient information, and turning to the full reference section at the end of the paper is not necessary. And even readers unfamiliar with the field will recognize the same source if it is repeatedly cited.

Citation form has been discussed following the Introduction section because that is where most citations appear. However, citations can appear in every section of a paper, and the rules for the form of citation are the same, regardless of the section.

Methods

The methods section is perhaps the most difficult to write. The major purpose of this section is to provide sufficient information about how the study was conducted to permit readers to decide how much credence to attribute to the results. Ideally, enough detail should be provided to enable a reader to repeat the study – that is, to copy the entire design and see whether the findings are replicable. In fact, however, it is almost never possible to describe all the detailed features of a design that would be necessary for a replication. One must settle for the most important characteristics.

Which points are most important to cover will vary somewhat from study to study. In most studies the following features of a research design will require explanation:

1) *Subjects*. It is important for the reader to be told the number of subjects included in a study and any attributes that they shared (for example, members of some voluntary organization). The way they were selected should be noted (for example, a random sample), along with any circumstance that may alter the degree to which they are representative of a population. For example, what was the refusal rate, and did those who refused differ in any way from those who participated? Even if an investigator utilizes data that were gathered elsewhere (that is, secondary analysis), it is still important to provide some descriptive information of this type. (The appendix to Chapter 6 includes the AAPOR transparency requirements, and it provides a very complete checklist of items to consider including in this section.)

2) *Data collection instrument*. Interview schedules, questionnaires, or observational procedures need to be described. Specifically, this entails noting such details as whether a questionnaire was self-administered, how long interviews took on average, and when the data were obtained. The operationalizations of major variables should be described in detail. For example, if answers to a particular question were used to assign scores to respondents, the exact wording of the question should be indicated as well as the way responses were coded. (Questionnaires, observation codes and the like should be included in an appendix.)

3) *Setting or conditions*. In field studies it is important to adequately note the kinds of settings in which observations and interviews took place. Natural experiments require similar descriptions. When studies of any

type are conducted in distinctive settings, this portion of the methods section will usually be rather lengthy in order to provide the reader with an adequate mental picture of the research setting.

4) *Techniques of analysis.* If data are analyzed in a conventional manner and if it is unproblematic to assume that the data meet the requirements of the analysis, then little description of the analysis is necessary in the methods section. The nature of the analysis will be self-evident in the results section. However, if the analysis involves innovative techniques, unconventional assumptions, or the like, then it may be viewed as part of the investigator's strategy and should be discussed in the methods section; in other words, readers should be fully prepared for the results before they reach that section of a report.

The major difference between the Methods section in a scientific research paper and an agency- or client-driven research paper is length. Ideally, readers of a scientific paper would like to be able to replicate the study, from the information provided. Clients and agencies usually have no such interest, so they require less detail, but it still should be sufficient to enable them to critique the way the project was conducted. In conjunction with descriptions of methods, it may also be important to itemize the cost of various procedures in order to justify funding.

Results

This section is devoted, as completely as possible, to presenting the findings – divorced from a discussion of what those findings may mean. The separation of results and interpretation serves the reader in a number of ways. First, it gives the reader an opportunity to scrutinize the findings independently, that is, without being told by the writer what to make of them. Second, some portions of the results that are of only incidental interest to the investigator may be of substantial interest to some readers. If results are presented in conjunction with interpretation, the writer might neglect to include these portions of the results.

Almost any analysis will generate more findings than an investigator will be able to present. Some difficult decisions will have to be made concerning what is most important to include. Tables, charts, and the like are helpful because they present a great deal of information in condensed form, thereby allowing more of the total findings to be included. When in doubt about what results to present, good advice is to return to the introduction section and reread it. The writer's own description of the problem, if it is well done, should provide helpful orientation to the results that are most relevant.

Discussion

The bulk of a discussion section is ordinarily devoted to an analysis of the original hypothesis in light of the results that have been obtained. To what degree was it supported, to what degree not? In addition, if the results support the hypothesis, an investigator should consider, in writing, the possibility that the results are a by-product of some unanticipated, but fortunate, occurrence. If so, would it affect the possibility of the study being replicated?

On the other hand, if the results do not support the hypothesis, then the writer should consider whether it is because of the effects of some other variable(s) not anticipated and hence not controlled, or accounted for, in the study. Or, was it due to some defect in the research design that was employed? In other words, the discussion section entails a critical appraisal of the results, from which an investigator offers a conclusion concerning whether or not the hypothesis should be rejected.

After conducting a study, investigators usually know a good deal more about the phenomenon in question and about how to study it than they did at the onset. This increased sophistication should be shared with the reader in the discussion section. Correspondingly, it is commonplace to include, near the end of this section, the investigator's suggestions for how others might fruitfully pursue further research. Especially in a lengthy report an investigator may also wish to include a summary as a last paragraph in the Discussion section; but in most cases, the abstract will suffice.

Recommendations

With a non-scientific paper, the discussion section may be termed Discussion and Recommendations, or there may be a separate Recommendations section. In any case, this is a crucial part of a research report prepared for an agency or a client. The purpose of this type of research, after all, is to suggest solutions to a vexing problem. At this point in the report, therefore, the investigator needs to address that problem. How has the research clarified what is going on? Can the causes of the problem be better explicated? Based upon what has been learned from the research, what remedies for the problem may be suggested, and what is the prognosis for alternative remedies?

The major recommendations of the study should also be summarized in bullet points, as though it was to be presented in PowerPoint, regardless of whether or not it will be. This means putting only one key point in each bullet, and keeping it brief. Remember, it is a summary, not intended to explain everything. Each bullet point, on a slide or on paper, should express a key conclusion/recommendation that the investigators want the "audience" (whoever that is) to take from the presentation.[5]

If in the course of conducting the project, the investigator came across some previous research that was helpful, it may be of benefit to sponsors or others to note those studies. They can be included at the end of the recommendations section or at the very end of the paper in a section entitled "Bibliography" or "Suggestions for Additional Reading."

References

In the final section of a research paper, the cited references are presented in alphabetical order. Here they are presented in full, as opposed to their abbreviated form in the body of the research paper. Specifically, the most widely expected (APA) style is to list a cited author's last name first, followed only by initials. The date of publication is next, in parentheses. The first letter of the first word in the title of the publication is in capitals, the remainder is all in lower case. The name of the book or journal is italicized, and if it is a journal, the volume follows the name of the journal and the pages on which the article can be found is the final entry. Box 8.2 illustrates what the beginning of such a section might look like.

Writing style

The primary objectives of the narrative of a research report are clarity and precision. These objectives provide the criteria against which one should make all presentation discussions. In the following pages we will review a number of features of effective writing, in general, and of formal writing styles, in particular. These stylistic rules will ordinarily enhance the overall clarity and precision of a research report. Occasionally, however, a particular situation arises in which adherence to appropriate form may detract from the clarity or precision of a report. In such situations, stylistic considerations should be subordinated.

Box 8.2 Reference section sample

Adams, P. (2013). The effect of city size on city budgets. *Urban Research Quarterly, 22,* 119–122.

Burrows, R. J., Kline, V., and Phillips, B. N. (2006). A review of the world's major urban centers. New York, NY: Wiley.

Charlene, R.J. (2015). An investigation into funding of Michigan's smaller cities. (Unpublished honors thesis, University of Michigan, Ann Arbor, MI).

(If a journal article or other publications was retrieved on-line, the hypertext address should be noted at the very end of the citation.)

As a general rule, the less attention that readers pay to matters of writing style the better. In other words, the writer wants the reader to concentrate on content – the description of procedures, findings, and the like presented in the report. If the mode of presentation passes unnoticed – that is, never interferes with the reader's ability simply to read through the report – then it is successful. With this goal in mind, the writer of a report will do well to keep the writing simple. Avoid flowery prose and unnecessary metaphors or analogies because they can make the style obtrusive, thereby detracting from the content. For similar reasons it is desirable to minimize the number of long and complex sentences which contain many clauses and phrases because only a limited number of ideas can be effectively presented in a single sentence as this particular sentence is intended to illustrate! Short sentences tend to be clearer. They cannot convey complex ideas, though. Reading one short, simple sentence after another can also become boring. Therefore, some variety is desirable.

It is helpful to remember that most sentences have a beginning, a middle, and an end. It is the beginning and the end of a written sentence that are most salient. Readers will tend, consciously or unconsciously, to de-emphasize the middle portion of a complex sentence. Recognizing this, writers must decide what they want to emphasize in a sentence and place it accordingly. Consider the following sentences as concrete examples:

1) Most subjects expressed satisfaction, though there were exceptions, and indicated a willingness to continue to participate.
2) Most subjects expressed satisfaction, in the post-experiment interview, and indicated a willingness to continue to participate.

In both of the above examples, attention is drawn to the fact that most subjects expressed satisfaction and were willing to continue. If that was the writer's intent, then these parts of the sentence were properly placed at the beginning and the end. In example 1, however, the middle clause is redundant. Most implies less than everyone. The sentence would be better without this middle clause. The people who were exceptions could then be described in a subsequent sentence.

The structure of paragraphs should resemble the structure of sentences. Specifically, this means that the beginning and end of a paragraph should state (and sometimes restate) its main points. In addition, paragraphs should build upon each other or logically interconnect. Sometimes this requires an opening sentence that explicitly relates to the preceding paragraph. In other cases adjoining paragraphs cannot be connected no matter what a writer tries to do. That is often an indication that one of

the paragraphs is out of place and should be moved to another portion of the report. When one paragraph does not seem to follow another, it can also indicate that the first paragraph completes a set of ideas. It may then be helpful to place a section heading or subheading after that paragraph to inform the reader that the report is about to move in a different direction.

Formality

A research report calls for a formal writing style. It differs primarily from an informal style – the way people ordinarily e-mail their friends, for example – in that a formal style entails a series of proscriptions. Among the most important things to avoid are (1) contractions (such as don't and can't), (2) slang expressions that are in vogue at the moment, and (3) use of the first person pronoun, I (as well as my, mine, and the like).

Contractions are generally avoided because their meanings are not always evident – that is, it is sometimes unclear what word(s) they signify. Normal speech patterns are full of contractions, and writers sometimes feel self-conscious about writing out words that they verbally contract. It may feel awkward to write out "do not" when one is accustomed to saying "don't." However, there is a marked difference between printed and spoken words, and the absence of contractions will not seem clumsy to readers. (There is one important exception to this rule, namely, when actual quotations from respondents are presented. If they said "aren't" or "they'll," put it in quotations and report it as they said it.)

Slang expressions (again, unless quotations) should be avoided completely because their meanings tend to be momentary. A research report, by contrast, is expected to be enduring. Years later, the readers of a research report are likely to be thoroughly confused by slang expressions that were in vogue when the report was written.

First person reference (that is, "I") is to be avoided because it is associated with subjectivity, and objectivity is the goal of a research report. Furthermore, the use of I, my, and the like is usually redundant because it is already implied. Thus, it is obviously the writer who followed the described procedures, obtained the reported findings, offered the interpretations, and so on.

In their efforts to avoid the first person pronoun, however, writers often back into the passive voice. In this mode, the subject of a sentence is described as the object of the action – for example, "The student was observed cheating," rather than, "I observed the student cheating." Passive sentences are often confusing. They are usually lifeless and boring. It would frequently be preferable to use "I" than to make extensive use of the passive mode.

The research report

There is one notable exception to the rule of avoiding first person references. In action research, introduced in Chapter 1, the investigator-author is typically an advocate for particular positions, which will serve to benefit disadvantaged groups in the community. To be authentic, the writer's explicit use of first-person references is sometimes recommended.[6]

Even though the English language is full of examples of males being equated with everyone (e.g. "mankind"), the use of a generic "he," when no specific gender is implied by the content, is not satisfactory. There are several ways to avoid it that are generally considered acceptable. One possibility is to include both pronouns, for example: "he or she is able to. . ." and to alternate which comes first so the next relevant sentence might state: "she or he found this. . ." Another possibility that has recently gained favor is to utilize "they" as though it were singular. While it clearly violates customary usage, the singular they does enable a writer to avoid generic pronouns in an efficient manner.

Finally, the beginning writer must realize that almost no one is able to prepare a well-written report in the first draft. It is not until after something has been written once and then read that it is even possible to tell that paragraphs seem out of sequence or that some sentences do not seem to emphasize the intended points. Thus, in outlining the time schedule for writing a research paper, one should allot sufficient time not only to write the paper, but to re-write the paper. It may actually be more realistic to assume that several drafts will be required.

Notes

1 For further discussion of the executive summary, see Margaret Greenhall, *Report Writing Skills Training Course*. University of Learning, Ltd, 2013.
2 See Gabe T. Wang and Keumjae Park, *Student Research and Report Writing*. Wiley-Blackwell, 2016.
3 See American Psychological Association, *The Publication Manual of the American Psychological Association* (6th Ed.). APA, 2011.
4 See American Sociological Association, *Style Guide* (5th Ed). ASA, 2014.
5 For an insightful, and sometimes humorous, discussion of bullet point presentations, see Simon Guest, *File>New>Presentation*. Amazon Digital, 2013.
6 See Jean McNiff, *Writing and Doing Action Research*. Sage, 2015.

Index

Index